Human Rights Watch

World Report

2004

Human Rights and Armed Conflict

Human Rights Watch

Addresses for Human Rights Watch

350 Fifth Avenue, 34th Floor, New York, NY 10118-3299

Tel: (212) 290-4700, Fax: (212) 736-1300, E-mail: hrwnyc@hrw.org

1630 Connecticut Avenue, N.W., Suite 500, Washington, DC 20009

Tel: (202) 612-4321, Fax: (202) 612-4333, E-mail: hrwdc@hrw.org

2nd Floor, 2-12 Pentonville Road London N1 9HF, UK

Tel: (44 20) 7713 1995, Fax: (44 20) 7713 1800, E-mail: hrwuk@hrw.org

15 Rue Van Campenhout, 1000 Brussels, Belgium

Tel: (32 2) 732-2009, Fax: (32 2) 732-0471, E-mail: hrwatcheu@skynet.be

8 rue des Vieux-Grenadiers, 1205 Geneva

Tel: (41 22) 320 5590, Fax: (41 22) 320 5511, Email: hrwgva@hrw.org

Web Site Address: http://www.hrw.org

Listserv address: To receive Human Rights Watch news releases by email, subscribe
to the HRW news listserv of your choice by visiting http://hrw.org/act/subscribe-
mlists/subscribe.htm

Human Rights Watch is dedicated to
protecting the human rights of people around the world.

We stand with victims and activists to prevent
discrimination, to uphold political freedom, to protect people from
inhumane conduct in wartime, and to bring offenders to justice.

We investigate and expose
human rights violations and hold abusers accountable.

We challenge governments and those who hold power to end abusive
practices and respect international human rights law.

We enlist the public and the international
community to support the cause of human rights for all.

HUMAN RIGHTS WATCH

Human Rights Watch conducts regular, systematic investigations of human rights abuses in some seventy countries around the world. Our reputation for timely, reliable disclosures has made us an essential source of information for those concerned with human rights. We address the human rights practices of governments of all political stripes, of all geopolitical alignments, and of all ethnic and religious persuasions. Human Rights Watch defends freedom of thought and expression, due process and equal protection of the law, and a vigorous civil society; we document and denounce murders, disappearances, torture, arbitrary imprisonment, discrimination, and other abuses of internationally recognized human rights. Our goal is to hold governments accountable if they transgress the rights of their people.

Human Rights Watch began in 1978 with the founding of its Europe and Central Asia division (then known as Helsinki Watch). Today, it also includes divisions covering Africa, the Americas, Asia, and the Middle East. In addition, it includes three thematic divisions on arms, children's rights, and women's rights. It maintains offices in Brussels, Geneva, London, Los Angeles, Moscow, New York, San Francisco, Tashkent and Washington. Human Rights Watch is an independent, nongovernmental organization, supported by contributions from private individuals and foundations worldwide. It accepts no government funds, directly or indirectly.

The staff includes Kenneth Roth, executive director; Carroll Bogert, associate director; Allison Adoradio, operations director; Michele Alexander, development director; Steve Crawshaw, London director; Barbara Guglielmo, finance director; Lotte Leicht, Brussels office

Human Rights Watch mourned the sudden passing this year of two much-loved colleagues, Mike Jendrzejczyk and Alison Hughes. Mike J., known for his extraordinary energy and passion for social justice, was Washington D.C. director of our Asia Division and had been a staff member for thirteen years at his death on May 1. He was a pioneer who helped shape human rights advocacy as we know it today, developing tools and innovative new approaches that have become standard practice. Alison Hughes, Washington, D.C.-based advocacy associate, was only 26 when she died on October 26. A bright light in our office, she was committed, talented, and brought to her work an infectious sense of humor and a deep sense of justice. We remember Mike and Alison with great warmth and sadness.

ACKNOWLEDGEMENTS

The World Report contributors would like to acknowledge the following individuals, who provided valuable assistance during the writing of the essays: Elizabeth Andersen, Georges Berghezan, Ilhan Berkol, Carroll Bogert, Widney Brown, Grace Chon, Joanne Csete, Rachel Denber, Alison DesForges, Richard Dicker, Bonnie Docherty, Malcolm Dort, Corinne Dufka, Shiva Eftekhari, Jamie Fellner, Isaac Flattau, Kate Fletcher, Barbara Frey, Arvind Ganesan, Marc Garlasco, Steve Goose, Christopher Keith Hall, Julie Hassman, Mark Hiznay, Bogdan Ivanisevic, LaShawn Jefferson, Pascal Kambale, Elise Keppler, Juliane Kippenberg, Edward Laurance, Leslie Lefkow, Darryl Li, Diederik Lohman, Lora Lumpe, Tara Magner, Erin Mahoney, Anjana Malhotra, Bronwen Manby, Geraldine Mattioli, Nobuntu Mbelle, Fiona McKay, Marianne Mollmann, Elizabeth Morrow, Anna Neistat, Alison Parker, Vikram Parekh, Wendy Patten, Alexander Petrov, Sara Rakita, Ahmad Rashid, Yolanda Revilla, Jim Ross, Barney Rubin, Rebecca Schleifer, John Sifton, Brigitte Suhr, Veronika Leila Szente Goldston, Jennifer Trahan, Anneke Van Woudenberg, Nisha Varia, Alex Vines, Janet Walsh, Benjamin Ward, Mary Wareham, and Brian Wood.

Joseph Saunders edited this report, with the assistance of Iain Levine. Jim Ross and Wilder Tayler conducted the legal review. Layout and production assistance was provided by Gil Colon, John Emerson, Sobeira Genao, Fitzroy Hepkins, Andrea Holley, Manu Krishnan, Jose Martinez, Veronica Matushaj, and Jagdish Parikh. Mike Bochenek, Ami Evangelista, Kate Fletcher, Leila Hull, Suneeta Kaimal, Erin Mahoney, Kay Seok, Dana Sommers, and Liz Weiss proofread the report.

Table of Contents

Preface

This year's Human Rights Watch World Report offers something new. Past volumes have featured summaries of human-rights-related developments in each of the seventy or so countries and themes we cover in-depth each year. This year, to mark the twenty-fifth anniversary of Human Rights Watch, we have chosen a single theme—human rights and armed conflict—and have produced a series of more analytical, reflective essays. Each essay takes stock of developments in a specific area and offers suggestions on the way forward.

The focus this year on armed conflict was influenced by events, most obviously the war in Iraq and continuing armed conflict in Africa, particularly in the Great Lakes region and in West Africa. 2003 also saw renewed bloodshed in Russia (Chechnya) and Indonesia (Aceh), to name only two of the many conflicts that continued to destroy civilian lives and the institutions and infrastructure on which they depend: justice, education, health, water. Almost without exception, the world's worst human rights and humanitarian crises take place in combat zones.

The United States-led war in Iraq was the major international political event of the year, and will continue to raise important challenges for human rights and international humanitarian law. As Kenneth Roth argues in the keynote essay of this volume, while the Bush administration has repeatedly cited the human rights crimes of the Saddam Hussein government to justify the war retrospectively, this never was a war that could be justified on strictly humanitarian grounds.

1

In their essay on conditions in post-Saddam Iraq, Joe Stork and Fred Abrahams note that the United States and its coalition partners have treated rights issues as matters of secondary importance. Themes that they identify in Iraq—from failure to provide troops with essential training in securing law and order to insufficient attention to justice for past serious crimes—echo themes identified by Sam Zia-Zarifi in his essay on post-conflict Afghanistan. Zia-Zarifi notes that, in Afghanistan, the focus of coalition forces on defeating remnant Taliban and al-Qaeda forces as quickly as possible led to reliance on warlords, many with long records of rights abuses. The result has been a deteriorating human rights situation, deepening fear among Afghans and growing insecurity in much of the country.

The human rights implications of the global campaign against terrorism, often portrayed by those who wage it as a new kind of war, loom large in a number of the essays. Entries on the United States and Russia (Chechnya) in particular demonstrate a clear and troubling trend: an assault on human rights in the name of counter-terrorism. Jamie Fellner and Alison Parker describe various ways in which the Bush administration is citing threats to national security as a justification for putting executive action above the law in the United States. The Bush Administration's indifference to norms of accountability that are at the core of the U.S. governmental structure as well as the international human rights framework is deeply troubling internationally and for the American public as well. Rachel Denber's essay on Chechnya shows how the international community, despite well-intended words on the importance of human rights and humanitarian law, has failed dismally to engage with the Russian government over its appalling human rights record in Chechnya, a conflict now justified by Russian authorities as their contribution to the global war on terror.

In his essay on the conduct of counter-terrorism operations, Kenneth Roth notes the unclear boundaries of what the Bush administration calls its war on terror. As Roth notes, if "war" were meant metaphorically, like the war on drugs, it would be an uncontroversial hortatory device, a way of rallying support to an important cause. But the administration seems to mean it literally, invoking the extraordinary power of a government at war to detain suspects without trial and even to kill them, despite distance from any traditional battlefield such as Afghanistan or Iraq. Roth also examines Israel's practice of targeted killings of alleged armed militants. He concludes that, even in war, law enforcement rules should presumptively apply away from a traditional battlefield, and war rules should be a tool of last resort, certainly not applicable when a functioning criminal justice system is available.

War in the Democratic Republic of the Congo (DRC), addressed by many of the essays here, is a profound, multi-faceted human rights crisis. Though neglected by virtually all of the world powers and major international media, an estimated 3.3 million civilians have lost their lives in the war since 1998—more than in any conflict since World War Two. These deaths are a combination of often brutal killings and the loss of access to food, health care, and other essentials of life as populations have been forced to flee and aid agencies have been overwhelmed by the needs of inaccessible populations in often insecure areas. The international system has coped with difficulty with a war which has

3

involved six other African states, over a dozen rebel groups, and dozens of companies and individuals seeking to exploit the country's natural resources.

One hopeful development, analyzed by Binaifer Nowrojee in her essay on recent armed conflicts in Africa, is the emergence of new regional bodies such as the African Union that could play a more active role in insisting on rights protections in conflict prevention initiatives. Although the African regional framework is still nascent and rights have remained marginal in regional peacekeeping interventions to date, African leaders have now committed on record to take a more active role in curbing regional armed conflict and associated rights abuses. As Nowrojee notes, international engagement and assistance will continue to be critically important even as such regional initiatives get underway.

An important theme that emerges in many of the essays here is the extraordinary and awful gap between existing international legal standards and practice. In the last few years, new standards have included the Mine Ban Treaty, the Guiding Principles on Internal Displacement, the Optional Protocol to the Convention on the Rights of the Child banning the use of child soldiers, and the establishment of the International Criminal Court. Yet we seem no closer to preventing the brutality of DRC and so many other conflicts.

A number of essays highlight the critical importance of the U.N. Security Council, the key international body tasked with the maintenance of international peace and security. The council has passed resolutions and established mechanisms that often put commitments to protect rights at the center of the U.N. system's response to international crises. Yet time and time again these commitments to protect children, to hold perpetrators accountable, to address arms flows, and to scrutinize the behavior of international companies are forgotten, ignored, or neglected in the face of political pressures.

As Jo Becker demonstrates in her survey of current developments in the global effort to stop the use of child soldiers, even innovative efforts such as Secretary-General Kofi Annan's public naming of armed groups and governments that recruit or use children will not succeed in changing the practices of the named parties without more systematic follow-through. Strict application of Security Council resolutions and concrete action against violators is required to ensure that the council's commitments are more than empty promises to those caught up in brutal and chronic conflicts.

In parts of the former Yugoslavia—notably Croatia, Bosnia and Herzegovina, and Kosovo—the failure of international and domestic efforts to promote the return of refugees and displaced persons has left substantially in place the wartime displacement of ethnic minorities. As Bogdan Ivanisevic's essay on ethnic minority returns in the region concludes, the Balkan experience offers an important lesson for other post-conflict situations: unless displacement and "ethnic cleansing" are to be accepted as permanent and acceptable outcomes of war, comprehensive and multi-faceted return strategies—with firm implementation and enforcement mechanisms—must be an early priority for peace-building efforts. When such elements are present, minority returns progress; when they are absent, returns stall.

LaShawn Jefferson's essay on sexual violence highlights an important point: the violations of human rights that we witness in conflict are often rooted in forms of prejudice, discrimination, marginalization, and impunity that were present long before the conflict began. Jefferson argues that women and girls are continuously at risk for wartime sexual violence because of women's subordinate status and abuses in peacetime, using as examples the brutal and insidious sexual violence that has characterized conflicts in Sierra Leone, Liberia, and DRC in recent years, and in Bosnia and Rwanda in the 1990s. Survivors of sexual violence often face daunting obstacles in post-conflict periods. Civil society groups have tried to step into the breach, but governments often fail to provide necessary services, and, in reconstruction and development plans, women's voices are all too often conspicuous by their absence.

The availability of natural resource wealth, particularly when paired with corrupt, unaccountable government, forms an important part of the backdrop of many armed conflicts. Though economists and political scientists continue to argue over the genesis of many of today's civil conflicts—greed or grievance?—the role of corruption, lack of transparency, and private and public sector profiteering merits renewed attention. Arvind Ganesan and Alex Vines's essay on conflict and resources addresses just such issues. Lisa Misol's discussion of the role of arms-supplying governments and private traffickers who supply weapons to known rights abusers highlights, among other things, the dangers of governments abrogating their responsibilities to regulate the actions of private actors.

Misol's essay also reminds us that although we have many of the necessary laws in place to protect non-combatants, there is still room for improvement. A proposed international arms trade treaty, spearheaded by civil society groups, would prohibit arms transfers where the authorizing government knows or ought to know that the weapons will be used to commit genocide, crimes against humanity, serious human rights abuses, or serious violations of international humanitarian law.

Steve Goose, in his essay on the damage to innocent civilians wrought by cluster munitions both during and after armed conflict, similarly notes the importance of developing new legal tools. Cluster munitions are particularly dangerous to civilians because they are inaccurate, scattering explosive submunitions across wide areas, and because of the long-term lethal threat posed by landmine-like submunition duds. Cluster munitions have already been used in sixteen countries and existing stockpiles likely include well over two billion submunitions. As Goose explains, in the past decade the international community has banned two weapons—antipersonnel landmines and blinding lasers—on humanitarian grounds; cluster munitions now stand out as the weapon category most in need of stronger regulation to protect civilians during and after armed conflict.

Armed conflict continues to pose some of the most urgent questions for the international community and for the human rights movement in particular. The range of abuses associated with warfare— killings and maiming of civilians, sexual violence, poor conditions for refugees and internally displaced people, illicit arms flows to abusers, use of child soldiers, and so on—reflects the complexity of most conflicts. Add to the mix the difficulties of dealing with rebel movements (ranging from de facto civil administrations to Hobbesian thugs such as the Lord's Resistance Army), neighboring governments, diaspora communities, and the corporate sector—and the complexity increases.

It is easy for activists and people of goodwill to lose hope or question the continued relevance of human rights arguments. Reed Brody, reflecting on 25 years of the human rights movement, quotes Michael Ignatieff as asking "whether the era of human rights has come and gone." Yet much has been achieved and, as Brody's essay reminds us, human rights discourse and institutions are now fixtures of the international relations landscape.

U.N. Secretary General Kofi Annan has said "we must do more to move from words to deeds, from the elaboration of norms to an era of application." Many of the norms and commitments to which he refers are in place. Most of the laws required to protect in conflict are on the statute books. Even the mechanisms for holding perpetrators accountable are being put in place through the International Criminal Court and some of the ad hoc international tribunals that have been set up to try crimes committed in Rwanda, the former Yugoslavia, and Sierra Leone.

As Richard Dicker and Elise Keppler note in their overview of international justice mechanisms, the developing system of international justice that grew up in the 1990s faces a more difficult environment today. They offer an assessment of successes and failures to date and identify obstacles ahead. Still, the importance of justice to a society's health and long-term stability, coupled with the fact that national court systems, particularly in post-conflict settings, will likely continue to fall far short of minimally acceptable standards, strongly argues the need for consolidating gains to make international mechanisms more effective.

This volume provides but a snapshot of Human Rights Watch's work in seeking to protect the victims of conflict. It does not cover some key issues we regularly work on such as refugees and the displaced, or the special problems of dealing with armed groups; it does not address some of the conflicts we watched closely in 2003, including Colombia, Aceh, and Israel and the Occupied Territories. We offer it as a contribution to the current thinking on protecting human rights in conflict.

The essays here make clear that what is needed is the political will to implement existing commitments and the creativity to draw on past successes and failures to devise new institutional responses to the human rights challenges posed by pervasive armed conflict. Such change will require renewed activism to name and shame those who, by sins of omission or commission, are responsible for or complicit in the kinds of acts described in this volume. Activists must work to remind the world of the promises that have been made to women, to children, to the displaced, to the sick and the hungry, to ethnic and racial minorities and other vulnerable groups—the laws, the norms, the

9

standards, the resolutions, and the policies that are meant to ensure their protection and the preservation of their lives, their well being, and their dignity.

At a mass gravesite in al-Hilla, Iraq, a U.S. marine holds a video camera while desperate families dig up graves in an attempt to identify the remains of loved ones. Families waited in vain for direction from U.S. and U.K. authorities as to how the Coalition intended to exhume gravesites and preserve evidence for possible criminal proceedings. © 2003 Geert van Kesteren

War in Iraq: Not a Humanitarian Intervention
By Ken Roth

Humanitarian intervention was supposed to have gone the way of the 1990s. The use of military force across borders to stop mass killing was seen as a luxury of an era in which national security concerns among the major powers were less pressing and problems of human security could come to the fore. Somalia, Haiti, Bosnia, Kosovo, East Timor, Sierra Leone—these interventions, to varying degrees justified in humanitarian terms, were dismissed as products of an unusual interlude between the tensions of the Cold War and the growing threat of terrorism. September 11, 2001 was said to have changed all that, signaling a return to more immediate security challenges. Yet surprisingly, with the campaign against terrorism in full swing, the past year or so has seen four military interventions that are described by their instigators, in whole or in part, as humanitarian.

In principle, one can only welcome this renewed concern with the fate of faraway victims. What could be more virtuous than to risk life and limb to save distant people from slaughter? But the common use of the humanitarian label masks significant differences among these interventions. The French intervention in the Democratic Republic of Congo, later backed by a reinforced U.N. peacekeeping presence, was most clearly motivated by a desire to stop ongoing slaughter. In Liberia and Côte d'Ivoire, West African and French forces intervened to enforce a peace plan but also played important humanitarian roles. (The United States briefly participated in the Liberian intervention, but the

13

handful of troops it deployed had little effect.) All of these African interventions were initially or ultimately approved by the U.N. Security Council. Indeed, in each case the recognized local government consented to the intervention, though under varying degrees of pressure.

By contrast, the United States-led coalition forces justified the invasion of Iraq on a variety of grounds, only one of which—a comparatively minor one—was humanitarian. The Security Council did not approve the invasion, and the Iraqi government, its existence on the line, violently opposed it. Moreover, while the African interventions were modest affairs, the Iraq war was massive, involving an extensive bombing campaign and some 150,000 ground troops.

The sheer size of the invasion of Iraq, the central involvement of the world's superpower, and the enormous controversy surrounding the war meant that the Iraqi conflict overshadowed the other military actions. For better or for worse, that prominence gave it greater power to shape public perceptions of armed interventions said by their proponents to be justified on humanitarian grounds. The result is that at a time of renewed interest in humanitarian intervention, the Iraq war and the effort to justify it even in part in humanitarian terms risk giving humanitarian intervention a bad name. If that breeds cynicism about the use of military force for humanitarian purposes, it could be devastating for people in need of future rescue.

Human Rights Watch ordinarily takes no position on whether a state should go to war. The issues involved usually extend beyond our mandate, and a position of neutrality maximizes our ability to press all parties to a conflict to avoid harming noncombatants. The sole exception we make is in extreme situations requiring humanitarian intervention.

Because the Iraq war was not mainly about saving the Iraqi people from mass slaughter, and because no such slaughter was then ongoing or imminent, Human Rights Watch at the time took no position for or against the war. A humanitarian rationale was occasionally offered for the war, but it was so plainly subsidiary to other reasons that we felt no need to address it. Indeed, if Saddam Hussein had been overthrown and the issue of weapons of mass destruction reliably dealt with, there clearly would have been no war, even if the successor government were just as repressive. Some argued that Human Rights Watch should support a war launched on other grounds if it would arguably lead to significant human rights improvements. But the substantial risk that wars guided by non-humanitarian goals will endanger human rights keeps us from adopting that position.

Over time, the principal justifications originally given for the Iraq war lost much of their force. More than seven months after the declared end of major hostilities, weapons of mass destruction have not been found. No significant prewar link between Saddam Hussein and international terrorism has been discovered. The difficulty of establishing stable institutions in Iraq is making the country an increasingly unlikely staging ground for promoting democracy in the Middle East. As time elapses, the Bush administration's dominant remaining justification for the war is that Saddam Hussein was a tyrant who deserved to be overthrown—an argument of humanitarian intervention. The administration is now citing this rationale not simply as a side benefit of the war but also as a prime justification for it. Other reasons are still regularly mentioned, but the humanitarian one has gained prominence.

Does that claim hold up to scrutiny? The question is not simply whether Saddam Hussein was a ruthless leader; he most certainly was. Rather, the question is whether the conditions were present that would justify humanitarian intervention—conditions that look at more than the level of repression. If so, honesty would require conceding as much, despite the war's global unpopularity. If not, it is important to say so as well, since allowing the arguments of humanitarian intervention to serve as a pretext for war fought mainly on other grounds risks tainting a principle whose viability might be essential to save countless lives.

In examining whether the invasion of Iraq could properly be understood as a humanitarian intervention, our purpose is not to say whether the U.S.-led coalition should have gone to war for other reasons. That, as noted, involves judgments beyond our mandate. Rather, now that the war's proponents are relying so significantly on a humanitarian rationale for the war, the need to assess this claim has grown in importance. We conclude that, despite the horrors of Saddam Hussein's rule, the invasion of Iraq cannot be justified as a humanitarian intervention.

The Standards for Humanitarian Intervention

Unusual among human rights groups, Human Rights Watch has a longstanding policy on humanitarian intervention. War often carries enormous human costs, but we recognize that the imperative of stopping or preventing genocide or other systematic slaughter can sometimes justify the use of military force. For that reason, Human Rights Watch has on rare occasion advocated humanitarian intervention—for example, to stop ongoing genocide in Rwanda and Bosnia.

Yet military action should not be taken lightly, even for humanitarian purposes. One might use military force more readily when a government facing serious abuses on its territory invites military assistance from others—as in the cases of the three recent African interventions. But military intervention on asserted humanitarian grounds without the government's consent should be used with extreme caution. In arriving at the standards that we believe should govern such nonconsensual military action, we draw on the principles underlying our own policy on humanitarian intervention and on our experiences in applying them. We also take into account other relevant literature, including the report of the Canadian government-sponsored International Commission on Intervention and State Sovereignty.

In our view, as a threshold matter, humanitarian intervention that occurs without the consent of the relevant government can be justified only in the face of ongoing or imminent genocide, or comparable mass slaughter or loss of life. To state the obvious, war is dangerous. In theory it can be surgical, but the reality is often highly destructive, with a

17

risk of enormous bloodshed. Only large-scale murder, we believe, can justify the death, destruction, and disorder that so often are inherent in war and its aftermath. Other forms of tyranny are deplorable and worth working intensively to end, but they do not in our view rise to the level that would justify the extraordinary response of military force. Only mass slaughter might permit the deliberate taking of life involved in using military force for humanitarian purposes.

In addition, the capacity to use military force is finite. Encouraging military action to meet lesser abuses may mean a lack of capacity to intervene when atrocities are most severe. The invasion of a country, especially without the approval of the U.N. Security Council, also damages the international legal order which itself is important to protect rights. For these reasons, we believe that humanitarian intervention should be reserved for situations involving mass killing.

We understand that "mass" killing is a subjective term, allowing for varying interpretations, and we do not propose a single quantitative measure. We also recognize that the level of killing that we as a human rights organization would see as justifying humanitarian intervention might well be different from the level that a government might set. However, in either circumstance, because of the substantial risks inherent in the use of military force, humanitarian intervention should be exceptional—reserved for the most dire circumstances.

If this high threshold is met, we then look to five other factors to determine whether the use of military force can be characterized as humanitarian. First, military action must be the last reasonable option to halt or prevent slaughter; military force should not be used for humanitarian purposes if effective alternatives are available. Second, the intervention must be guided primarily by a humanitarian purpose; we do not expect purity of motive, but humanitarianism should be the dominant reason for military action. Third, every effort should be made to ensure that the means used to intervene themselves respect international human rights and humanitarian law; we do not subscribe to the view that some abuses can be countenanced in the name of stopping others. Fourth, it must be reasonably likely that military action will do more good than harm; humanitarian intervention should not be tried if it seems likely to produce a wider conflagration or significantly more suffering. Finally, we prefer endorsement of humanitarian intervention by the U.N. Security Council or other bodies with significant multilateral authority. However, in light of the imperfect nature of international governance today, we would not require multilateral approval in an emergency context.

Two Irrelevant Considerations

Before applying these criteria to Iraq, it is worth noting two factors that we do not consider relevant in assessing whether an intervention can be justified as humanitarian. First, we are aware of, but reject, the argument that humanitarian intervention cannot be justified if other equally or more needy places are ignored. Iraqi repression was severe, but the case might be made that repression elsewhere was worse. For example, an estimated three million or more have lost their lives to violence, disease, and exposure in recent years during the conflict in the eastern Democratic Republic of Congo (DRC), yet intervention in the DRC was

late and, compared to Iraq, modest. However, if the killing in Iraq
warranted military intervention, it would be callous to disregard the
plight of these victims simply because other victims were being
neglected. In that case, intervention should be encouraged in both
places, not rejected in one because it was weak or nonexistent in the
other.

Second, we are aware of, but reject, the argument that past U.S.
complicity in Iraqi repression should preclude U.S. intervention in Iraq
on humanitarian grounds. This argument is built on the U.S.
government's sordid record in Iraq in the 1980s and early 1990s. When
the Iraqi government was using chemical weapons against Iranian troops
in the 1980s, the Reagan administration was giving it intelligence
information. After the *Anfal* genocide against Iraqi Kurds in 1988, the
Reagan and first Bush administrations gave Baghdad billions of dollars
in commodity credits and import loan guarantees. The Iraqi
government's ruthless suppression of the 1991 uprising was facilitated
by the first Bush administration's agreement to Iraq's use of helicopters
– permission made all the more callous because then-President Bush
had encouraged the uprising in the first place. In each of these cases,
Washington deemed it more important to defeat Iran or avoid Iranian
influence in a potentially destabilized Iraq than to discourage or prevent
large-scale slaughter. We condemn such calculations. However, we
would not deny relief to, say, the potential victims of genocide simply
because the proposed intervener had dirty hands in the past.

The Level of Killing

In considering the criteria that would justify humanitarian intervention, the most important, as noted, is the level of killing: was genocide or comparable mass slaughter underway or imminent? Brutal as Saddam Hussein's reign had been, the scope of the Iraqi government's killing in March 2003 was not of the exceptional and dire magnitude that would justify humanitarian intervention. We have no illusions about Saddam Hussein's vicious inhumanity. Having devoted extensive time and effort to documenting his atrocities, we estimate that in the last twenty-five years of Ba`th Party rule the Iraqi government murdered or "disappeared" some quarter of a million Iraqis, if not more. In addition, one must consider such abuses as Iraq's use of chemical weapons against Iranian soldiers. However, by the time of the March 2003 invasion, Saddam Hussein's killing had ebbed.

There were times in the past when the killing was so intense that humanitarian intervention would have been justified—for example, during the 1988 *Anfal* genocide, in which the Iraqi government slaughtered some 100,000 Kurds. Indeed, Human Rights Watch, though still in its infancy and not yet working in the Middle East in 1988, did advocate a form of military intervention in 1991 after we had begun addressing Iraq. As Iraqi Kurds fleeing Saddam Hussein's brutal repression of the post-Gulf War uprising were stranded and dying in harsh winter weather on Turkey's mountainous border, we advocated the creation of a no-fly zone in northern Iraq so they could return home without facing renewed genocide. There were other moments of intense killing as well, such as the suppression of the uprisings in 1991. But on the eve of the latest Iraq war, no one contends that the Iraqi government was engaged in killing of anywhere near this magnitude, or had been for some time. "Better late than never" is not a justification for humanitarian intervention, which should be countenanced only to stop mass murder, not to punish its perpetrators, desirable as punishment is in such circumstances.

But if Saddam Hussein committed mass atrocities in the past, wasn't his overthrow justified to prevent his resumption of such atrocities in the future? No. Human Rights Watch accepts that military intervention may be necessary not only to stop ongoing slaughter but also to prevent future slaughter, but the future slaughter must be imminent. To justify the extraordinary remedy of military force for preventive humanitarian purposes, there must be evidence that large-scale slaughter is in preparation and about to begin unless militarily stopped. But no one seriously claimed before the war that the Saddam Hussein government was planning imminent mass killing, and no evidence has emerged that it was. There were claims that Saddam Hussein, with a history of gassing Iranian soldiers and Iraqi Kurds, was planning to deliver weapons of mass destruction through terrorist networks, but these allegations were entirely speculative; no substantial evidence has yet emerged. There were also fears that the Iraqi government might respond to an invasion with the use of chemical or biological weapons, perhaps even against its own people, but no one seriously suggested such use as an imminent possibility in the absence of an invasion.

That does not mean that past atrocities should be ignored. Rather, their perpetrators should be prosecuted. Human Rights Watch has devoted enormous efforts to investigating and documenting the Iraqi government's atrocities, particularly the *Anfal* genocide against Iraqi Kurds. We have interviewed witnesses and survivors, exhumed mass graves, taken soil samples to demonstrate the use of chemical weapons, and combed through literally tons of Iraqi secret police documents. We have circled the globe trying to convince some government—any government—to institute legal proceedings against Iraq for genocide. No one would. In the mid-1990s, when our efforts were most intense, governments feared that charging Iraq with genocide would be too provocative—that it would undermine future commercial deals with Iraq, squander influence in the Middle East, invite terrorist retaliation, or simply cost too much money.

But to urge justice or even criminal prosecution is not to justify humanitarian intervention. Indictments should be issued, and suspects should be arrested if they dare to venture abroad, but the extraordinary remedy of humanitarian intervention should not be used simply to secure justice for past crimes. This extreme step, as noted, should be taken only to stop current or imminent slaughter, not to punish past abuse.

In stating that the killing in Iraq did not rise to a level that justified humanitarian intervention, we are not insensitive to the awful plight of the Iraqi people. We are aware that summary executions occurred with disturbing frequency in Iraq up to the end of Saddam Hussein's rule, as did torture and other brutality. Such atrocities should be met with public, diplomatic, and economic pressure, as well as prosecution. But before taking the substantial risk to life that is inherent in any war, mass slaughter should be taking place or imminent. That was not the case in Saddam Hussein's Iraq in March 2003.

The Last Reasonable Option

The lack of ongoing or imminent mass slaughter was itself sufficient to disqualify the invasion of Iraq as a humanitarian intervention. Nonetheless, particularly in light of the ruthlessness of Saddam Hussein's rule, it is useful to examine the other criteria for humanitarian intervention. For the most part, these too were not met.

As noted, because of the substantial risks involved, an invasion should qualify as a humanitarian intervention only if it is the last reasonable option to stop mass killings. Since there were no ongoing mass killings in Iraq in early 2003, this issue technically did not arise. But it is useful to explore whether military intervention was the last reasonable option to stop what Iraqi abuses were ongoing.

It was not. If the purpose of the intervention was primarily humanitarian, then at least one other option should have been tried long before resorting to the extreme step of military invasion—criminal prosecution. There is no guarantee that prosecution would have worked, and one might have justified skipping it had large-scale slaughter been underway. But in the face of the Iraqi government's more routine abuses, this alternative to military action should have been tried.

An indictment, of course, is not the same as arrest, trial, and punishment. A mere piece of paper will not stop mass slaughter. But as a long-term approach to Iraq, justice held some promise. The experiences of former Yugoslav President Slobodan Milosevic and former Liberian President Charles Taylor suggest that an international indictment profoundly discredits even a ruthless, dictatorial leader. That enormous stigma tends to undermine support for the leader, both at home and abroad, often in unexpected ways. By allowing Saddam Hussein to rule without the stigma of an indictment for genocide and crimes against humanity, the international community never tried a step that might have contributed to his removal and a parallel reduction in government abuses.

In noting that prosecution was not tried before war, we recognize that the U.N. Security Council had never availed itself of this option in more than a decade of attention to Iraq. The council's April 1991 resolution on Iraq (resolution 688), in condemning "the repression of the Iraqi civilian population in many parts of Iraq," broke new ground at the time as the first council resolution to treat such repression as a threat to international peace and security. But the council never followed up by deploying the obvious tool of prosecution to curtail that repression. Yet if the U.S. government had devoted anywhere near the attention to justice as it did to pressing for war, the chances are at least reasonable that the council would have been responsive.

Humanitarian Purpose

Any humanitarian intervention should be conducted with the aim of maximizing humanitarian results. We recognize that an intervention motivated by purely humanitarian concerns probably cannot be found. Governments that intervene to stop mass slaughter inevitably have other reasons as well, so we do not insist on purity of motive. But a dominant humanitarian motive is important because it affects numerous decisions made in the course of an intervention and its aftermath that can determine its success in saving people from harm.

Humanitarianism, even understood broadly as concern for the welfare of the Iraqi people, was at best a subsidiary motive for the invasion of Iraq. The principal justifications offered in the prelude to the invasion were the Iraqi government's alleged possession of weapons of mass destruction, its alleged failure to account for them as prescribed by numerous U.N. Security Council resolutions, and its alleged connection with terrorist networks. U.S. officials also spoke of a democratic Iraq transforming the Middle East. In this tangle of motives, Saddam Hussein's cruelty toward his own people was mentioned—sometimes prominently—but, in the prewar period, it was never the dominant factor. This is not simply an academic point; it affected the way the invasion was carried out, to the detriment of the Iraqi people.

To begin with, if invading forces had been determined to maximize the humanitarian impact of an intervention, they would have been better prepared to fill the security vacuum that predictably was created by the toppling of the Iraqi government. It was entirely foreseeable that

Saddam Hussein's downfall would lead to civil disorder. The 1991
uprisings in Iraq were marked by large-scale summary executions. The
government's Arabization policy raised the prospect of clashes between
displaced Kurds seeking to reclaim their old homes and Arabs who had
moved into them. Other sudden changes of regime, such as the
Bosnian Serb withdrawal from the Sarajevo suburbs in 1996, have been
marked by widespread violence, looting, and arson.

In part to prevent violence and disorder, the U.S. army chief of staff
before the war, General Eric K. Shinseki, predicted that "several"
hundreds of thousands of troops would be required. But the civilian
leaders of the Pentagon dismissed this assessment and launched the war
with considerably fewer combat troops—some 150,000. The reasons
for this decision are unclear, but they seem due to some combination of
the U.S. government's faith in high-tech weaponry, its distaste for
nation-building, its disinclination to take the time to deploy additional
troops as summer's heat rose in Iraq and the political heat of opposition
to the war mounted around the world, and its excessive reliance on
wishful thinking and best-case scenarios. The result is that coalition
troops were quickly overwhelmed by the enormity of the task of
maintaining public order in Iraq. Looting was pervasive. Arms caches
were raided and emptied. Violence was rampant.

The problem of understaffing was only compounded by the failure to
deploy an adequate number of troops trained in policing. Regular
troops are trained to fight—to meet threats with lethal force. But that
presumptive resort to lethal force is inappropriate and unlawful when it
comes to policing an occupied nation. The consequence was a steady

stream of civilians killed when coalition troops—on edge in the face of regular resistance attacks, many perfidious—mistakenly fired on civilians. That only increased resentment among Iraqis and fueled further attacks. Troops trained in policing—that is, trained to use lethal force as a last resort—would have been better suited to conduct occupation duties humanely. But the Pentagon has not made a priority of developing policing skills among its troops, leaving relatively few to be deployed in Iraq.

To top it all off, L. Paul Bremer III, the U.S. administrator in Iraq, disbanded the entire Iraqi army and police force. That left the occupying authorities without a large pool of indigenous forces that could have helped to establish the rule of law. We recognize that security forces or intelligence agencies that had played a lead role in atrocities, such as the Special Republican Guard or the Mukhabarat, should have been disbanded and their members prosecuted. Some members of the Iraqi army and police were also complicit in atrocities, but the average member had significantly less culpability; there was no penal justification for disbanding these forces en masse rather than pursuing the guilty on an individual basis. The blanket dismissal took a toll on Iraqi security.

The lack of an overriding humanitarian purpose also affected Washington's attitude toward the system of justice to be used to try Iraqi officials' human rights crimes. The Bush administration, like many other people, clearly would like to see those responsible for atrocities in Iraq brought to justice, but its greater distaste for the International Criminal Court (ICC) has prevented it from recommending the justice mechanism that is most likely to succeed. The administration has insisted that accused Iraqi officials be tried before an "Iraqi-led process." In theory, it is certainly preferable for Iraq to try its own offenders. But after three-and-a-half decades of Ba`th Party rule, the Iraqi judicial system has neither a tradition of respect for due process nor the capacity to organize and try a complex case of genocide or crimes against humanity. Were such prosecutions to proceed in Iraqi courts, there is much reason to believe that they would be show trials.

The obvious solution to this problem is to establish an international criminal tribunal for Iraq—either a fully international one such as those established for Rwanda and former Yugoslavia, or an internationally led tribunal with local participation such as the special court created for Sierra Leone. Although the Bush administration has supported these pre-existing tribunals, it adamantly opposes an international tribunal for Iraq. The reason appears to lie in the ICC. The ICC itself would be largely irrelevant for this task since its jurisdiction would begin at the earliest in July 2002, when the treaty establishing it took effect. Most crimes of the Saddam Hussein government were committed before that. But the administration so detests the ICC that it opposes the creation of any international tribunal for Iraq, apparently out of fear that such a new tribunal would lend credibility to the entire project of international justice and thus indirectly bolster the ICC. An overriding concern with the best interests of the Iraqi people would have made it less likely that this ideological position prevailed.

Compliance with Humanitarian Law

Every effort should be made to ensure that a humanitarian intervention is carried out in strict compliance with international human rights and humanitarian law. Compliance is required in all conflicts—no less for an intervention that is justified on humanitarian grounds. The invasion of Iraq largely met this requirement, but not entirely. Coalition forces took extraordinary care to avoid harming civilians when attacking fixed, pre-selected targets. But their record in attacking mobile targets of opportunity was mixed.

As Human Rights Watch reported in detail in its December 2003 report on the war, U.S. efforts to bomb leadership targets were an abysmal failure. The 0-for-50 record reflected a targeting method that bordered on indiscriminate, allowing bombs to be dropped on the basis of evidence suggesting little more than that the leader was somewhere in a community. Substantial civilian casualties were the predictable result.

U.S. ground forces, particularly the Army, also used cluster munitions near populated areas, with predictable loss of civilian life. After roughly a quarter of the civilian deaths in the 1999 NATO bombing of Yugoslavia were caused by the use of cluster bombs in populated areas, the U.S. Air Force substantially curtailed the practice. But the U.S. Army apparently never absorbed this lesson. In responding to Iraqi attacks as they advanced through Iraq, Army troops regularly used cluster munitions in populated areas, causing substantial loss of life. Such disregard for civilian life is incompatible with a genuinely humanitarian intervention.

Better Rather Than Worse

Another factor for assessing the humanitarian nature of an intervention is whether it is reasonably calculated to make things better rather than worse in the country invaded. One is tempted to say that anything is better than living under the tyranny of Saddam Hussein, but unfortunately, it is possible to imagine scenarios that are even worse. Vicious as his rule was, chaos or abusive civil war might well become even deadlier, and it is too early to say whether such violence might still emerge in Iraq.

Still, in March 2003, when the war was launched, the U.S. and U.K. governments clearly hoped that the Iraqi government would topple quickly and that the Iraqi nation would soon be on the path to democracy. Their failure to equip themselves with the troops needed to stabilize post-war Iraq diminished the likelihood of this rosy scenario coming to pass. However, the balance of considerations just before the war probably supported the assessment that Iraq would be better off if Saddam Hussein's ruthless reign were ended. But that one factor, in light of the failure to meet the other criteria, does not make the intervention humanitarian.

U.N. Approval

There is considerable value in receiving the endorsement of the U.N. Security Council or another major multilateral body before launching a humanitarian intervention. The need to convince others of the appropriateness of a proposed intervention is a good way to guard against pretextual or unjustified action. An international commitment to an intervention also increases the likelihood that adequate personnel and resources will be devoted to the intervention and its aftermath. And approval by the Security Council, in particular, ends the debate about the legality of an intervention.

However, in extreme situations, Human Rights Watch does not insist on Security Council approval. The council in its current state is simply too imperfect to make it the sole mechanism for legitimizing humanitarian intervention. Its permanent membership is a relic of the post-World War II era, and its veto system allows those members to block the rescue of people facing slaughter for the most parochial of reasons. In light of these faults, one's patience with the council's approval process would understandably diminish if large-scale slaughter were underway. However, because there was no such urgency in early 2003 for Iraq, the failure to win council approval, let alone the endorsement of any other multilateral body, weighs heavily in assessing the intervenors' claim to humanitarianism.

We recognize, of course, that the Security Council was never asked to consider a purely humanitarian intervention in Iraq. The principal case presented to it was built on the Iraqi government's alleged possession of and failure to account for weapons of mass destruction. Even so, approval might have ameliorated at least some of the factors that stood in the way of the invasion being genuinely humanitarian. Most significantly, a council-approved invasion is likely to have yielded more troops to join the predominantly American and British forces, meaning that preparation for the post-war chaos might have been better.

Conclusion

In sum, the invasion of Iraq failed to meet the test for a humanitarian intervention. Most important, the killing in Iraq at the time was not of the exceptional nature that would justify such intervention. In addition, intervention was not the last reasonable option to stop Iraqi atrocities. Intervention was not motivated primarily by humanitarian concerns. It was not conducted in a way that maximized compliance with international humanitarian law. It was not approved by the Security Council. And while at the time it was launched it was reasonable to believe that the Iraqi people would be better off, it was not designed or carried out with the needs of Iraqis foremost in mind.

In opening this essay, we noted that the controversial invasion of Iraq stood in contrast to the three African interventions. In making that point, we do not suggest that the African interventions were without problems. All suffered to one degree or another from a mixture of motives, inadequate staffing, insufficient efforts to disarm and demobilize abusive forces, and little attention to securing justice and the rule of law. All of the African interventions, however, ultimately confronted ongoing slaughter, were motivated in significant part by humanitarian concerns, were conducted with apparent respect for international humanitarian law, arguably left the country somewhat better off, and received the approval of the U.N. Security Council. Significantly, all were welcomed by the relevant government, meaning that the standards for assessing them are more permissive than for a nonconsensual intervention.

However, even in light of the problems of the African interventions, the extraordinarily high profile of the Iraq war gives it far more potential to affect the public view of future interventions. If its defenders continue to try to justify it as humanitarian when it was not, they risk undermining an institution that, despite all odds, has managed to maintain its viability in this new century as a tool for rescuing people from slaughter.

The Iraq war highlights the need for a better understanding of when military intervention can be justified in humanitarian terms. The above-noted International Commission on Intervention and State Sovereignty was one important effort to define these parameters. Human Rights Watch has periodically contributed to this debate as well, including with this essay, and various academic writers have offered their own views. But no intergovernmental body has put forth criteria for humanitarian intervention.

This official reticence is not surprising, since governments do not like to contemplate uninvited intrusions in their country. But humanitarian intervention appears to be here to stay—an important and appropriate response to people facing mass slaughter. In the absence of international consensus on the conditions for such intervention, governments inevitably are going to abuse the concept, as the United States has done in its after-the-fact efforts to justify the Iraq war.

Human Rights Watch calls on intergovernmental organizations, particularly the political bodies of the United Nations, to end the taboo on discussing the conditions for humanitarian intervention. Some consensus on these conditions, in addition to promoting appropriate use of humanitarian intervention, would help deter abuse of the concept and thus assist in preserving a tool that some of the world's most vulnerable victims need.

In 2002, villagers fled their homes in Ituri province, northeastern Congo, where fighting among local militias serving as proxies for the Rwandan, Ugandan, and Congolese governments has resulted in the death of some 50,000 people. It is estimated that, in the past five years, war-related violence, disease, and displacement have killed 3.3 million people in the Democratic Republic of Congo. © 2002 Marcus Perkins/Tearfund

Africa on its Own: Regional Intervention and Human Rights

By Binaifer Nowrojee[1]

Despite the continued gloomy reality of much reporting from Africa, the current moment is in fact one of hope for the continent. Though a quarter of Africa's countries were affected by conflict in 2003, several long-running wars have recently ended, including the twenty-five year war in Angola. In the Democratic Republic of Congo (DRC) all the major actors signed agreements and began a period of political transition, although scattered military activity continued in the east. In Burundi the government and the leading rebel force reached agreement in October and November 2003, but the government continued to fight against a smaller rebel movement in areas near the capital. Talks to end the brutal wars in Sudan and Liberia appeared likely to bear fruit.

Perhaps more importantly, new continental institutions and policy frameworks are creating the political space needed to discuss openly the roots of conflict—the source of Africa's worst abuses—in threats to democracy, human rights, and the rule of law. The transformation of the Organization of African Unity (OAU) into the African Union (A.U.) in 2002 offers unprecedented opportunities to begin to address the

---

[1] The writing of this essay was coordinated by Binaifer Nowrojee, but relies heavily on contributions from all members of the Human Rights Watch Africa Division, particularly Bronwen Manby, Alison DesForges, Anneke Van Woudenberg, Corinne Dufka, Leslie Lefkow, Sara Rakita, Nobuntu Mbelle, and Kate Fletcher.

reasons why Africa has been such a troubled continent since most of its states achieved independence forty or so years ago.

At the level of peacekeeping or "peace enforcement," military intervention in conflict-affected countries sponsored by African continental or sub-regional institutions is increasingly becoming a reality. The major world powers have not given the United Nations (U.N.) the capacity to respond effectively to Africa's wars. And, though Africa's former colonizers have sent troops in recent years to areas ravaged by conflict—including the 2000 British intervention in Sierra Leone and the ongoing French engagement in Côte d'Ivoire since late 2002—the major powers have repeatedly made it clear that they will not make the necessary commitment to prevent the massive human rights violations in Africa that result from conflict (Rwanda, the DRC, Burundi, and the Central African Republic being some examples of such neglect). The European Union intervention in the northeastern region of Ituri was an exception, prompted by fear of genocide and strictly limited in time to the period necessary for the U.N. to increase its forces in that troubled region. In this context, African states have no choice but to take up the challenge.

At both international and continental levels, the historical response to war in Africa has been hand-wringing when hostilities break out, but little if anything in the way of serious preventive action. Yet there are often obvious signs that war may be coming—in particular official policies that violate human rights through systematic discrimination and disregard for the rule of law, stolen elections (if any are held at all), and impunity for gross abuses. At least on paper, the A.U. and initiatives it has adopted—including the New Partnership for Africa's Development (NEPAD) and the Conference on Security, Stability, Development and Cooperation in Africa (CSSDCA)—provide a means for African states that are committed to furthering respect for human rights and acting to preempt conflict to apply pressure to governments that abuse their power.

This essay outlines the new institutions of the A.U. and the commitments to human rights that they make. It then considers four recent military peacekeeping interventions—in Burundi, Liberia, Côte d'Ivoire, and the DRC—that have been endorsed by African regional institutions. Although these interventions were undertaken with explicitly humanitarian motives, the human rights component has continued to be inadequate. Finally, the essay considers how, despite their commitments on paper, African states have yet to act on the commitments made in the Constitutive Act of the A.U. to ensure respect for democracy, human rights, and the rule of law in all states of the continent—the most important conflict prevention measure available.

Building Institutional Capacity to Intervene: the A.U. and Conflict Prevention

African leaders have recently reformed, fairly radically, the continent's institutions and policies. In 2002, the forty-year-old OAU was dissolved and reconstituted as the A.U. In contrast to the OAU, the A.U. is provided with the Constitutive Act that envisages a more integrated level of continental governance, possibly eventually paralleling that of the

European Union. Under the OAU, state sovereignty was paramount: non-interference in the internal affairs of member states was its trademark. Regional or sub-regional interventions like those by the Economic Community of West African States (ECOWAS) in conflicts in Liberia and Sierra Leone were the exception, not the rule.

Under the A.U.'s Constitutive Act, there is a commitment to "promote and protect human and peoples' rights," and it specifies that "governments which shall come to power through unconstitutional means shall not be allowed to participate in the activities of the Union." It also provides for a fifteen-member Peace and Security Council to replace the OAU's Mechanism for Conflict Prevention, Management, and Resolution. Once established, the council will facilitate the A.U.'s response to crises and will "promote and encourage democratic practices, good governance and the rule of law, protect human rights and fundamental freedoms, respect for the sanctity of human life and international humanitarian law, as part of efforts for preventing conflicts." As of October 2003, seventeen African countries, of the twenty-seven needed, had ratified the A.U. Protocol on Peace and Security, which would set up the Peace and Security Council. The A.U. Protocol explicitly authorizes the organization to "intervene in a Member State ... in respect of grave circumstances, namely: war crimes, genocide and crimes against humanity."

At the same time as the process establishing the A.U. was ongoing, African governments—led by South Africa, Nigeria, Senegal and Algeria—created another new mechanism to promote good governance and economic development: the New Partnership for Africa's

40

Development (NEPAD), and the related African Peer Review Mechanism. NEPAD is focused on economic development, but unusually, explicitly recognizes that: "Peace, security, democracy, good governance, human rights, and sound economic management are conditions for sustainable development." It proposes systems for monitoring adherence to the rule of law that can promote respect for human rights, in addition to perhaps serving as a check to prevent conditions in a given country from deteriorating to the point of insurgency or conflict. NEPAD has now been adopted as a formal program of the A.U.

One of the proposed systems for monitoring adherence to the rule of law is NEPAD's African Peer Review Mechanism (APRM). Under the APRM, a group of African "eminent persons" is to conduct periodic reviews of members' "policies and practices" "to ascertain progress being made towards achieving mutually agreed goals." Membership in the APRM is not mandatory. Rather, states choose peer review by signing an additional memorandum of understanding, adopted in March 2003. At this writing, a dozen countries have joined.

The Conference on Security, Stability, Development and Cooperation in Africa—on which the A.U. also adopted a Memorandum of Understanding in 2002—includes a set of undertakings on a wide range of issues related to human rights, democracy, and the rule of law. The CSSDCA, loosely modeled on the Organization for Security and Cooperation in Europe (OSCE), has a peer review implementation mechanism that resembles but in some respects is stronger than NEPAD's. There are obvious areas of overlap between the CSSDCA and NEPAD, and there is now an attempt to coordinate the two processes, with ongoing discussions about harmonizing the standards used and division of responsibilities under the different review systems.

NEPAD has been endorsed by virtually all international agencies and bilateral donors, from the U.N. General Assembly to the European Union (E.U.), Japan, and the United States (U.S.), as the general framework around which the international community should structure its development efforts in Africa. Perhaps most important among these endorsements is that of the Group of Eight (G8) industrialized countries, which adopted an Africa Action Plan at its 2002 summit. The G8 plan sets out a detailed list of engagements in support of the A.U.'s priorities, focusing on human rights and political governance as well as on economic issues. The G8 plan included some good—though carefully limited—language on the promotion of peace and security in Africa; the only G8 promise with a hard deadline was "to deliver a joint plan, by 2003, for the development of African capability to undertake peace support operations, including at the regional level." A report on progress in implementing the Africa Action Plan was duly presented to the 2003 G8 summit. But though the report reads as if much has been achieved, in practice there have been more words than action or financial support. The promised plan for the development of African capacity in peace support operations itself acknowledged freely that "it will take time and considerable resources to create, and establish the conditions to sustain, the complete range of capabilities needed to fully undertake complex peace support operations and their related activities."

Regional Interventions

We are likely to see more African interventions to stem conflict in the coming years. Though they can make a useful contribution, as the examples below demonstrate, there are also many possible pitfalls; as these and other cases have already shown. A regional intervention may ignore critical post-conflict components such as justice, demobilization, and restructuring the armed forces. Regional politics may interfere with and undermine the humanitarian nature of the intervention. Funding limitations may hinder a timely and effective intervention. Peacekeepers may be recruited from national armies that regularly commit abuses against their own citizens; and in some cases from neighboring countries that have an interest in the conflict they are supposed to be policing. The intervention may fail to establish mechanisms of accountability to punish peacekeepers that commit human rights violations and thus itself further contribute to an environment of impunity.

Lastly, African regional interventions may encourage the wider international community in its tendency to abdicate its responsibility to respond to African crises. The reality is that Africa's peacekeeping capabilities cannot in the short run equal those of wealthier countries. Even if wealthier countries make a more serious financial commitment to peacekeeping in Africa than has historically been the case—that is, even if the G8's promises are fulfilled—Africa should not be expected to take sole charge of the burden of attempting to prevent or respond to war on the continent.

In 2003, regional and continental African bodies demonstrated an increased willingness to respond both militarily and politically to regional

43

crises. Of all the sub-regional bodies, the West African group ECOWAS continued to play the most prominent role in addressing conflicts in Côte d'Ivoire and Liberia. In May, the ECOWAS security committee resolved to create a rapid response military force to tackle sub-regional crises, and also agreed to strengthen the regional arms moratorium. ECOWAS is also in the process of establishing early warning centers in the troubled West African region.

The trend towards greater regional intervention was most evident in four countries:

- Burundi, where the A.U. mounted its first peacekeeping operation in 2003.

- Côte d'Ivoire, where some 1,300 ECOWAS troops coordinated with 3,800 French forces in monitoring the fragile cease-fire that ended the civil war sparked in September 2002.

- Liberia, where, after President Charles Taylor stepped down, 3,500 ECOWAS peacekeepers deployed in and around the capital, Monrovia, pending the arrival of U.N. forces. ECOWAS also brokered an August 2003 ceasefire and an agreement to establish an interim government.

- Democratic Republic of Congo, where the Southern African Development Community (SADC) justified intervention on the grounds that a SADC member state was fighting an extra-territorial threat. The intervention included attempts to mediate peace in DRC and the deployment of troops.

All of these interventions were prompted by conflict that has caused massive suffering to civilian populations. Yet their human rights component remained marginal.

Burundi

The decade-long civil war in Burundi was sparked when an elected Hutu president was assassinated in 1993 by soldiers from the Tutsi-dominated government army. The war has claimed more than 200,000 lives and has been marked by daily violations of international humanitarian law by all sides: killings, rape, and torture of civilians, the use of child soldiers, and the forced displacement of populations.

After a series of ceasefire agreements between the government and three of four rebel movements, a transitional government took power. Legislators passed several laws important for delivering justice, including a long-promised law against genocide, war crimes, and crimes against humanity; and the country received a new infusion of foreign aid. But the government and the leading rebel movement, the Forces for the Defense of Democracy (FDD), continued combat sporadically until October and November 2003 when they signed protocols renewing their commitment to a cease-fire and began incorporating FDD members into the government and the army. The final ceasefire protocol included guarantees of unlimited and undefined "provisional immunity" from prosecution for both forces, calling into question all previous efforts to ensure accountability for violations of international humanitarian law. Meanwhile the war continued between government

troops and a smaller rebel movement, the Forces for National
Liberation, that held territory around the capital.

The A.U.'s initial intervention in Burundi was a traditional peacekeeping
mission, deployed to enforce the 2000 Arusha Peace Accords rather
than to curtail an immediate crisis. It was based on and expanded a
smaller force of South African troops present to protect opposition
political leaders under the terms of the Arusha Accords. In January
2003, the A.U. authorized the dispatch of a small military observer
mission to monitor the ceasefire. A month later, at an extraordinary
summit, the A.U. approved a larger peacekeeping mission, the African
Mission in Burundi (AMIB). The A.U. mandated AMIB to disarm,
demobilize, and reintegrate into society all rebel troops and to monitor
the country's post-war transition to democracy. By October, a 3,500-
strong force had been deployed to Burundi, largely from South Africa,
Ethiopia, and Mozambique. However, delays in donor funding,
bureaucratic inertia, and the absence of a political agreement initially
frustrated the A.U. peace effort. In addition, there was growing concern
that inadequate facilities and arrangements for the cantonment of Hutu
rebels would undermine the implementation of the ceasefire.

The Burundi peacekeeping mission charged peacekeepers with
protecting government buildings, facilitating rebel demobilization, and
paving the way for elections in 2004. The mandate says nothing about
protecting civilians, but its rules of engagement do provide for
intervention in the event of massive violence against civilians. Still
largely confined to the capital at this writing in December 2003, AMIB
soldiers had not played a role in limiting abuses against non-combatants.

46

Although the mission did not have a human rights mandate, it did include election-related issues, a first for A.U.-initiated interventions.

As with any such endeavor, difficulties and challenges abounded. Because the parties to the peace process failed to resolve issues such as the restructuring of the national army, the peacekeepers could not move forward with programs to demobilize and reintegrate combatants.

Regional leaders, led initially by Tanzania and Uganda, had long attempted to end the war, but without success. South Africa assumed a greater role after the Arusha Accords were signed. When the United Nations, designated by the Accords to provide troops to protect opposition leaders, refused to do so until there was an effective ceasefire, South Africa provided the necessary soldiers for implementation to go forward. South Africa paid the cost of these soldiers, who later became the core of the AMIB force while other contributors to AMIB, Ethiopia and Mozambique, received support from the United States and the United Kingdom to help cover their expenses. South Africa pushed vigorously for the October and November 2003 protocols ending combat between the government and the FDD rebels, in part because it could then ask the United Nations to send peacekeepers to replace its own troops and end its expensive commitment to peacekeeping in Burundi. In welcoming the protocols, South African leaders said nothing about the guarantee of provisional immunity. Other international leaders—including U.N. Secretary-General Kofi Annan—equally anxious to end combat in Burundi, also remained silent about the indefinite delay in demanding justice for crimes against civilians.

47

Liberia

Liberia has seen ECOWAS-led peacekeeping operations since 1990. The flow of arms and combatants, including mercenaries, across its porous borders has destabilized the country for over a decade and its conflict has spilled over into neighboring Sierra Leone and Côte d'Ivoire, as well as into Guinea. Liberia is likely to remain a source of regional instability for some time, despite ECOWAS's efforts and its successful brokering of a peace agreement.

The ECOWAS military intervention at the start of civil war in 1990 was a Nigerian-led operation that remained in Liberia for nine years. It successfully set up a haven of relative peace around the capital city and protected civilians within the perimeter of its control—though the peacekeepers also committed abuses against civilians or suspected rebels on occasion. The peacekeepers also provided economic and arms support to factions opposed to Charles Taylor (leader of one of the most successful and most abusive armed groups), thereby contributing to the proliferation of rebel groups. In 1997, with support from the United Nations, ECOWAS promoted a peace plan and oversaw the highly flawed elections that brought Charles Taylor to office as head of state. In 1999, the ECOWAS troops left Liberia.

Prompted by the 1990 intervention, ECOWAS began to strengthen its institutional conflict-response mechanisms. In 1993, ECOWAS expanded its founding treaty to include peace and security in its mandate. ECOWAS subsequently created a Mediation and Security Council with the authority to deploy military forces by a two-thirds vote.

It was not long before ECOWAS dispatched a peacekeeping force to Sierra Leone. Following a 1997 insurgency by the Revolutionary United Front (RUF), a rebel group supported by Charles Taylor, by then Liberian president, ECOWAS sent forces to Sierra Leone to quell its decade-long civil war. In 1998, ECOWAS troops helped to restore to power the elected government of President Ahmad Tejan Kabbah. The ECOWAS mandate in Sierra Leone ended in 1999, when the United Nations deployed peacekeepers. Most of the ECOWAS contingents were absorbed into the U.N. mission. In 2000, Sierra Leone collapsed back into war for another two years, as the RUF returned to the bush, but a bilateral intervention by the United Kingdom and a beefed up U.N. presence eventually contributed to the ending of the war and the holding of elections in 2002. U.N. troops, as well as a small British contingent, remained in a post-war Sierra Leone as of late 2003.

Liberia once again descended into civil war in 2000. The two rebel groups, Liberians United for Reconciliation and Democracy (LURD) and the Movement for Democracy in Liberia (MODEL), and government forces each committed widespread atrocities. But not until 2003 did ECOWAS finally redeploy peacekeepers to Liberia. The situation in Liberia deteriorated in the latter half of 2003 as LURD and MODEL fought their way to the capital Monrovia, indiscriminately shelling civilian areas. Under the auspices of ECOWAS, President John A. Kufour of Ghana began hosting peace talks in June 2003. A ceasefire was signed in mid-June but fighting continued. In early August, Taylor resigned his presidency and fled to Nigeria, where he was offered shelter, despite an indictment for war crimes by the Special Court for Sierra Leone. After two-and-a-half months, the Ghana talks culminated in the signing of a peace agreement on August 18, 2003.

The first of the new contingent of ECOWAS peacekeepers arrived in Liberia on August 4, 2003. ECOWAS shifted troops from Sierra Leone in order to deploy some 3,000 West African ECOMIL (ECOWAS Military Mission in Liberia) peacekeepers. The ECOMIL troops brought much needed calm to the capital, and led the way for the deployment of a 15,000-strong U.N. peacekeeping force approved by the U.N. Security Council in early September. The mission deployed in October, and the ECOMIL troops became the first contingent of U.N. troops in Liberia.

Given its historic ties to Liberia, the United States seemed the obvious candidate to lead an international peacekeeping mission, as the United Kingdom and France had done in Sierra Leone and Côte d'Ivoire, respectively. Yet the U.S. refused to assume any risk or responsibility for curtailing the crisis in Liberia. After much debate, the U.S. made only a weak, largely symbolic intervention: some 2,000 U.S. Marines were stationed on vessels off-shore, but a mere 200 landed in Monrovia. These 200 troops landed only after ECOMIL had taken control of Monrovia and the rebels had withdrawn from the immediate area. They stayed on shore only a few days and the entire U.S. force withdrew from the area roughly ten days later. The U.S.'s paltry intervention came as a huge disappointment; many believed that the presence of U.S. troops would have calmed significantly the volatile situation and enabled West African peacekeepers to deploy outside the capital where serious abuses were continuing. It also would have made recruiting forces for the U.N. peacekeeping force much easier.

The A.U.'s role in Liberia has been disappointing on the question of justice. The A.U. remained silent regarding the Special Court for Sierra

Leone's indictment of Taylor for war crimes in connection with his support for the RUF. The A.U. took no position when the indictment was unsealed and Ghana's President Kufour chose not to arrest Taylor during the peace talks in Accra. Neither the A.U. nor ECOWAS has called on Nigeria's President Obasanjo, who offered Taylor refuge in Nigeria, to arrest Taylor and transfer him to Sierra Leone for trial. The ECOWAS-brokered Liberian peace agreement made no clear recommendations for or commitments to justice; it is uncertain what kind of justice mechanisms, if any, will be established to address crimes committed during the war. Given the dangerous regional nature of the Liberian crisis, with Guinea and Côte d'Ivoire providing ongoing support to Liberian rebel groups, the AU should also take steps to denounce Liberia's neighbors and others providing support to abusive armed insurgency groups. The A.U. appointed a special envoy for Liberia, who could and should urge respect for human rights.

Côte d'Ivoire

Since September 19, 2002, Côte d'Ivoire has been gripped by an internal conflict that has paralyzed the economy, split the political leadership, and illuminated the stark polarization of Ivorian society along ethnic, political, and religious lines. It is a conflict that has been characterized by relatively little in the way of active hostilities between combatants, but by widespread and egregious abuses against civilians. It is a conflict that, while primarily internal, developed regional dimensions when both the Ivorian rebel groups and the government of Côte d'Ivoire recruited Liberian mercenary fighters to support their forces in the west.

ECOWAS quickly recognized the gravity of the Ivorian situation, touching as it did the economic heart of the region, and began mediation efforts within days of the initial uprising. ECOWAS concerns largely centered on the economic and humanitarian impact of the crisis and the risks to regional stability posed by the conflict. In October 2002, ECOWAS mediators brokered a ceasefire, and both the Ivorian government and the main rebel group, the Patriotic Movement of Côte d'Ivoire (Mouvement Patriotique de la Côte d'Ivoire, MPCI) authorized an ECOWAS monitoring mission. However, the ECOWAS commitment to send troops was hampered by funding constraints and stalled for more than two months after it was made. In the interim, France agreed to fill the gap, expanding its longstanding military presence and extending its mandate from protection of French nationals to ceasefire monitoring.

Despite these efforts, the Ivorian conflict intensified with the opening of the western front, the involvement of Liberian forces on both sides, and the proliferation of rebel groups in December 2002. ECOWAS military engagement remained minimal until early 2003, despite consistent efforts to broker cease-fires, set up peace negotiations, and bring the parties to conflict together. As ECOWAS efforts stalled, French concern deepened and France's contributions increased on both the military and political fronts. By early 2003, there were over 2,500 French troops in Côte d'Ivoire working in conjunction with over 500 ECOWAS forces, and a French-brokered peace agreement, the Linas-Marcoussis accords, had been signed by the government and all three rebel groups. ECOWAS and A.U. officials continued to apply pressure to both the Ivorian government and rebel forces, with Ghana's president, John Kufuor, playing a particularly prominent role as head of ECOWAS.

Additional ceasefire agreements and negotiations led to an officially-proclaimed end to the conflict in July 2003, but implementation of the Linas-Marcoussis accords was slow. Working in conjunction with a small U.N. political and military liaison mission, MINUCI, and some 4,000 French troops, the ECOWAS operation helped monitor compliance with the peace agreement between the Ivorian government and rebel forces. As of late-May 2003, approximately 1,300 ECOWAS troops were in place in the country. However, insufficient resources remained a serious constraint.

In spite of intense regional and French efforts, Côte d'Ivoire's hopes for peace remained deadlocked as of November 2003. At this writing, disarmament has still not taken place, and the government of reconciliation formed by the peace accord has been handicapped by continuing splits between the warring parties. The growth of a vocal, violent, pro-government militia movement with links to the state armed forces, has done little to ease tensions. Abuses against civilians, both in Abidjan and rural areas, have continued, albeit on a lesser scale than during the "official" war.

Continuing impunity remains a fundamental problem. Despite domestic, regional, and international recognition of the serious abuses that took place during the conflict and in election-related violence in 2000, to date there have been no significant steps taken to bring perpetrators of abuses to justice. Key human rights provisions in the peace accords included the establishment of a national human rights commission and an international commission of inquiry, yet neither has materialized. In February 2003, the A.U. called for an investigation by the African Commission on Human Rights, but has since remained silent on the subject. Yet impunity remains one of the key underlying causes of the conflict in Côte d'Ivoire. Long-term resolution of the conflict will require not only political and military engagement by ECOWAS and the A.U., but resolute action to condemn human rights abuses and use financial and political leverage to restore the rule of law.

From the start of the conflict, the U.N. deferred to France on political and military matters concerning Côte d'Ivoire. A Security Council resolution in February 2003 condemned human rights abuses in the conflict and conferred authority on French and ECOWAS forces to intervene. The U.N. Mission in Côte d'Ivoire (MINUCI) was proposed in late April and approved in early May 2003. Initially, the mission included military observers and liaison officers and a vital human rights monitoring component. But the Security Council cut human and financial resources for the mission's civilian components, based mainly on U.S. concerns over the budget and staffing. In advocating such cuts, the U.S. displayed serious short-sightedness: the multitude of abuses in Côte d'Ivoire amply underscored the urgent need for a human rights monitoring component to be included in the peacekeeping effort. The international and donor communities must press aggressively for accountability and respect for human rights, including the use of sanctions and the conditioning of aid. Even where African leaders are taking the initiative, there is still an important continuing role for the international community.

Democratic Republic of Congo (DRC)

From August 1998 until 2003, the DRC was enmeshed in Africa's most devastating and large-scale war, at one point pitting the armies of Rwanda, Uganda, and Burundi together with Congolese rebel groups against the government of DRC supported by Zimbabwe, Angola, and Namibia. Despite three peace agreements aimed at ending the war as well as the creation of a new transitional government that started work in July 2003, sporadic fighting in eastern DRC continued until the end of 2003. It has been estimated that the war led directly or indirectly to the deaths of more than three million civilians, making it more deadly to civilians than any other conflict since World War II.

The conflict in the DRC has presented critical challenges to African leaders. For the A.U., it was a fundamental test of its commitment to conflict prevention, management, and resolution in Africa. For the Southern African Development Community (SADC), the war created significant regional political problems, as member states Zimbabwe, Namibia, and Angola joined, under the SADC umbrella, the former government in Kinshasa to fight the invasion of Uganda and Rwanda. Questions were also raised regarding the legality of the SADC intervention and whether proper authorization procedures were followed by SADC's Organ on Politics, Defense and Security, led at the time by Zimbabwean President Robert Mugabe.

Under the leadership of President Thabo Mbeki, the inaugural chair of the A.U., South Africa brokered talks aimed at a peace agreement between the former Kinshasa government and Rwanda. The talks culminated in the Pretoria Peace Accords of 2002. South Africa also hosted the lengthy inter-Congolese dialogue that paved the way for an eventual government of national unity. South Africa further provided a substantial military contribution to the U.N. peace operation in DRC, agreeing to place some 1,500 South African troops in a forward base in the volatile east.

While crediting the willingness of South Africa to take a leading role in trying to resolve the conflict, critics remarked that its leaders failed to denounce numerous human rights violations by all parties to the war. Some questioned South Africa's neutrality, accusing it of having economic ambitions in DRC and a close partnership with Rwanda. South Africa was also ineffective in its role as a neutral observer for the Third Party Verification Mission (TPVM), a mechanism for implementing the accords that was finally dissolved in late 2003.

Despite the appearance that peace is closer now than ever, immense challenges still confront the new government of national unity in Kinshasa, among them the need for justice for massive human rights violations committed in Congo by all warring parties—domestic and international. Congolese civil society groups have been vocal in demanding an end to impunity. The international community, including the U.N. Security Council, has repeatedly stated that perpetrators will be held responsible for crimes committed during the war. Yet, as of this writing, no mechanism is in place to prosecute crimes committed before July 2002. July 2002 marks the official inauguration of the International Criminal Court (ICC) which Congo has ratified, and crimes committed thereafter fall under its jurisdiction. The A.U.'s ability to respond effectively to the many remaining post-conflict problems in the DRC may be the most challenging test of its commitment to taking a more proactive, continent-wide role.

Conclusion

The A.U.'s growing, if tentative, involvement in some of Africa's worst conflicts is a welcome development. However, its interventions must include a stronger human rights component fully integrated into all aspects of peacekeeping operations. As the cases highlighted in this essay show, African peacekeeping forces need both better training and stronger mandates to protect civilians. There is also an obvious need to integrate African peacekeeping initiatives with U.N. efforts, including by ensuring that the A.U.'s Peace and Security Council is closely linked to the U.N. Security Council, and to increase international—including U.N. and G8—support for peacekeeping initiatives on the continent. It is ironic that it is on the poorest continent that peacekeeping is increasingly being devolved to regional rather than international institutions.

Peacekeeping, moreover, is a limited remedy. Peacekeeping interventions usually engage conflict late and focus primarily on providing short-term, often geographically limited military solutions. While such interventions can save lives and bring about significant improvements in short-term security, they do not in themselves necessarily address the underlying structural causes of conflict, including ensuring respect for human rights, accountable government, and the rule of law.

Among the most difficult of these issues is that of ending impunity for past and ongoing human rights crimes, an area where the A.U. has not been as strong as it should be. Although the OAU Council of Ministers endorsed in 1996 a "Plan of Action Against Impunity in Africa" adopted by the African Commission on Human and Peoples' Rights earlier that year, there has been no real political will to implement this largely NGO-drafted document. African leaders have made a commitment (in a declaration on the CSSDCA adopted in 2000) to "condemn genocide, crimes against humanity and war crimes in the continent and undertake to cooperate with relevant institutions set up to prosecute the perpetrators"—yet a member state of the A.U.—Nigeria—is currently refusing to hand over to justice former President Charles Taylor to the Special Court for Sierra Leone. No A.U. voice has been raised to protest this refusal.

NEPAD proposes four key areas for building Africa's capacity to manage all aspects of conflict, including the need to strengthen regional institutions for conflict prevention, management, and resolution; for peacekeeping; for post conflict reconstruction; and for "combating the illicit proliferation of small arms, light weapons and landmines." Nobody could argue that these are not urgent matters, but in the absence of a strategy to deal with deeper causes they are unlikely to be successful. These deeper causes include widespread impunity not only for the worst atrocities but also for the more mundane large-scale theft of public funds; the illegal extraction and sale of Africa's primary resources; and systematic discrimination on ethnic or regional grounds.

Ultimately the A.U. must strengthen its institutional commitment and capacity to monitor and address human rights violations on a regular basis—and it must act before things deteriorate to a crisis point and require military intervention. Although the documents setting up the new African institutions, including the A.U. Constitutive Act, NEPAD, and the CSSDCA, include many bold statements about the importance of good governance and the rule of law, African leaders have yet to show the will to condemn publicly abuses by their peers and insist that measures are taken to end the abuses. The NEPAD and CSSDCA peer review processes should in theory help correct this problem. The international community has a responsibility to ensure that they have the resources to do so and that African civil society groups are able to monitor them as they begin their work.

The opportunities presented by these new African regional initiatives—this moment of hope—should not be thrown away.

A U.S. soldier checks Afghan women villagers for weapons. Kandahar, Afghanistan, May 2003. (c) 2003 Agence France Presse

Losing the Peace in Afghanistan
By Sam Zia-Zarifi

"Failure is not an option." From President George W. Bush on down, this is how American officials describe their policy toward Afghanistan. This statement crops up so often that it sounds like a mantra, as if simply repeating it enough times will guarantee success. Recently, leaders of the North Atlantic Treaty Organization (NATO) have also taken to this statement, reflecting the extent to which NATO officials believe that the organization's future depends on its success in bringing security to Afghanistan.

Yet repetition of the statement alone does not remove the suspicion, oft-heard in Afghanistan, that it reflects more a political calculation of the cost of failure to U.S. and western interests than it does a commitment to the well-being of the Afghan people. Unless the United States, the de facto leader of the international community in Afghanistan, develops and implements policies that take into account and protect the rights and well-being of Afghans, failure is a very real possibility.

U.S. officials have increasingly referred to Afghanistan as a success story that can serve as a model for Iraq. There are successes to point to in Afghanistan. When the United States and its Coalition partners helped oust the Taliban, they opened a window of opportunity for ordinary Afghans to resume their lives. In the first year after the fall of the

Taliban, some two million Afghans who had fled their country returned (although millions more remain refugees); girls and children regained the possibility of attending school or holding jobs; and the voices of civil society, silenced by over two decades of repression and fighting, again emerged around the country.

Long-term success in Afghanistan (as in other post-conflict situations) will mean protecting and expanding these developments until they become stable and sustainable. This is what Afghans hoped and believed the international community, led by the world's lone superpower, would help them do. But key elements of the U.S. approach in Afghanistan— relying on regional power brokers (warlords) and their troops to maintain order, and downplaying human rights concerns—have in fact slowed the pace of progress and, in many instances, stopped or even reversed it. It is this failure to grasp the opportunities provided in Afghanistan that makes U.S. policies there more of a model of what to avoid than what to replicate.

Failure is never far from the minds of Afghans. For the past two years, wherever Human Rights Watch has been in Afghanistan, Afghans have ranked insecurity as their greatest worry. When they talk about insecurity, Afghans often speak of their fear that the current international project will fail. They fear a return to the mayhem of the warlords or the harsh rule of the Taliban, and they fear new troubles sure to arise from a criminal economy fueled by booming heroin production. Afghans are keenly aware that they are only accidental recipients of international support.

Despite the self-congratulatory liberation rhetoric emanating from Washington, London, and other western capitals, Afghans know that it wasn't humanitarian concern, but the September 11 attacks and Osama bin Laden's unwanted residence in Afghanistan that prompted the international community to take notice of Afghanistan again. Afghans fear that the world outside will fail them and banish them again to insecurity, conflict, and chaos, as happened after the Afghan mujahideen's success in driving out the Soviet Union. Failure following quickly upon proclaimed liberation is an option that Afghans have experienced before, and have no wish to repeat.

Afghans are right to worry. The signs are troubling. Despite the initial enthusiasm for rebuilding the country, the world seems to have forgotten them. International support has been scarce. Comparisons with recent peacekeeping and nation-building exercises are troubling. As pointed out by the humanitarian organization CARE International, in Rwanda, East Timor, Kosovo, and Bosnia, donors spent an average of $250 per person annually in aid. If that average were applied in Afghanistan, the country would receive $5.5 billion in aid every year for the next four years. Instead, it has received pledges amounting to less than one-fourth of that sum. The Henry L. Stimson Center, a Washington, D.C.-based think-tank, has pointed out that in Kosovo the international community spent twenty-five times more money, on a per capita basis, than it has pledged in Afghanistan. Similarly, in Kosovo the international community committed fifty times more troops per capita than it has in Afghanistan. Comparisons with Iraq, of course, are even worse: while Iraq received U.S.$26 billion in reconstruction aid in 2003, Afghanistan received less than $1 billion.

World Report 2004

This inattention has had a tremendously negative impact. Taliban forces are resurgent and emboldened in their attacks on U.S. troops as well as on the government of President Hamid Karzai and the foreign community supporting him. Warlords, militias, and brigands dominate the entire country, including the city of Kabul. Many women and girls, freed from the Taliban's rule, have again been forced out of schools and jobs due to insecurity. Poppy cultivation has soared to new highs, providing billions of dollars to the Taliban, warlords, and petty criminals who resist the central government. Foreign states with long, mostly destructive histories of interference in Afghanistan's affairs—Pakistan, Iran, Saudi Arabia, India, Uzbekistan, and Russia—are again picking local proxies to push their agendas.

What explains the lack of commitment to Afghanistan? A major reason is that the United States, like previous foreign powers in Afghanistan, sees the country as endemically violent and thus excessively relies on a military response to the country's problems. Viewing the country through a prism of violence has contributed to a number of erroneous policies in Afghanistan, to wit: focusing on the short-term defeat of Taliban and al-Qaeda forces with little regard for long-term security concerns; the resultant reliance on warlords on the national and local levels without regard for their legitimacy with the local population; and the shortchanging of nonmilitary measures. This skewed understanding of Afghanistan's problems and their solutions has persisted despite recent indications that Washington policy-makers now recognize the continuing threats posed in Afghanistan and understand some of the mistakes of their past policies.

What would failure mean in Afghanistan? For the community of nations dedicated to the machinery of global order created after the Second World War, abandoning Afghanistan again would constitute a defeat with repercussions well beyond Afghanistan's borders. The country might once again become a training ground for terror.

President Bush declared in April 2002 that he envisioned nothing short of a Marshall Plan for Afghanistan. The whole world is gauging how the United States and other international actors perform in Afghanistan. For NATO, which has just taken over the responsibility of providing security in parts of Afghanistan, failure would mean losing a raison d'être in a world without a Soviet threat. Failure in Afghanistan would be a sign of the global community's impotence and insincerity in transforming failed states. For most Afghans, failure would mean a return to warfare, chaos, and misery.

The goal of creating a stable, civilian government in Afghanistan faces four different but interlinked challenges: increasingly powerful regional warlords, resurgent Taliban forces, growth of the poppy trade and other criminal activity, and a continuing threat of meddling regional powers, in particular Pakistan, Iran, Saudi Arabia, and Russia. All of these challenges have grown more pressing due to international inattention, and all are likely to become even more threatening as Afghanistan enters a politically charged election year, with a constitutional process recently completed and a presidential election set for June of 2004. Failure to meet any of these challenges will greatly increase the chances of failure in Afghanistan and a return to a conflict that savages the Afghans and destabilizes Central Asia, the Middle East, South Asia, and, by providing a haven for criminals and terrorists, the world.

Such an outcome is not inevitable in Afghanistan. Nearly all observers, Afghan and international, agree that progress can be made in Afghanistan. It requires an increased, consistent commitment by the international community. It requires integration of military and economic reconstruction efforts. Most basically, and most crucially, it requires listening to ordinary Afghans who seek international assistance so they can work toward peace and prosperity. A serious commitment to Afghanistan has to be made, and made clearly. There are signs that in some quarters of the U.N. and, most importantly, of the U.S. leadership, this need is now understood. However, this commitment is still not being felt in Afghanistan. Without it, failure is likely.

Shortchanging the Peace

There is widespread agreement among Afghans and international observers that there can be no reconstruction without security, and there can be no security without reconstruction. In Afghanistan, as in other post-conflict situations, construction crews cannot build roads, clinics, or schools if they face threatening forces; armed groups will not give up the way of the gun unless they can make a living and protect their families and livelihood without it.

This is by no means an intractable problem; rather, it points out how international support should be used to help a country emerging from conflict regain a stable peace. International financial aid supports the task of reconstruction, while international security assistance allows hostile groups to stop fighting long enough for reconstruction to help them. The financial aid has to be sufficient in scope to spark reconstruction and generate a self-sustaining cycle of economic growth. The security assistance must be robust enough to discourage forces opportunistically, or intractably, opposed to peace from spoiling the reconstruction. This model has gained widespread acceptance in the past two decades over the course of major reconstruction efforts throughout the world. This was broadly the model promised to Afghans as the U.S. was ousting the Taliban. The international community signaled its commitment to this model in the Bonn Agreement and at the Tokyo donors' conference.

Despite grandiose promises, the international community has been stingy with Afghans. In a shocking display of political short-sightedness, countries that have declared war on terror and on drugs—Afghanistan's two biggest exports in the recent past—have failed or refused to marshal the resources necessary to combat the resurgence of armed groups and drug lords in Afghanistan. Afghans will be the first to pay the price for this failure, but they will not be the last.

President Bush repeatedly invoked the Marshall Plan as a model for U.S. support for Afghanistan. Certainly such a sweeping reconstruction effort, modeled on the United States' largesse and support for Europe after the Second World War, is what is needed in Afghanistan. The country is one of the poorest in the world, with little infrastructure surviving three decades of conflict, no major developed natural resources, and staggeringly poor health care. According to UNICEF, an average of 1,600 women die in Afghanistan for every 100,000 live births. This figure is 12 times worse than in neighboring Iran, and 130 times higher than in the United States. In the northeastern province of Badakhshan, in particular, the area where the country's strongest warlords come from, the mortality rate is 6,500 per 100,000 live births—the highest maternal-mortality ratio ever documented in the world. The mind can barely comprehend the level of human misery now, much less if the current international reconstruction effort fails.

Far easier to grasp is the level of financial assistance necessary and adequate for the job of reconstructing Afghanistan: most estimates suggest that at least $15-20 billion U.S. dollars will be needed over the next five years. The Afghan government believes it needs even more: some $30 billion. These are relatively small sums, as recent peacekeeping and reconstruction efforts go. By comparison, recent reconstruction budgets in Kosovo, Bosnia, and East Timor were up to fifty times greater when measured on a per capita basis. The amount pledged by donors for Afghanistan is also significantly smaller than the $26 billion sum pledged for the reconstruction of Iraq by the United States this year alone. (And, as *The Economist* magazine has pointed out, Afghanistan is larger than Iraq in terms of population, area, and need.)

Not many of those who control the purse strings in the international community seem to have listened to the call for assistance. Despite the call for $20 billion over five years, the international community has pledged only $7 billion ($1.6 billion from the United States).

Of this $7 billion sum, the international community has to date actually provided only $4 billion. Only a third of this amount has made its way to Afghanistan over the last two years. And of that amount, only some $200 million has resulted in completed projects.

So: two years after the fall of the Taliban, during a period when international and local experts have suggested that five to eight billion dollars worth of international aid was necessary for reconstructing Afghanistan, only some two to five percent of the amount has been delivered to Afghanistan. This hardly seems like the formula for success.

Wanted: Peacekeepers

Two years after the fall of the Taliban, security remains poor in much of the country, with most indicators pointing downward and upcoming elections likely only to aggravate the insecurity. The U.S. has simultaneously pursued two policies in Afghanistan. These could be complementary, but instead they conflict with each other: fighting the war against remnants of the Taliban and al-Qaeda, and creating a stable civilian government in Kabul that could eventually bring peace to the whole country. For much of the first year, the first issue dominated, making a mess for the second.

As part of "Operation Enduring Freedom," the United States currently has some 10,000 troops in Afghanistan, with another 2,000 from the United Kingdom, Australia, and other Coalition members. The mandate of these troops is to combat the Taliban, not to provide security for

Afghans. In fact, as of this writing, these troops freely engage and support local warlords and military commanders who ostensibly will fight the Taliban, with little or no regard for how the warlords treat the local citizenry. These troops have no mandate to protect civilians in case of fighting between rival militias; they will not act to enforce the writ of the central government against recalcitrant warlords.

The mandate to help support the central government (but not Afghan civilians directly) falls to the five thousand strong International Security Assistance Force (ISAF), which has had a completely distinct command and control structure from the U.S. forces. Of the five thousand, some one thousand are devoted to protecting embassies and other important foreign institutions.

A comparison with recent post-conflict situations, put forward by CARE International, illuminates the limited scope of the international community's commitment to Afghanistan: while in Kosovo, Bosnia, and East Timor the international peacekeeping force amounted to one peacekeeper per seventy or so people, in Afghanistan that ratio was one peacekeeper per five thousand people.

There is no question that ISAF has been modestly successful in increasing security in Kabul, hence helping support the remarkable economic development that the city has witnessed over the last two years, and demonstrating how quickly Afghans can and will work toward creating a civil society if given the space to do so. But even in Kabul and its immediate environs ISAF did not (or could not) carry out one of its central missions, which was to rid Kabul of factional militias. Armed men, particularly those associated with the forces of Defense Minister Marshall Fahim and fundamentalist warlord Abdul Rasul Sayyaf, still roam the streets by day and engage in robbery and banditry by night.

Afghans outside Kabul have been clamoring for two years to share in the benefits of international security assistance. From the first moments that Human Rights Watch researchers traveled around Afghanistan after the U.S. rout of the Taliban, Afghans told us that they wanted foreign peacekeepers. The chief U.N. representative to Afghanistan, Lakhdar Brahimi, eventually took up this call for expanded security. President Hamid Karzai joined in the clamor too, after his initial bursts of misplaced optimism were taken advantage of by U.S. officials, who claimed that Afghanistan was secure and needed no more aid in that regard.

Many senior European officials also generally accepted the argument for greater security forces. But they said their countries did not have adequate forces to offer; or if they did, they didn't have the ships or airplanes to get them to Afghanistan; or if they did, they lacked the trucks and helicopters necessary to transport them around the country. Meanwhile, the United States—which possessed the only readily available logistical force capable of providing security throughout Afghanistan—kept asking why Europe could not contribute more to the Afghan cause.

This state of affairs lasted until mid-2003. By then, it had become apparent that the security situation in Afghanistan was seriously deteriorating. The Taliban had resurfaced as a military threat in the south and the southeast, while serious clashes were taking place between different factional forces on a regular basis in the northwest and the west. Given this reality, those European allies of the United States that had refused to cooperate with the attack on Iraq felt compelled to contribute to the operations in Afghanistan.

After squandering the first year after the fall of the Taliban, the international community signaled its growing seriousness about dealing with the security problems of Afghanistan. These signals have yet to be translated into concrete results.

The first tentative step was the creation of so-called Provincial Reconstruction Teams. These teams combine some 300 to 400 military and intelligence personnel with reconstruction specialists. The U.S. initially fielded four such teams to Gardez (in the southeast), Kunduz (the north), Mazar-i Sharif (northwest), and Bamiyan (center). As of this writing, the U.K., Germany, and New Zealand have agreed to take over one PRT each, and four other PRTs are scheduled to join them by early 2004 in Herat (the west), Parwan (center), Jalalabad (southeast), and Kandahar (south).

By most accounts, the PRTs have somewhat improved security conditions, although this should not be exaggerated: the city of Mazar-i Sharif, for instance, is still a flashpoint of local conflict despite the presence of a well-regarded British PRT. But the real problem with the PRT program is that it is a bandage being touted as a cure. After months of claiming that no expansion of ISAF was possible because it would require thousands of (unavailable) armed troops, it seems dishonest of the U.S. and the European powers to now claim that a few hundred lightly armed reconstruction teams will suffice to secure Afghanistan. The security mandate of the U.S. PRTs is more focused on force protection than the protection of Afghans. And, at least some military experts have warned that sending the relatively small PRTs out across Afghanistan without adequate military support raises the possibility of leaving them vulnerable to hostile action—threatening repetition of problems encountered in Bosnia, where U.N. peacekeepers effectively became hostages to Serb forces and were unable to protect the civilians under their purview.

Humanitarian aid organizations, which still provide for many of the basic needs of the Afghan people, vociferously oppose the PRTs' confusion of military and aid missions. Such blurring of distinctions poses a real threat to civilian aid workers, who become viewed as agents of the military forces instead of as independent actors, and thus become targets for attack.

It remains to be seen how the PRTs will interact with the newly reconstituted ISAF under NATO command. Clearly, the Afghanistan operation is a major undertaking for NATO. It constitutes NATO's first combat operation outside of Europe, and it signals a possible new direction for an international alliance whose original mission—countering the Soviet threat to Europe—no longer exists. Lord

Robertson, NATO's chairman, powerfully expressed his vision of a new, leaner and meaner NATO that can serve as a global force. He criticized the alliance's current force configuration, where the 1.4 million men in arms of NATO's non-U.S. members can field only 55,000 troops. Whether NATO can overcome its institutional weaknesses remains to be seen. Several military and civilian NATO officials have voiced concerns about the coalition's lack of sufficient logistical and communication equipment in Afghanistan. Such shortcomings could render NATO forces, as well as the PRTs, vulnerable to attack.

Fear, Drugs, and the Taliban

Criminality, particularly poppy cultivation and the heroin trade, has blossomed again in Afghanistan, generating billions of dollars for forces outside the control of any legitimate authority. Much of this trade and the money it generates is under the control, or at least the influence, of various major and minor military commanders, who use this money to increase their military capability and gain independence from the central government and any international troops working with them. The Taliban, too, has used this trade to finance its increasingly sophisticated and brazen attacks. These problems could have been avoided, had the U.S. and the international community acted more responsibly in Afghanistan. All these problems are still resolvable, if the world acts quickly and seriously.

In the absence of the Taliban, which in some years managed to stop nearly all poppy production, or any other limiting authority, opium cultivation has again exploded in Afghanistan. Farmers who have waited futilely for agricultural assistance from the central government or the international community have turned to poppy cultivation. As a result, Afghanistan has regained its position as the world's leading producer of heroin. According to the U.N. Office on Drugs and Crimes, the country's 3,000 metric tons of opium production in 2003 constituted two-thirds of the world's supply and generated revenues of $2.3 billion for Afghan warlords, corrupt provincial authorities, and even the Taliban. Both the absolute and the proportionate impact of drug trafficking is expected to be still higher in 2004 because the laboratories used to transform poppies into opium and heroin are now increasingly located in Afghanistan. This sum—equivalent to nearly half of the legitimate gross domestic product—finances forces opposed to central authority.

Criminality in general—including smuggling of timber and other goods to and from the Middle East, Central Asia, and South Asia—generates large sums of unregulated income. The lure of illicit income is especially strong in the absence of legitimate economic outlets due to failures of reconstruction. Not surprisingly, there are strong indications that the regional armed leaders—the warlords—are extensively involved in the drug and smuggling trade. The more powerful warlords, those with a major political base, do not even need to rely on drug trafficking, confident that they can avoid such potentially problematic sources of income.

The Rule of the Warlords

Who are these warlords? Warlord is not a technical word. In Afghanistan, it is a literal translation of the local phrase "jang salar," and it has simply come to refer to any leader of men under arms. The country has thousands of such men, some deriving their power from a single roadblock, others controlling a town or small area, and still others reigning over large districts. At the apex of this chaotic system are some six or seven major warlords, each with a significant geographic, ethnic, and political base of support. Over the last two years, Human Rights Watch has documented criminality and abuses by commanders small and large, and by nearly all of the major warlords: General Atta and General Dostum in the north, Ismail Khan in the west, Gul Agha Shirzai in the south, Abdul Rasul Sayyaf in the center, and, the most powerful, Marshall Fahim, the senior vice president and minister of defense.

Fahim's background and current behavior illustrates why these men inspire such fear among Afghans. Fahim was one of the mujahideen who fought the Soviets for years under the predominantly Tajik Northern Alliance and the group's fabled leader, Ahmad Shah Massoud. When the mujahideen forced out the Soviets, he became the chief of security for the government of Burhanuddin Rabbani. He inherited the command of the Northern Alliance on September 9, 2001, when suicide bombers assassinated Massoud.

As the fortuitous leader of the last remaining credible force fighting the Taliban, Fahim found himself in a strong position to negotiate with grateful American military forces and to gain an important position in the transitional Afghan authority. Thus his innovative approach to the post of minister of defense: he brought his own army with him. The Northern Alliance forces, estimated to include about 70,000 troops, possess heavy artillery, land and air transport vehicles, and armored vehicles; and they have no loyalty to President Karzai or any other civilian government in Afghanistan. With this force behind him, Fahim bullied Karzai, the United Nations, and the United States into giving him the vice presidency.

Marshall Fahim put this advantage to good use. He immediately began placing fellow Tajiks from the small Panjshir valley north of Kabul in important positions. As he reconstituted the Afghan army, with American and European assistance, he amassed a large cache of weapons and supplies intended for the national army. It is clear that he did not envision the army as facing a foreign threat or even a significant local threat from the Taliban. At the end of 2002, Kabul and the area directly controlled by Fahim (northeast of the capital) housed fourteen divisions. In the north, there were at least ten divisions. By contrast, the west received only four divisions, while the south got another four, and the southeast and the east each received five. The center received two. Of the thirty-eight generals chosen for the new army by Fahim, thirty-seven were Tajiks (the other was Uzbek). Of the thirty-seven Tajiks, thirty-five were linked to Fahim's political group; of a total of one hundred generals appointed by Fahim in early 2002, ninety were from his group.

Fahim's reach extended beyond political and military power. Like many other senior political and military officials, Fahim has reportedly enriched himself through an extensive patronage network that perpetuates and extends his power. Not surprisingly, this network displays nepotism familiar from the Tajik-controlled military.

And yet none of this power translates into improved conditions even for Fahim's fellow Tajiks in Badakhshan, which remains one of the poorest, most oppressed areas in Afghanistan. In Badakhshan, women suffer from the lowest standards of health care in the world, poppy cultivation is rising exponentially, and criticism of the state of affairs is not tolerated.

Despite this sorry record, U.S. military officials defend Fahim as a stalwart ally against the Taliban and a heroic fighter against the Soviets. This is how the warlords cast themselves, and how the U.S. has treated them: mujahideen, defenders of the faith and homeland, who fought against the Soviets and the Taliban until, with American support, they liberated Afghanistan.

In its unwavering support for Marshall Fahim and the other warlords, the United States pretends to forget that they ruled the country for four ruinous, devastating years—years so bad that many Afghans were relieved when the Taliban routed the warlords. The warlords, in their public pronouncements, never refer to what they did from 1992 to 1995, but no Afghan fails to recall these years without a shudder. Marshall Fahim himself has been personally implicated in various purges and atrocities committed by Northern Alliance forces during the civil war that killed some 10,000 civilians in Kabul in 1992 and 1993. Other warlords, like Abdul Rasul Sayyaf, Ismail Khan, General Dostum, and Gul Agha have essentially similar bloody backgrounds.

Furthermore, these warlords and U.S. officials neglect to mention that on October 6, 2001, when the United States began attacking the Taliban, there were almost no warlords left in Afghanistan. By that time, the Taliban had either co-opted the major warlords, or destroyed them. Arbitrary and criminal rule by local warlords had for the most part been replaced by the brutal authoritarian rule of the Taliban, until the September 11 attacks on the United States once again drew the attention of the United States to Afghanistan.

The American attack assumed a military strategy that avoided ground combat and the resulting threat to U.S. forces. The strategy of aerial bombardment, while capable of punishing the Taliban, lacked the ground troops necessary to secure territory. To carry out this task, the United States needed local troops, and for this the United States physically brought back the warlords, rearmed them, financed them, supported them militarily, and reinstalled them in power. The CIA simply handed suitcases of cash to warlords around the country. This investment allowed local commanders to resume their former positions and rearm themselves, ostensibly to take on the Taliban. It also gave them the seed money to become self-sufficient by engaging in smuggling, drug trafficking, and general criminal activity. Predictably, their rule has been nasty and brutal, as grimly documented in numerous accounts gathered by Human Rights Watch researchers and others from throughout Afghanistan over the past two years.

Just as predictably, the warlords have performed as poor proxies in the fight against the Taliban. Most famously, local troops subcontracted by American forces are believed to have allowed Osama bin Laden to escape capture in the mountains of southeastern Afghanistan in the immediate aftermath of the Taliban's retreat. In the time since, these ostensible allies have attacked their personal rivals by providing false information to goad or trick U.S. forces into attack. The depredations and lawlessness perpetrated by these armed thugs have fueled the drug trade, fostered resentment that has renewed the appeal of the Taliban's harsh brand of justice, and squandered the good will of the Afghan people toward the international community.

Take the case of Hazrat Ali, the warlord of Nangarhar province, based in the southeastern city of Jalalabad, astride the main road between Kabul and Pakistan. Hazrat Ali is an ally of Marshall Fahim; in fact, Fahim imposed Hazrat Ali on the province, favoring him over a local candidate in 2002. Wanton looting, sexual assault on women, girls, and boys, intimidation of critics, and brigandage have been the hallmarks of Hazrat Ali's rule—though such abuses are by no means unique to the area under his command.

Press reports consistently link Hazrat Ali to the burgeoning opium trade and smuggling networks now choking Jalalabad. When Human Rights Watch publicly criticized Hazrat Ali, he responded by publicly threatening Human Rights Watch's researchers. But U.S. and U.K. officials have confirmed that Hazrat Ali has received (and likely continues to receive) direct payments for his role in fighting the Taliban and maintaining order in his sector. Meanwhile, the British government, which has taken the lead in the anti-narcotic effort, has failed to provide adequate resources for the job in the area under Hazrat Ali. Afghan anti-narcotic officers have complained about the lack of financial and military support from American and British forces on the crucial trunk road between Kabul and Pakistan.

The Return of the Taliban

The warlords' reemergence and blatant misrule, and the international community's seeming acquiescence, has created fear and despair around Afghanistan, but nowhere more so than among the rural Pashtun of the south. The Pashtun are Afghanistan's largest ethnic group, comprising about 40 percent of the population. They formed the backbone of the Taliban movement, in part reflecting the greater prevalence of conservative religious beliefs among Pashtuns, and in part reflecting their fear of non-Pashtun groups, such as the Northern Alliance, gaining control over Afghanistan. The dominance of Tajik forces in Kabul, personified by Marshall Fahim, has further stoked the Pashtuns' sense of marginalization from political developments in Afghanistan. Thus the Pashtun areas of southern and southeastern Afghanistan have witnessed an upsurge in activity by the Taliban and forces under the command of Gulbuddin Hekmatyar, a long-active extremist warlord with links to Pakistani security forces and Saudi Arabian Wahhabist groups.

The result of this upsurge has been an absolute breakdown in security in the Pashtun areas and increasing human rights violations. The United Nations and international non-governmental organizations now consider nearly two-thirds of the Pashtun-belt as no-go areas. The assassination on November 16, 2003, of Bettina Goislard, a young French staffer for the U.N. High Commissioner for Refugees, underscored this terrible threat. Goislard was the first U.N. worker killed in Afghanistan, but by September 2003, an average of some three- dozen Afghan and international staff members of various aid agencies and reconstruction teams were coming under armed attack. The targeting of foreign and local humanitarian groups suggests a troubling change in tactics by the Taliban and other groups opposed to the central government in Afghanistan.

The resurgent Taliban has exhibited even more violence and less tolerance than during its previous incarnation. Attacks on aid groups in the period between May and August 2003 occurred nearly three times as often as during any period in the previous year. Flush with income from the drug trade (which previously the Taliban seems to have avoided and actively combated), the Taliban can now outspend and outman not just the weak central government in Kabul, but even the U.S. forces: In areas around the southern city of Kandahar, the Taliban is reportedly paying their fighters as much as $70 a week, going up to $120 a week for fighters who attack American forces. The United States is reportedly paying its local warlord allies $60 a week. Not surprisingly, the Taliban now claims to hold large portions of several southern and southeastern provinces.

One thing that unites the Taliban and local warlords who are ostensibly allied with Karzai's government or U.S. forces is their opposition to any legitimate political process in Afghanistan that could return peace and civility to the country. Human Rights Watch documented numerous instances of warlords intimidating local representatives during the constitutional drafting process, which ended in December. These warlords are intent on imposing their own representatives on the upcoming Afghan government and thus completing their entrenchment as sources of power, a process that they began during the emergency *loya jirga* (grand council) in June 2002. As presidential elections slated for June of 2004 approach, it is likely that the warlords will also step up their efforts to grab power.

The Taliban has exhibited less interest in influencing the electoral process than in simply stopping it. It has declared the constitutional process invalid, instead offering its own limited version of religious law. Through "night letters" (surreptitiously distributed pamphlets) and, increasingly through public pronouncements, the Taliban has threatened to harm candidates as well as those who vote in the elections. The Taliban has reserved special venom for those Afghan women daring enough to stand as candidates, threatening not only them, but also their families.

The impact of Taliban intimidation has been dramatic. Compared with elections preceding the emergency loya jirga—which itself faced serious intimidation and intrusion by warlords, participation in elections has dropped across Afghanistan, with the lowest levels seen in the south. The United Nations has reported that popular participation in elections to pick representatives for the constitutional process was so low in some precincts as to challenge the legitimacy of the elections.

The Failure Option

The degenerating security situation has already seriously hampered Afghanistan's political and economic reconstruction. Nevertheless, the electoral process, dictated by the Bonn Agreement, marches on. International experience suggests caution before embarking on a national election where national security has not been established. In Bosnia and Liberia, for instance, the election process aggravated political power rivalries and fostered violence.

The Afghan government is responsible for providing security for elections, but currently lacks the requisite capability. The Afghan National Army, with at most 7,000 effective troops, is still under the command of Marshall Fahim, and lacks the military capacity or the political legitimacy to protect voting booths. The Afghan police force, even more necessary than the army for providing security in cities and towns and along the main roads in Afghanistan, is even worse off than the army. The United Nations Development Fund has established a Law and Order Trust Fund (LOTFA) to gather the estimated $350 million necessary to reform and fund the Afghan police force over the next five years. As of this writing, only $10 million had been delivered to LOTFA by the international community. (The European Union, shocked by the lack of security and the burgeoning drug trade, has reportedly agreed on another $50 million, but this sum had not been delivered at this writing). Police officers, many of whom complain that their salaries have not been paid, cannot reasonably be expected to protect Afghan voters and candidates.

In short, at present there appears to be no alternative to the international community assuming the burden of providing security in the run-up to elections—a responsibility familiar from efforts in the Balkans and in East Timor. Yet inexplicably, the United States and the international community as a whole seem to be ignoring this lesson. The shortage of international security forces, discussed above, is particularly acute when considered in the context of the 2004 elections: Not a single international trooper is mandated to protect the election process. The American forces lack this mandate, the PRTs lack this mandate, and even ISAF (even if expanded under NATO command) lacks this mandate. Although NATO performed an important role in securing elections in Kosovo, apparently the organization's planners have not yet considered such a responsibility in Afghanistan.

Afghans and international observers agree that international assistance is essential to safeguard Afghanistan during this political season, yet international assistance has still not been offered. Without such assistance, a weak Karzai government will likely find itself hostage to the competing demands of ethnically based warlords and the external threat of the Taliban. Afghanistan may return to conditions similar to those that prevailed a decade ago, with several ethnically based militias vying with the Tajiks for control of Kabul while the Taliban, thriving on Pashtun resentment, threatens from the south. Such an outcome would, of course, constitute a failure of the worst kind for Afghans and Afghanistan.

Even if the election takes place without serious incident, there are dangers for Afghanistan—the most obvious is international apathy. With its attention diverted to developments in Iraq, for example, the international community could declare the election a success, usher in a new Afghan government, applaud, and then leave. Under these conditions, the inevitable face-off between the entrenched warlords would begin in earnest as soon as the last foreign soldier left the country.

The Road Forward

A better future for Afghanistan is possible, but it requires international commitment and resources sufficient to begin to set the country on a better course and give Afghans time to prepare to shoulder the burden themselves.

First, the international community must provide economic assistance commensurate to the task of rebuilding Afghanistan. Every step of the reconstruction of Afghanistan has been hampered by a lack of financial assistance. The international community should begin by at least honoring existing pledges to Afghanistan, and then considering new and greater pledges at the upcoming donor conference in Tokyo.

Second, the international community must take responsibility for providing security beyond Kabul. The expanded PRTs are a move in the right direction in terms of improving security, but they hardly suffice. Their mandate needs to be expanded geographically (to cover more areas of Afghanistan) and focused to concentrate on security and leave reconstruction to other organizations. NATO, whose own credibility is on the line, must reassess its mission in Afghanistan, greatly bolster its military capability, and assume rules of engagement that focus on protecting the rights of the Afghan people. Afghan warlords, while they may have thousands of armed men at their command, can hardly stand up to a serious western military force, as amply demonstrated by the much-vaunted Taliban's rapid dissolution in the face of sustained force. The warlords know this, as do many mystified Afghans, who cannot understand why the United States and international institutions seem so cowed by the warlords.

Military experts have repeated that Afghanistan's reconstruction needs a "robust spine"—a military force, relying on air power and quick deployment, that can support the legitimate central government and the reconstruction project. Its existence, and the commitment it signifies, would suffice in many areas to bring into line the majority of regional commanders, whose chief impetus right now is opportunistic profit at the cost of the central government.

Meanwhile, groups intractably opposed to a civilian government in Afghanistan—so-called total spoilers, such as the Taliban, Gulbuddin Hekmatyar, and even some warlords temporarily allied with the central government, like Sayyaf—must be dealt with as a real military threat for some time to come. No Afghan army can or should be expected to assume this burden alone in the near future. Nor should a poorly thought out Afghan army be created as an ostensible cure-all or excuse for international disengagement, as such an army would almost certainly become just another tool in the power struggle between competing factions. For the time being, the responsibility for security rests with the United States and its coalition partners.

Finally, the international community should give greater priority to deploying human rights monitors to gauge conditions on the ground and listen to what the Afghan people are saying. The United States seems to have very little official capacity for engaging the Afghan people directly. The PRTs, for instance, do not have a human rights protection mandate and, as far as is known, do not include any monitors dedicated to human rights protection. The U.N. too lacks this capacity. The United Nations has adopted an admirable policy of operating with a light footprint, but there is a time when the print can be too light. Afghanistan is in such a period now. Only eight human rights monitors are envisioned for covering all of Afghanistan, as opposed to the hundreds that monitored the post-conflict period in Guatemala, East Timor, or the Balkans. Even worse, of these eight, only five positions are filled. U.N. officials claim they simply cannot find qualified candidates for these posts. At a policy level, this seems to violate one of the tenets of Lakhdar Brahimi's own blueprint for U.N. operations, namely that bureaucratic obstacles should not be allowed to hobble operational needs. On a more practical level, however, this obvious failure of management bolsters the suspicion that the United Nations may be reluctant to listen to what Afghans have to say, lest it upset the carefully balanced (though ultimately unstable) political structure maintained in Afghanistan by the United States and the United Nations.

The international community should also support emergent voices for accountability and the rule of law in Afghanistan, such as the brave but beleaguered Afghan Independent Human Rights Commission (AIHRC). Created by the Bonn Agreement, the Commission has performed admirably to date, listening to ordinary Afghans and voicing their concerns, even as each report it issues on abuses by members of the current government is followed by threats to AIHRC members.

One thing AIHRC members have asked for, repeating the demands of ordinary Afghans, is justice for past and current abuses. As mentioned above, many of the senior members of the current cabinet have bloody hands. They should be investigated, arrested, prosecuted. They should be kept out of politics, as was envisioned by the Bonn Agreement. The international community shamefully failed to follow the will of the Afghan people when they allowed warlords into the emergency loya jirga process. They are making the same mistake during the constitutional process. It is essential to begin a process of securing justice for the worst crimes, demonstrating that a repeat of the past will not be tolerated. Ignoring this issue, which consistently tops the list of demands by ordinary Afghans, will aggravate insecurity, decrease legitimacy, and perpetuate longstanding conflicts. The international community should help by providing funding, expertise and, most importantly, political support to create a justice mechanism capable of helping Afghans grapple with their bloody past.

More specifically, the United States must promote respect for the rule of law in Afghanistan. The U.S. military must cease cooperation with regional warlords outside the purview of the central government. U.S.

forces must assume a mandate that respects and protects the rights of Afghan civilians against abusive local warlords.

Perhaps more importantly, U.S. military forces must abide by international human rights and humanitarian law while conducting operations in Afghanistan. The use of excessive force during military operations in residential areas has generated tremendous resentment against the international community. The U.S. practice of detaining Afghans without charge or other due process rights at ad hoc prisons in Bagram and other locations around Afghanistan has made a mockery of respect for justice. Such rights violations are a festering sore for many Afghans and a terrible example for a country where every two-bit warlord runs a private prison.

Success or failure in Afghanistan is ultimately not a military issue, or at least not only a military issue. Current international policies toward Afghanistan demonstrate very little integration of the military and reconstruction efforts. Continuing in this manner is to court failure.

Mustafa Subhi Hassan al-Qubaisi, 12, holds a photo of his twin brother Muhammad, shot by U.S. troops from the 82nd Airborne on June 26 in the Hay al-Jihad neighborhood of Baghdad. September 23, 2003. © 2003 Fred Abrahams/Human Rights Watch

Sidelined: Human Rights in Postwar Iraq
By Joe Stork and Fred Abrahams[2]

Human rights have had an inconsistent place in the Iraq crisis of 2003.
The Bush administration's campaign to build domestic and international
political support in the lead-up to war sometimes invoked the appalling
human rights record of Saddam Hussein's government, though few
believed this was a significant motivating factor behind the decision to
go to war. After the battlefield successes of March and April, as its
claims of Iraqi weapons of mass destruction lost credibility, the
administration more insistently cited human right crimes to justify the
war retrospectively.

In the military occupation of Iraq and counterinsurgency operations,
however, the United States and its partners have treated human rights
issues as matters of secondary importance, demonstrating ambivalence
toward human rights and humanitarian law concerns. They have too
often set aside lessons from past international interventions that
demonstrate the importance of rights monitoring and protection.

This essay examines three aspects of this problem: the failure to deploy
sufficiently trained and equipped forces for law enforcement
responsibilities; the failure initially to protect mass grave sites or to

---

[2] Fred Abrahams, a former staff member, is currently a consultant and conducted research for Human Rights Watch in Iraq in 2003.

ensure that professional forensic exhumations were conducted to preserve evidence of past atrocities; and the dogged resistance of the U.S. to any international role in efforts to address responsibility for serious past crimes in Iraq.

The despotic and abusive rule of Saddam Hussein is gone, and Iraqis today can express themselves without fear of arbitrary detention, torture, or execution. Political parties and civic associations have emerged quickly, and many of the new associations are dedicated to one or another aspect of a larger human rights agenda, such as documenting cases of the "disappeared" or safeguarding and cataloguing documents of the myriad security agencies that were the infrastructure of Ba`thist repression. But the rule of law has not arrived, and as of this writing, seven months into the occupation, the country is still beset by the legacy of human rights abuses of the former government, as well as new ones that have emerged under the occupation.

Meeting Law Enforcement Responsibilities

The problematic human rights dimension of U.S. policy in Iraq stood out clearly in April and May, with the failure of war planners to address post-war obligations of the U.S.-led coalition to respect civilian lives and property, including public property, and provide basic security for Iraqi residents. Initially, such security extended to little beyond the Ministry of Oil, which was well-guarded while other government buildings were looted. The occupying power neglected to provide sufficient and suitable forces for this task and failed to order troops to take steps to halt the widespread and protracted looting, therefore not meeting its international humanitarian law obligations.[3] U.S. Defense Secretary Donald Rumsfeld appeared to dismiss such concerns with his "freedom's untidy" comment,[4] perhaps reflecting his own share of the responsibility for this failure. Subsequent accounts of the Pentagon's dismissal of postwar plans developed by other government agencies, such as the State Department-sponsored Future of Iraq Project, reinforced such perceptions.[5] Lt. Gen. (Ret.) Jay Garner, who headed the U.S. stabilization and reconstruction effort for the first month after major combat ceased, said that the Future of Iraq Project's report "was good work" but that it "wasn't well received" by the Pentagon's civilian leadership.[6]

One irony was the failure to stop the looting of Iraqi military arsenals. Human Rights Watch researchers in Iraq came across caches of antitank and antipersonnel mines, and even missiles. It is not clear why the occupying forces did not more actively collect the weapons that

---

[3] The Hague Regulation of 1907, to which the U.S. is party, provides that the occupying power "shall take all steps in his power to re-establish and insure, as far as possible, public order and safety...." Art. 43.

[4] "DoD News Briefing – Secretary Rumsfeld and Gen. Myers," transcript, p. 7, www.defenselink.mil/transcripts/2003/tr20030411-secdef0090 (retrieved December 2, 2003).

[5] The project brought together several hundred Iraqi expatriates under State Department auspices beginning in April 2002 to assess Iraqi societal and infrastructure needs and propose reconstruction plans in various sectors.

[6] Garner also said he tried to recruit the project's director, Tom Warrick, to his team, but that Warrick apparently "just wasn't acceptable" to the Pentagon. See Frontline documentary "Truth, War and Consequences," www.pbs.org/wgbh/pages/frontline/shows/truth/interviews/garner (retrieved December 2, 2003).

insurgents might be using against them now. "There were a couple of areas that we were concerned about—nuclear plants and that type of thing, for obvious reasons," Lt. Gen. James Conway, Commander of the First Marine Expeditionary Force, told the U.S. public television news program Frontline. "But the things that came down for us to protect were very few in number in the early going. Not a very extensive list at all."[7]

Eventually the looting slowed, when all that remained was dust and debris. But security remained a problem in many cities, with thefts, car-jackings, kidnappings, and sexual assaults on women and girls an ongoing concern. As with the looting, this problem had been foreseen. Recent experience from Kosovo, East Timor, and Afghanistan made clear that professional police forces are required after an armed conflict to patrol streets and maintain civic order. Also needed are jails and judges—the basics of a criminal justice system. Many experts warned well before the war that, in the words of the Future of Iraq Project report, "the period immediately after regime change might offer these criminals the opportunity to engage in acts of killing, plunder and looting."[8]

Security was not merely desirable, but reflected the legal obligation of the occupying power under international humanitarian law to restore

---

[7] Ibid., see http://www.pbs.org/wgbh/pages/frontline/shows/truth/interviews/conway.html

[8] "U.S. study foresaw pitfalls in Iraq" by Eric Schmitt and Joel Brinkley, *New York Times*, October 20, 2003.

and maintain public order. It was a chaotic post-conflict scene, as U.S. commanders say, but the conditions did not absolve the U.S. and its coalition partners of their responsibilities under international humanitarian law.

Problematic adherence to human rights norms in Iraq since major combat operations ended has been especially evident in the deployment of combat forces for policing tasks. Human Rights Watch investigations of civilian deaths have raised serious concerns regarding the failure to deploy sufficient numbers of appropriately trained and equipped forces in this regard. These serious shortcomings have been exacerbated by a systematic failure to undertake sufficiently high-level investigations in cases of civilian deaths that may have resulted from excessive or indiscriminate use of lethal force by U.S. troops.[9]

The death of `Adil `Abd al-Karim al-Kawwaz is a case in point. On August 7, al-Kawwaz was driving home from his in-law's house in Baghdad with his wife and four children just prior to the evening curfew. It was dark and he did not see the U.S. soldiers from the 1st Armored Division operating a checkpoint with armored vehicles and heavy-caliber guns. No signs or lights indicating their presence were visible, and al-Kawwaz did not understand he was supposed to stop. He drove too close and the soldiers opened fire, killing him and three of his children, the youngest of whom was eight years old.

---

[9] *Violent Response: The U.S. Army in al-Falluja*, Human Rights Watch, June 2003; *Hearts and Minds: Post-war Civilian Casualties in Baghdad by U.S. Forces*, Human Right Watch, October 2003.

This shooting was not an isolated event. At checkpoints, during raids, or after roadside attacks, edgy U.S. soldiers have resorted to lethal force with distressing speed. Troops also have not been adequately equipped with non-lethal or less lethal equipment, such as tear gas and rubber bullets, for use in establishing control of a situation without recourse to live fire. When they have reason to use lethal force, soldiers sometimes respond in an excessive and indiscriminate way that put civilians at risk.

Compounding the problem is a lack of accountability for unlawful deaths. Coalition soldiers and civil authorities, and even independent non-Iraqi contractors engaged by them, are immune from Iraqi law, under the terms of Coalition Provisional Authority (CPA) Decree 17. This leaves it up to the member states of the U.S.-led coalition and their respective militaries to investigate such incidents and hold accountable anyone found to have used, or condoned the use of, excessive or indiscriminate force.

The U.S. military has asserted that all incidents involving suspicious or wrongful death are being properly investigated. In response to a Human Rights Watch report, a CPA statement said, "We have fully investigated all credible reports and have taken appropriate action considering the constitutional protections for all the soldiers involved, applicable military law, and the law of war."[10]

---

[10] Vivienne Walt, "Iraqi families want retribution for deaths; some charge U.S. soldiers unjustly shoot, kill civilians," *San Francisco Chronicle*, November 24, 2003.

But adequate investigations did not take place, contributing to an atmosphere of impunity in which soldiers feel they can pull the trigger without consequences if their actions resulted in wrongful death or injury. As of October 1, the U.S. military had announced completing only five investigations into allegedly unlawful civilian deaths. In all five investigations, the soldiers who fired were found to have operated within the military rules of engagement. In one case, the findings recommended that checkpoints be better marked--unfortunately that came in September, after another family had been killed in a car at a checkpoint.

Human Rights Watch investigated two of these five incidents and found evidence to suggest that soldiers had in fact used excessive force. In one case, from August 9, soldiers from the 1st Armored Division's 3rd Brigade mistakenly shot at an unmarked Iraqi police car as it chased suspected criminals in a van, killing two Iraqi policemen. A witness said one of the policemen was killed after he had stepped out of his car with his hands raised and shouting "No! Police!" U.S. soldiers beat a third policeman who was in the car.

The second case was the shooting of the al-Kawwaz family, recounted above. The U.S. military called that "a regrettable incident," but determined that soldiers from the 1st Armored Division's Alpha 2-3 Field Artillery had acted within the rules of engagement. The U.S. military gave the family $11,000 "as an expression of sympathy."

Human Rights Watch investigated civilian deaths in Baghdad as a result of U.S. fire after May 1, 2003, and estimated that as of September 30 there had been ninety-four cases in the capital alone that warranted an official investigation. The U.S. military does not even attempt to track how many civilians its soldiers have killed, saying it is "impossible for us to maintain an accurate account."[11] The failure to attempt even a rough tally suggests that Iraqi civilian loss of life or serious injury are not primary concerns.

U.S. military personnel acknowledge that one underlying problem is the reliance on combat troops to perform post-conflict policing tasks. Soldiers from the 82nd Airborne or the 1st Armored Division fought their way into Iraq and are now being asked to show patience and restraint in an increasingly risky environment. As one U.S. officer told Human Rights Watch, "it takes a while to get the Rambo stuff out." Military police, by contrast, are better suited to deal with these tasks, but the Bush administration is apparently reluctant to call up more reservists or National Guard forces that could perform these tasks.

The rules of engagement of U.S. troops in Iraq are not made public, due to security concerns. But Iraqis have a right to know how they can avoid walking into their own deaths. Through proper signs in Arabic and public service campaigns, they should know how they are expected to behave at checkpoints or during raids on their homes.

---

[11] *Hearts and Minds: Post-war Civilian Casualties in Baghdad by U.S. Forces*, Human Right Watch, October 2003.

U.S. soldiers have for the most part not had training to compensate for their understandably weak comprehension of Iraqi culture, not to mention an inability to speak or understand Arabic. For at least the first months of the occupation, most checkpoints and patrols did not have Arabic translators available. At checkpoints, soldiers used hand signals or verbal orders that Iraqis did not understand, sometimes with fatal results. Other misunderstandings were also damaging. Male U.S. soldiers sometimes searched Iraqi women, although this practice abated over time. Other soldiers put their feet on the heads of detainees, a serious affront to personal dignity.

As attacks on U.S. soldiers have grown more frequent and more intense, the danger of harm to civilians grows. After unknown attackers shot down a U.S. Blackhawk helicopter near Tikrit on November 7, killing six soldiers, the U.S. military responded with a "show of force" that included the use of tanks, howitzers and planes dropping 500-pound bombs. "We've lost six of our comrades today," a U.S. officer was quoted as saying. "We're going to make it unequivocally clear what power we have at our disposal."[12]

In Tikrit in mid-November U.S. forces reportedly used tank and artillery fire to destroy homes belonging to families of Iraqis who allegedly mounted attacks against U.S. forces. A spokesman for the U.S. Army's 4th Infantry Division said the demolitions were intended to "send a

---

[12] Anthony Shadid and Vernon Loeb ,"Another Copter Down in Iraq; 6 GIs Killed," *Washington Post*, November 8, 2003.

message" to the insurgents and their supporters.[13] While U.S. troops are entitled to suppress armed attacks against them, destroying civilian property as a reprisal or as a deterrent amounts to collective punishment, a violation of the 1949 Geneva Conventions.[14]

The escalating use of force reveals how the occupying powers have been unable to secure law and order, even when attacks on coalition troops were not a daily event. From the beginning of the occupation, U.S. troops have failed to communicate effectively with the local population on security issues, and to deploy sufficient numbers of international police or constabulary (*gendarme*) forces, and have relied on combat troops for policing duties without appropriate training.

Some military officers have acknowledged that soldiers were inadequately trained and equipped for what they call SASO—Stability and Support Operations. "The soldiers have been asked to go from killing the enemy to protecting and interacting, and back to killing again," one U.S. military commander wrote in an After Action Report. "The soldiers are blurred and confused about the rules of engagement,

---

[13] Rajiv Chandrasekaran and Daniel Williams, "U.S. Military Returns to War Tactics," *Washington Post*, November 22, 2003.

[14] Fourth Geneva Convention of 1949, art. 33.

which continues to raise questions, and issues about force protection while at checkpoints and conducting patrols."[15]

In some cases, soldiers did not have the right equipment, like construction and barrier materials, to establish checkpoints. Even interpreters were lacking, leaving the soldiers unable to communicate with the local population they were supposed to serve. "These interpreters are critical to the team's ability to interact with civilians, discern their problems, and broadcast friendly unit intentions," the After Action Report said. "Often times the unit had crowds and upset civilians to deal with and absolutely no way to verbally communicate with them."[16]

The failure to provide a secure environment seriously affects Iraq's vulnerable populations: women, children and minority groups. The widespread fear of rape and abduction among women and their families has kept women and girls at home, preventing them from taking part in public life. Iraqi police give a low priority to allegations of sexual violence and abduction. The victims of sexual violence confront indifference and sexism from Iraqi law enforcement personnel, and the U.S military police are not filling the gap.[17] Almost half of Iraq's

---

[15] "Subject: Operation Iraqi Freedom After Action Review Comments," April 24, 2003, conducted by TCM C/3-15 Infantry, Task Force 1-64 [declassified], http://www.strategypage.com/dls/articles/20030912.asp (retrieved October 17, 2003).

[16] Ibid.

[17] *Climate of Fear: Sexual Violence and abduction of women and girls in Baghdad*, Human Rights Watch, July 2003.

population is under the age of eighteen, and the war and its aftermath are exposing them to continued risk. Drugs are becoming more prevalent and the number of street kids has grown.

"You don't want troops to do policing but you have no choice," an Australian coalition official told Human Rights Watch. The coalition wants to hand law enforcement tasks over to the Iraqi police and army, he said, but these institutions are still weak and, despite improvements, they are not yet capable of performing the necessary tasks alone.

The training and reequipping of the Iraqi police and army must continue so that they can assume greater responsibility for law and order. But there are risks in the push to get Iraqi security forces on the street. Independent monitoring and redress systems must be in place from the beginning. And training must include thorough instruction in human rights law enforcement standards for crowd control, treatment of detainees, conduct of interrogations, and other areas where the Iraqi police have displayed shortcomings in the past. The occupying forces must also screen and vet local officials, police, and other security personnel to ensure that human rights abusers do not rejoin their ranks.

This extends to the judicial system. Major resources and efforts are needed to reestablish an independent judiciary and to retrain jurists, prosecutors, defense attorneys, police officers, and court personnel. Iraq's prisons, sites of grave human rights abuses in the past, must be brought up to international standards. While some steps have been taken to start this process, Iraqi laws that do not meet international due

process and fair trial standards must be repealed or brought into
compliance with international human rights and fair trial standards.

Mass Graves

On March 4, 1991, thirteen-year-old Khalid Khudayyir and his thirty-
three-year-old cousin Fu'ad Kadhim left their village in southern Iraq on
foot, headed for the city of al-Hilla to buy food. They never returned.

More than twelve years later, on May 16, 2003, the family learned of
their fate when their identification documents were found among
decomposed human remains in a mass grave near al-Mahawil military
base, some twenty kilometers north of al-Hilla. Like thousands of Iraqis
in the predominantly Shi`a southern part of the country, they had been
arrested and "disappeared" during the Iraqi government's brutal
suppression of the popular uprising that followed the Iraqi army's defeat
in Kuwait in 1991.

For the Khudayyir family, the gruesome discovery brought some closure
to a sad and horrific chapter in their lives. For Iraq's Shi`a population,
and other Iraqis as well, it helped mark a beginning of collective
reckoning with decades of state persecution and mass murder. Almost
immediately after the fall of the government in April, Iraqis began to
identify mass gravesites around the country.

The acting mayor of al-Hilla notified U.S. military authorities on May 3 of one of the smaller al-Hilla mass gravesites. The gravesite at al-Mahawil contained the remains of more than two thousand Iraqi victims. Another mass gravesite about five kilometers distant contained several hundred bodies. A third site just south of al-Hilla contained an additional forty bodies. In all three sites the bodies were buried en masse, in contact with one another, rather than in individual plots.

A U.S. assessment team from the Office of Reconstruction and Humanitarian Assistance (ORHA, the predecessor of today's Coalition Provisional Authority, or CPA), visited several days later and recommended that military troops secure the sites and arrange for exhumations by forensics experts. Instead, in the absence of a comprehensive strategy for assisting with mass grave exhumations, desperate families used shovels and mechanical backhoes to search fields, tumbling bodies into heaps of clothes and bones. U.S. Marines at the site, whose orders were simply to "assist local authorities," videotaped the exhumation and collected some testimonies. The family of Khalid and Fu'ad found what they sought, but hundreds, perhaps thousands, of others may be denied that closure due to the disorganized and unprofessional exhumations. After frantic digging at the largest site in the area, more than one thousand remains—approximately half of those originally interred—were reburied without identification in conditions that almost surely preclude subsequent identification.[18]

---

[18] *The Mass Graves of al-Mahawil: The Truth Uncovered*, Human Rights Watch, May 2003.

The experience at al-Mahawil was not unique. In the southern city of Basra and its environs, eyewitnesses to the killings of scores of young Shi`a men in 1999, in reprisal for street disturbances following the assassination of Ayatollah Muhammad Sadiq al-Sadr by government agents in February 1999, came forth to identify three of the numerous unmarked gravesites in the area. There, too, families waited in vain for direction from U.S. and U.K. authorities as to how the coalition intended to exhume the gravesites and preserve evidence for possible criminal proceedings. Relatives grew impatient as they combed through lists of executed prisoners recovered from looted government archives, and began to excavate some of the sites without professional direction or support. At the gravesite of al-Birigisia, thirty miles south of Basra near an oil refinery, the chaotic conditions at the exhumation precluded even rudimentary precautions against misidentification of remains.

Mass graves of this sort almost always indicate that the deaths were the result of natural disasters or mass atrocities. The random manner in which Khalid Khudayyir and Fu'ad Kadhim and thousands like them across Iraq were exhumed in those weeks after the fall of Saddam Hussein's government exposed a disturbing lack of planning by the U.S.-led coalition. Saddam Hussein's government "disappeared" at least 290,000 Iraqis over the years of its rule. Despite awareness of Saddam Hussein's crimes—indeed often using them to justify war—the occupying power did not secure the gravesites, provide forensic teams, or tell desperate Iraqis searching for their loved ones what procedures and mechanisms were being planned to address the crisis.

This failure to protect the mass gravesites had direct consequences, first of all for the families of victims, and the effects likely will be felt for years. The flawed exhumation at al-Mahawil rendered perhaps half the bodies unidentifiable. Bodies were mixed up and many corpses were dismembered. Identity documents were lost. There were also consequences for holding accountable those most responsible for these atrocities. These mass gravesites were crime scenes, and evidence that could have been crucial to future criminal prosecutions for crimes against humanity may have been tainted if not lost or destroyed.

Many mass gravesites remain undisturbed. Not all of the relevant evidence has been lost, by any means, and practices appeared to improve with time. According to U.S. officials with the Coalition Provisional Authority, the intervention of local rights activists, political parties, and community and religious leaders convinced many families and relatives of the need to conduct exhumations in a professional manner, with the help of trained forensic experts, in order to provide more reliable identifications and to preserve evidence for future criminal proceedings.

U.S. officials also told Human Rights Watch that they are working with Iraqi leaders to select some twenty key gravesites connected to the major incidents of atrocities, such as the 1988 Anfal campaign against Iraq's Kurds in the north and the 1991 and 1999 massacres of Shi`a in the south, based on assessments of international forensic teams that have visited the country. These sites would be the focus for forensic investigations in connection with trials of top leaders of the former government before a special tribunal.

Nevertheless, by failing to secure sites like those at al-Mahawil and al-Birigisia, the U.S. risked compromising the ability of Iraqis and the international community to hold accountable those responsible for serious past crimes such as genocide, crimes against humanity, and war crimes, at least with regard to the evidence of specific atrocities uncovered and now lost or ruined at those sites.

What Kind of Tribunal

The question of accountability for past atrocities and need to ensure some measure of justice for the victims and their survivors ranks as an issue of great concern to many Iraqis. How these matters are addressed by the CPA, and by the Iraqi Governing Council it appointed, has consequences not just for perpetrators and victims of serious abuses under the rule of Saddam Hussein. The decisions made—or avoided—today will affect as well the quality of Iraq's criminal justice system in the immediate and longer-term future. Those decisions will also potentially influence the future of international justice mechanisms as they emerged in the 1990s, namely the special criminal tribunals of former that Yugoslavia and that of Sierra Leone, and most recently the International Criminal Court.

So far, the steps taken by the CPA and the Iraq Governing Council, and the directions they have signaled, leave much to be desired.

Six months after the overthrow of the Saddam Hussein government, events have demonstrated the need to move swiftly on the justice front.

One indication is the steady pace of revenge killings of former government and Ba`th Party officials, killings that reportedly numbered in the "several hundred" in early November 2003.[19]

Other indicators are the murders of local Iraqi judges who were collecting evidence for criminal prosecutions. Muhan Jabr al-Shuwaili, the top al-Najaf governorate judge and one of a four-member investigative commission set up by al-Najaf's municipal council, had reportedly recorded 400 complaints and issued twelve arrest warrants in only a few months of work. On November 3, several men kidnapped him from his home, drove him to a deserted cemetery, and executed him with two shots to the head, saying "Saddam has ordered your prosecution."[20] The next morning Isma`il Yusif Sadiq, a judge from Mosul, was gunned down in front of his house.[21]

Despite this intimidation, other local investigative efforts are continuing, illustrating the strength of the search for accountability. The Iraqi Bar Association has reportedly registered some 50,000 claims for loss of lives and property at the hands of the former government. In the words

---

[19] Susan Sachs, "Iraqis Seek Justice, or Vengeance, for Victims of the Killing Fields," *New York Times*, November 4, 2003.

[20] The account is from one of the judge's associates, a prosecutor who was also kidnapped but released unharmed. See Nayla Razzouk, "Iraq judges probing Saddam-era cases angry at lack of US protection," Agence France-Presse, November 6, 2003 (retrieved December 2, 2003).

[21] Dan Murphy, "In the new Iraq, local officials put lives on the line," *Christian Science Monitor*, November 7, 2003 (retrieved December 2, 2003).

of district court judge Qais `Abbas Rida, "We have to let every single Iraqi file his case. We should broadcast these trials to the whole world." [22] Rida says he took testimony and forensic evidence from a man who had been tortured on orders of former Revolutionary Command Council deputy chairman `Izzat Ibrahim al-Duri and sent a warrant for al-Duri's arrest to all police stations in the country.

Iraqi human rights groups, like the Association of Victims in Basra, have emerged around the country—preserving documents, cataloguing names, identifying those names with various waves of repression. The groups have by and large refused to divulge the names of informers and intelligence agents, and thereby probably avoided a bloodbath. But for how long?

In Baghdad's Republican Palace, now the headquarters of the CPA, there are Americans and others who are serious about justice and accountability issues, but it is not clear how much resonance their views have in Washington policy-making circles. To date the Bush administration has firmly resisted calls to establish an independent repository to collect and safeguard evidence and set minimum standards for gathering documents, forensic evidence, and testimonies.

What should have happened, as it did in the case of former Yugoslavia and Rwanda (and in slightly different form in Cambodia and East

---

[22] Susan Sachs, "Iraqis Seek Justice, or Vengeance, for Victims of the Killing Fields," *New York Times*, November 4, 2003.

Timor), was a U.N. Security Council resolution authorizing the secretary-general to establish an international commission of some half-dozen experts, Iraqi and international in composition, with at least a four-month mandate, to

- establish an independent national central repository to receive documentary, forensic, and other forms of evidence (at least two international forensic teams reportedly declined to conduct exhumations in absence of an independent repository for evidence);

- coordinate international forensic efforts to train Iraqis to conduct exhumations and identification of remains ;

- establish a minimum-standards process for establishing the fate of the "disappeared;"

- develop minimum standards for gathering testimonies, documents, and forensic evidence (e.g., chain of custody standards);

- recommend mechanisms of accountability: the right mix of a special tribunal for those most responsible for the most serious offenses; necessary legal reforms to allow regular Iraqi criminal courts to handle the majority of alleged perpetrators of serious human rights crimes; a truth and justice mechanism to deal with lower-grade perpetrators and to establish a historical record; and vetting mechanisms to remove past abusers from government posts on the basis of individual accountability, in a way that doesn't add new rights violations;

- Recommend best practices for witness and victim protection.

Six months on, this is still missing. Security Council Resolution 1483 marks a key moment lost: that resolution's preamble "affirm[s] the need for accountability for crimes and atrocities committed by the previous Iraqi regime," but there is nothing in the operative paragraphs on how this is to happen, or who is responsible for developing policy. The main responsibility for this failure rests with the U.S. and U.K., but other Council member states failed to challenge them.

Human Rights Watch and colleague organizations have urged the secretary-general to initiate such a commission, based on the implicit authorization in 1483 which empowered the secretary-general's Special Representative for Iraq to "encourage[e] efforts to promote legal and judicial reform." Special Representative Sergio Vieira de Mello, in his meetings with the Security Council in late July, before he returned to Baghdad and his death, reportedly encountered opposition to this idea from the U.S. and found no appetite on the part of the secretary-general to take up the fight in the face of that opposition.

The "Iraqi-led" process as publicly endorsed by U.S. officials has effectively been translated by the Iraqi Governing Council as an "Iraqi-only" process, recognizing but then marginalizing the essential international dimension. With some assistance from a British legal advisor, the Judicial Commission set up by the Governing Council has drafted a statute that, once-approved by the Governing Council and ratified by CPA head Paul Bremer, will have the force of law. As of early December the draft was reportedly very close to completion but there were no indications that either the Governing Council or the CPA would make it public and invite comment, reflecting a distinct lack of transparency.

The draft statute incorporated many positive features, including international legal definitions of genocide, war crimes, and crimes against humanity as justiciable matters, largely reflecting the language of the Rome Statute of the International Criminal Court. But it also included violations of Iraqi criminal law, for the most part serious crimes like murder but also vaguely worded prohibitions against "abuse of position [of authority]," for example, and "use of the armed forces of Iraq against an Arab country." This seemed to reflect a determination to be able to punish former government officials even if the evidence did not support conviction on the most egregious offenses in the "crimes against humanity" categories. It also suggested an inclination to have the tribunal cast a wide net, to be able to bring within its purview whomever the present authorities wish to punish. Many of these people should be tried instead before ordinary (reformed) Iraqi criminal courts. This language left the proposed tribunal open to inefficiency if not outright abuse.

The draft statute recognized the need for an international component by mandating the president of the tribunal to appoint non-Iraqis as advisors to the separate chambers. The non-Iraqis, in addition to prior judicial or prosecutorial experience, must also have experience in international war crimes trials. For the Iraqi judges themselves there is not—there could not realistically be—any such requirement of international experience.

The draft statute also stipulated that the prosecutors and investigative judges—in the French-derived Egyptian model on which Iraq's judicial system is based, investigative judges conduct interrogations and inquiries to make the first determination of a prima facie criminal violation— must be Iraqi nationals, though again each of these departments was required to appoint non-Iraqi advisors.

The main impetus for this insistence that only Iraqis serve as judges and other key positions in the tribunal was the Iraqi Governing Council. This reflected in part an abiding distrust of the United Nations, blaming the world body for not taking stronger measures against Saddam Hussein's government despite its tyranny and awful crimes. There was also an Iraqi concern to preserve use of the death penalty, something that would not be possible in a U.N.-mandated tribunal.[23]

While Iraqi concerns must be taken seriously, it is also critical that the justice effort has integrity and credibility, which is not likely in an Iraqi-only process given the state of the Iraqi judiciary after decades of autocratic rule and the concerns detailed above. Even so, there has been little evident objection to the Governing Council plan from the Bush administration, which from the outset has manifested a largely instrumentalist approach to issues of accountability and justice in Iraq. The crimes of the former government have been duly recited and deplored, and justice promised, but the mechanism under consideration

---

[23] Coalition Provisional Authority Order Number 7, section 3, suspended use of the death penalty.

displays serious deficiencies. Several factors probably account for this, including the administration's aversion to anything hinting of "international justice," a concern that the jurisdiction of any justice mechanism be confined to crimes of Iraqi officials, and a desire to preserve some ability to trade prosecution deals for intelligence on weapons of mass destruction and other subjects of interest.

The most appropriate mechanism, drawing on the positive as well as negative experience of the existing international tribunals, would be a mechanism incorporating Iraqi and international expertise and experience, located if security conditions permit in Iraq, and using Arabic and Kurdish as the official languages of the tribunal. The presence of Iraqi jurists and prosecutors will help ensure that the composition of the tribunal and associated mechanisms reflects Iraqi society, whose interests are most directly at stake. At the same time, the presence of international jurists and prosecutors on the staff, not just as advisors but as integral members of the team of judges and lawyers at the core of the tribunal, would help ensure the necessary degree of credible impartiality and independence, competence in prosecuting and adjudicating extremely complex criminal proceedings, and familiarity with developments in international justice standards.

Ensuring Human Rights Accountability

An essential element of any reform and reconstruction process is transparency and accountability. In the short term, independent monitoring and reporting can curb abuses of power, provide a modicum of credibility and legitimacy, and offer a forum for grievances to be aired. In the long term, independent institutions are needed to ensure a government that is committed to the protection of basic human rights essential to a democratic society.

The Coalition Provisional Authority has a Human Rights and Transitional Justice division. Its mandate, however, does not include monitoring or reporting on current abuses, but only on abuses of the past. It does important work in the area of civil society development and human rights education, but the primary task is documenting Saddam Hussein's crimes, dealing with mass graves (which it has done better since the extremely problematic beginning) and assisting the establishment of a tribunal for past abuses. Its web page, like the entire website of the CPA, is primarily in English. It leaves an impression that its purpose is to show the outside world what the CPA is doing, rather than to inform Iraqis on how their country is being run and how their rights today can be protected.

The Governing Council—the interim body appointed by the CPA—included a Ministry of Human Rights in the cabinet it announced in early September 2003, but it remains untested. What is needed is a statutorily independent monitoring system, like an ombudsman's office or national human rights institution. International donors, who have committed $33 billion to Iraq since the war, should support the creation of such an institution with a mandate to cover the full range of human rights issues and the power to conduct investigations and make recommendations to both the occupying powers and any transitional Iraqi authority. It should have the necessary independence, diversity, resources, and geographic presence to do the job well.

Ultimately it is Iraqis who will best be able to ensure that the authorities in their country abide by international human rights standards, and the occupying powers and donor countries must do more to assist local nongovernmental organizations. The nascent human rights community in Iraq needs and desires training, management skills, and financial assistance from abroad. As the development of a local human rights community in Cambodia and East Timor has made clear, the United Nations and foreign donors can play an important role in fostering development of such groups.

In the meantime, the United Nations should better address the need for human rights protection, as security allows, by expanding the monitoring operations of the United Nations High Commissioner for Human Rights. The member states of the Commission for Human Rights, moreover, should make it a priority at its next annual meeting, in March-April 2004, to renew the mandate of the special rapporteur on Iraq and specify that the mandate includes on-going developments as well as past abuses. The work of the monitors and the special rapporteur alike could provide donors with authoritative information and analysis on the human rights situation within the country and make recommendations for remedial action, including long-term institutional reform.

Such monitoring missions have played a constructive role in other post-conflict transitions, like in Cambodia, East Timor, Bosnia-Herzegovina, and Kosovo. Security conditions may constrain United Nations efforts in Iraq, but this should not prevent donors from earmarking funding for this purpose, or the United Nations identifying suitable experts and preparing to extend its presence on the ground. Without such mechanisms to keep a check on abuses—to promote government transparency in general—Iraq's transitional period may proceed without the human rights grounding that is essential.

Toward that end, the United States and its allies should move quickly to address the serious human rights shortcomings of the occupation to date. The first is to carry out investigations of all cases where there are credible allegations or other reasons to suspect that use of lethal force by occupation troops may have led to wrongful death or injury to Iraqi civilians. The second is to establish an independent central depository to receive forensic evidence from mass graves as well as documentary evidence and eyewitness testimonies related to serious past human rights abuses. The third is to endorse publicly and support diplomatically the establishment of a special criminal tribunal for past crimes that incorporates experienced international as well as Iraqi judges and prosecutors in all key departments.

An elderly woman now lives in her basement after her house was destroyed in Grozny. Russia has used the "war on terrorism" to justify its brutal campaign in Chechnya. © 2002 Thomas Dworzak/Magnum Photos

"Glad to be Deceived": the International Community and Chechnya

By Rachel Denber

"It is so easy to deceive me, for I am glad to be deceived."

- Alexander Pushkin, "Confession" (1826)

The armed conflict in Chechnya, now in its fourth year, is the most serious human rights crisis of the new decade in Europe. It has taken a disastrous toll on the civilian population and is now one of the greatest threats to stability and rule of law in Russia. Yet the international community's response to it has been shameful and shortsighted.

The international community has a moral and political obligation to protect fundamental rights of people in and around Chechnya. It should with a unified voice be prevailing on the Russian government to halt forced disappearances, torture, and arbitrary detention, which Russian forces perpetrate on a daily basis. It should be compiling documentation about abuses into an authoritative, official record. It should be vigorously pressing for a credible accountability process for perpetrators of serious violations of international humanitarian law, and should think strategically about how to achieve this when the Russian court system fails to deliver justice. And it should stop Russia from forcing the return of displaced people to areas where their safety and well-being cannot be ensured.

But none of this has happened. The international community has instead chosen the path of self-deception, choosing to believe Russia's claims that the situation in Chechnya is stabilizing, and so be spared of making tough decisions about what actions are necessary to stop flagrant abuses and secure the well-being of the people of the region.

The year 2003 saw no improvement in the international community's disappointing response to the Chechen situation. All the international community could muster were well-intended statements of concern that were never reinforced with political, diplomatic, financial or other consequences.

Chechnya was placed on the agenda of the U.N. Commission on Human Rights, the highest human rights body within the U.N. system, but even there a resolution on Chechnya failed to pass. No government leader was willing to press for specific improvements during summits with Russian President Vladimir V. Putin. In late 2002 the Russian government closed the field office in Chechnya of the Organization for Security and Cooperation in Europe (OSCE). And to date the Russian government had still not invited U.N. special rapporteurs on torture and extrajudicial executions to visit the region. And unlike in other armed conflicts in Europe, few foreign missions in Russia sought to gather first-hand information about continuing human rights abuses.

It did not have to be this way. Events of the past decade have shown that however flawed their policies might be in many respects, concerned states and intergovernmental bodies can play a significant role in addressing human rights violations. Even in the Balkans, where the international community failed to stop horrific abuses as they were occurring, concerned states eventually supported the creation of the International Criminal Tribunal on the former Yugoslavia, a significant and likely long-lasting contribution to security and human rights in the region. Hundreds of OSCE monitors deployed to Kosovo in November 1998 were able to create official documentation of massacres and other human rights abuses.

To be sure, there are important political obstacles to affecting Russia's behavior in Chechnya. Because it is a permanent member of the United Nations Security Council, Russia was able to shield Chechnya from serious U.N. scrutiny, save for the U.N. Commission on Human Rights in 2000 and 2001. The U.S. and European governments have broad political and economic agendas with Russia, ranging from strategic missile defense to energy security to Russian policy in the Middle East. But none of these factors can justify or fully explain the international community's reluctance to promote human rights protections in and around Chechnya, or why Russia never has had to face significant consequences for abuses by its troops.

International disengagement on Chechnya became more marked after the September 11, 2001 attacks in the United States. Russia, which had since 1999 called the conflict in Chechnya a "counter-terror operation," soon began to argue that the war in Chechnya was its contribution to the U.S.-led global campaign against terrorism. Russia succeeded in further shielding the conflict from scrutiny in international forums and in Russia itself.

Western governments have emphasized the need for Russia to find a political solution to the conflict. But they fail to see the role that continuing abuses play in prolonging it. For this reason, the policy of disengagement is shortsighted. As abuses continue, and as there continues to be no credible accountability process, Chechens appear to be losing what faith or hope they may have had in the Russian government. Disengagement, particularly now, is untimely. Russia has spared little effort to present the situation as stabilizing. But it has proven incapable of ending the conflict; instead, in 2003 it began to spill into neighboring Ingushetia, with Russian forces perpetrating the same abuses there as they have in Chechnya.

In the long term, disengagement on Chechnya is a disservice to human rights in Russia. Having faced no diplomatic or other consequences for its crimes in Chechnya, the Russian government has certainly learned an important lesson about the limits of the international community's political will in pursuing human rights.

Unchecked patterns of abuse by Russia's forces in Chechnya will eventually affect the rest of Russian society. Tens of thousands of police and security forces have done tours of duty in Chechnya, after which they return to their home regions, bringing with them learned patterns of brutality and impunity. Several Russian human rights groups have begun to note a "Chechen syndrome" among police who served in Chechnya—a particular pattern of physical abuse and other dehumanizing treatment of people in custody. Russians already face serious risk of torture in police custody. The Chechnya experience is thus undermining efforts to promote the rule of law in Russia's criminal justice system.

Human Rights Abuses in the Chechnya Conflict

Russia's second armed conflict in Chechnya in the 1990s began in September 1999. Russia claimed it was a counter-terror operation, aimed at eliminating the chaos that had reigned in Chechnya since the end of the 1994-1996 Chechen war and at liquidating terrorist groups that had found haven there. Five months of indiscriminate bombing and shelling in 1999 and early 2000 resulted in thousands of civilian deaths. Three massacres, which followed combat operations, took the lives of at least 130 people. By March 2000, Russia's federal forces gained at least nominal control over most of Chechnya. They began a pattern of classic "dirty war" tactics and human rights abuses that continue to mark the conflict to this day. Russian forces arbitrarily detain those allegedly suspected of being, or collaborating with, rebel fighters and torture them in custody to secure confessions or testimony. In some cases, the corpses of those last seen in Russian custody were subsequently found, bearing marks of torture and summary execution, in dumping grounds or unmarked graves. More often, those last seen in custody are simply never seen again—they have been forcibly disappeared. Make no mistake, Chechen rebel forces too have committed grave crimes, including numerous brutal attacks targeting civilians in and outside of Chechnya, killing and injuring many. Rebel fighters were also responsible for assassinations of civil servants cooperating with the pro-Moscow Chechen administration of Chechnya. Anti-personnel land mines laid by fighters and Russian forces claimed the lives of federal soldiers and civilians alike.

125

At the height of the Chechen war in 2000, as many as 300,000 people had been displaced from their homes, with most living in the neighboring republic of Ingushetia. Of these, 40,000 resided in tent camps.

By 2003, the cycle of arbitrary detention, torture, and forced disappearance was well entrenched, and the crisis of forced disappearances appeared to have become a permanent one. According to unpublished governmental statistics, 126 people were abducted and presumed "disappeared" in January and February 2003 alone. In mid-August, the Chechen Ministry of Internal Affairs said that nearly 400 people had "disappeared" in Chechnya since the beginning of the year. Local officials in 2003 have also admitted the existence of forty-nine mass graves containing the remains of nearly 3,000 civilians.

As noted above, the conflict increasingly has spilled over the Chechen border into Ingushetia, still a haven for tens of thousands of displaced Chechens, and Russian operations there have been as abusive as they are in Chechnya. In June 2003, Russian and pro-Moscow Chechen forces conducted at least seven security operations in Ingushetia, five of them in settlements for Chechen displaced persons. The operations involved numerous cases of arbitrary arrest and detention, ill-treatment, and looting. As with abuses committed in Chechnya, authorities failed to diligently investigate the violations and hold perpetrators accountable.

Russian authorities in Ingushetia also have kept up steady pressure on displaced people living in tent camps to return to Chechnya.

Throughout 2003, as in 2002, federal and local migration authorities intermittently cut off gas, electricity, water, and other infrastructure services to several of the camps and removed hundreds of people from camp registration lists, causing them to be evicted. In addition, officials threatened the displaced people with arrests on false charges such as drugs and weapons possession, and impending security sweeps. Migration authorities closed one camp in the middle of winter in 2002, another in October 2003, and as of this writing seemed set to close yet a third; meanwhile, authorities blocked the construction of alternative shelters in Ingushetia.

Closing the tent camps, which at this writing housed more than 12,000 displaced Chechens, and pressuring people to return to Chechnya is part of a larger government strategy to put the Chechnya "problem" back inside Chechnya so that authorities can claim that the situation there is "normalizing." Such claims, in turn, are used to support Russia's position that international scrutiny of the republic is no longer justifiable.

The International Response

The international community was poorly positioned to respond effectively to these developments because it had acquiesced in Russia's efforts to keep outside observers from being deployed to Chechnya. In late 2002 the Russian government refused to renew the mandate of the OSCE Assistance Group, effectively closing the organization's important field presence in Chechnya. Since mid-2001, the Assistance Group had reported on human rights conditions, facilitated

humanitarian relief, and promoted a peaceful resolution of the crisis in
Chechnya. Negotiations over renewing the OSCE mandate collapsed
after Russia insisted that the mission relinquish its human rights and
political dimensions. To its credit, the OSCE refused. After the closure,
the Dutch chairmanship pressed for a new OSCE presence with a
human rights component, but did not receive support from other OSCE
participating states necessary to make the effort successful.

As already noted, a resolution sponsored by the European Union on
Chechnya failed to pass at the 2003 session of the U.N. Commission on
Human Rights for the second year in a row. It was rejected in part
because the European Union seemed to will it to fail: as in 2002, it used
the threat of a resolution only as a bargaining chip to coax the Russian
government into agreeing to a much weaker chairman's statement. This
strategy was misguided in its optimism, given that the Russian
government had ever since the beginning of the conflict vehemently
rejected international criticism of its conduct of the war and mobilized
diplomatic resources to keep the Chechnya issue out of the U.N. When
Russia predictably walked away from the chairman's statement
negotiations, the E.U. introduced the resolution but then purposively
failed to advocate for its adoption, and refused to share information
about its strategy with third party states.

In January 2003, the Chechnya rapporteur for the Parliamentary
Assembly of the Council of Europe (PACE) Lord Judd put forward a
resolution calling on Russia to postpone a constitutional referendum for
Chechnya planned for March, citing the escalating conflict and
persistence of human rights abuses and a poor security environment.

After a hot debate, PACE rejected this proposal, and instead called on Russia to ensure appropriate conditions for the referendum. Lord Judd resigned in protest. In April, PACE adopted a highly critical resolution on the human rights situation and the lack of accountability in Chechnya.

UNHCR worked hard to ensure protection for displaced persons in Ingushetia in 2002-03, and protested Russian government efforts to force them back. As authorities moved to close camps, UNHCR was able to prevent eighty families from being left homeless in Ingushetia. UNHCR's efforts are admirable. But Russia's intent to close tent camps could not be clearer, and UNHCR's efforts will not be sufficient unless U.N. member states also seek and obtain political commitments from Russia that ensure protection for displaced persons.

At the bilateral level, little apparent effort was made at the highest levels to press Russia to improve human rights protections in the region. President Putin received a ringing endorsement from governments around the world who helped him celebrate the 300th anniversary of the founding of St. Petersburg. Chechnya was at the bottom of the agendas in summits with British Prime Minister Tony Blair and U.S. President George W. Bush. Speaking on behalf of the Italian presidency of the European Union, Silvio Berlusconi even went so far as to praise the Chechen presidential elections, which nearly every independent observer said were rigged.

Antecedents to Inaction

Many analysts attribute international diffidence with respect to abuses in Chechnya to changing international priorities after September 11, 2001, particularly the increasing focus on global security. But in fact the antecedents to inaction go much farther back, even to the early months of the war. The international community deserves credit for the strong and forthright criticism it mounted at that time, and for efforts to bring diplomatic pressure to bear to convince the government to rein in abusive troops and allow access to the region. But the effort for the most part was half-hearted and short-lived, ending soon after Vladimir Putin, who became acting president upon Boris Yeltsin's resignation on December 31, 1999, was elected president in March 2000.

In the early months of the war, Russian forces razed Grozny in indiscriminate bombing, killing thousands, arrested thousands more, and summarily executed more than 130 detained persons in post-battle sweep operations. International criticism was sharp. The OSCE in 1999 insisted on a reaffirmation of its mandate in Chechnya, and in April 2000, the Parliamentary Assembly of the Council of Europe suspended Russia's voting rights, restoring them only in January 2001. In late 1999, the EU adopted a decision to freeze certain technical assistance programs because of Chechnya and recommended that embassy personnel travel to the region and gather information on events there. But after Yeltsin's resignation the EU toned down its rhetoric; the recommendation to send in diplomats was never implemented.

The limits the international community set for itself in this early period would set the parameters for years to come. Only the PACE recognized massacres of noncombatants as war crimes. International actors apparently were not prepared to follow through on the consequences that recognizing the massacres as war crimes would entail.

No government or multilateral institution was willing to consider linking financial benefits to improvements on the ground in Chechnya or the creation of a credible accountability process. The World Bank, which arguably had the most leverage and a mandate to withhold aid on human rights grounds, released U.S. $450 million in structural adjustment loan payments to Russia during the first year of the war, which went directly to the Russian government for unrestricted general budgetary spending.

Multilateral institutions and their member states also resisted pressing for an accountability process that had any international involvement, putting their faith in the Russian government to establish a credible domestic monitoring and accountability process. Council of Europe member states did not act on PACE's recommendation that they file an interstate complaint against Russia with the European Court of Human Rights.

In 2000 and 2001 the U.N. Human Rights Commission adopted strong resolutions condemning human rights abuses in Chechnya and calling on Russia to invite U.N. thematic mechanisms to the region. But it stopped short of calling for an international commission of inquiry, requiring instead that Russia establish a national commission of inquiry.

The Russian government bitterly opposed the resolution, and vowed not to cooperate with its recommendations. At the time, Human Rights Watch and others urged the Commission to call for an international commission of inquiry, which could operate, albeit in a limited capacity, in the face of Russian objections. We had serious doubts that the Russian government would establish a thorough and impartial monitoring or accountability process.

The Russian government established a human rights office in Chechnya, headed by President Putin's special envoy on human rights in Chechnya. A national commission of inquiry was formed, in name only. Neither institution had the authority to investigate or prosecute violations of humanitarian law or human rights law, and neither produced an official record of the abuses committed by both sides of the conflict.

In April 2001, at the request of PACE, the Russian government made available a list of criminal investigations related to the Chechnya conflict. This list revealed the extent of the impunity for crimes committed in the conflict: the vast majority of criminal cases were not under active investigation; no cases had made it to the courts; and there was no investigation into widespread torture, one of the key abuses of the conflict.

The international community had an important role to play in documenting abuses, both to inform policy toward Russia and, ultimately, to produce an official record of the abuses committed in the conflict. In 1999, the EU instructed heads of embassies of its member states to visit the region to gather information on humanitarian assistance. In sharp contrast to its efforts in Kosovo prior to March 1999, the instruction was not implemented, and working-level visits by diplomats to the region were few and far between.

The OSCE's Assistance Group to Grozny was the best equipped institution to lead a documentation effort on Chechnya. It had documented abuses in the 1994-1996 Chechnya conflict, played a crucial role in negotiating an end to it, and was still on the ground as late as 1998. The OSCE subsequently had gained institutional expertise in documenting humanitarian law violations in Kosovo. Its book, *As Seen as Told,* remains to this day one of the most authoritative accounts of the abuses that occurred in Kosovo prior to March 1999. It could not apply this experience to Chechnya, as Russia's prodigious efforts at presenting obstacles caused the Assistance Group to postpone its redeployment until May 2001. And even after its redeployment, the Assistance Group was constrained in its reporting.

In 2000, the Council of Europe seconded experts for Putin's special representative for human rights in Chechnya, but they spent most of the year in Strasbourg. After a bomb exploded near the experts' passing car in Chechnya in April 2003, they deemed the security situation too volatile to return. Even prior to that date, the work of the experts in Chechnya had been severely inhibited by their limited mandate, which prevented them from freely moving around Chechnya and conducting investigations of key incidents on their own initiative. The reporting of the experts generally contained little information that could not be found in other sources and information on human rights abuses was often of a general nature. The quality of reporting had improved in late 2002, but since April 2003 the experts have been forced to do their work in Strasbourg, which has made it impossible for them to directly monitor the situation on the ground.

As prime minister, Putin had staked his political career on the "counterterror" operation in Chechnya. Under his presidency the government, and he personally, greeted international criticism of the campaign, no matter how mild, with outbursts, threats, and indignation. If the strategy aimed to dampen Russia's interlocutors' enthusiasm for constructive intervention, it was successful. By mid-2000, Western leaders understood that Putin, until then a political unknown, had consolidated power and would lead Russia for at least four more years. They generally ceased to press Russia for concessions on Chechnya. This meant that the international community's most important multilateral achievements on Chechnya—resolutions at the United Nations Human Rights Commission, resolutions by the PACE, and the like—received no reinforcement at the bilateral level, and so went unheeded.

Russia, Chechnya, and the Global Campaign against Terror

By September 11, 2001, the war in Chechnya, its toll on civilians and its broader implications for the rule of law in Russia had fallen off the agenda of many of Russia's interlocutors. After the attacks in the United States, as noted above, Russia cast the conflict in Chechnya as its contribution to the global campaign against terrorism, pointing to links certain Chechen field commanders allegedly had to al-Qaeda.

Russia's cooperation was needed in the war in Afghanistan, and would later be sought in the U.S. war in Iraq. Several heads of state indicated outright that Russia's conduct in Chechnya would be seen in a new light. The horrific hostage-taking by Chechen rebels on a Moscow theater in October 2002 caused revulsion in Russia and throughout the world, and lent credence to Putin's assertions and, in the minds of some, seemed to confirm the existence of links between certain rebel groups and al-Qaeda. A series of suicide bombings in Chechnya and other parts of Russia in 2002 and 2003 killed and maimed hundreds more.

Already made a lower priority, Chechnya practically disappeared from governments' public agendas with Russia. Neither the European Union, its member states, nor the United States has had the political courage to mount strong criticism at key moments, or call publicly for accountability or for U.N. rapporteurs to be allowed to visit the region. Most governments have called publicly and in a coordinated fashion for Russia to desist from compelling displaced persons to return to Chechnya. But after so many years of criticism unmatched by a credible threat of sanction, such words yielded little effect.

In dealing with Chechnya today, governments and multilateral institutions for the most part stress the need for a political solution to the conflict, rather than pressing for an immediate end to human rights abuses, let alone holding Russia and Chechen rebels to account for them. Many argue that the abuses will end only when the conflict ends. The international community should not be reproached for seeking an end the conflict in Chechnya, but emphasizing this goal over all others overlooks the fact that it is the continuing cycle of abuses that fuel the conflict. To end the conflict, the Russian government has to build in the population of Chechnya an atmosphere of trust in Russia's institutions. But the daily grind of torture, arbitrary detention, and forced disappearances instead sows further mistrust. As people see their loved ones killed or disappeared they have less incentive not to join the rebel effort.

Russia's efforts at finding a political solution—at "normalizing" the situation—are not ending the conflict in Chechnya, but rather making the conflict less visible to the outside world. The constitutional referendum held in Chechnya in March 2003, and the subsequent presidential elections in October, were widely advertised by the Russian government as a final stage of stabilization of conditions in the republic. In reality, the referendum and elections took place against a background of continuing and escalating violence, and independent observers unanimously believed that the elections were rigged. Yet the Russian government has continued to use both elections to convince the outside world that the situation is normalizing through a political process, and to argue that international scrutiny or other involvement is no longer justified.

Ironically, as the Russian government is emphasizing the international implications of the Chechnya operation for the global campaign against terrorism, it is shutting the region to international scrutiny and cooperation. This discredits Russia's partners in the global campaign against terrorism among those inside Chechnya who suffer form lawlessness and abuse at the hands of Russia's forces and Chechen rebels.

As Russian forces enjoy impunity for crimes in Chechnya, and as Russia has escaped any significant diplomatic consequences for such crimes, the Russian government may come to expect nothing less than international disengagement on human rights more generally in Russia. The Russian public may conclude that it is acceptable for the government to be unaccountable for its actions. This will stunt progress on human rights in Russia for years to come, as the government learns to simply dismiss criticism of its broader human rights record, confident that words, no matter how tough, will never translate into action.

The Way Forward

Russia's sway within the international arena should not hinder a robust response from the international community on human rights abuses in Chechnya. The international community should consider that Russia's involvement in the war against terrorism raises rather than diminishes the stakes of its conduct in Chechnya. Russia's status as a permanent member of the U.N. Security Council, and its ability to remove Chechnya from the U.N.'s agenda, heightens the importance of regional mechanisms—the Council of Europe and the OSCE. To be effective, these institutions require first and foremost the support of their member governments in their bilateral relations with Russia. At the same time, U.N. officials, including the secretary-general, should press Russian authorities to allow U.N. institutions and mechanisms to play a role in monitoring and promoting human rights in Chechnya. This too is a message that must be reinforced in bilateral relations.

Russia's interlocutors should coordinate to deliver a unified message on the need for accountability for crimes against civilians, access to the region by human rights monitors, continued international assistance to displaced persons, and an end to involuntary returns to Chechnya. They should use summits and multilateral meetings as opportunities to press for specific benchmarks—including an updated, detailed list of investigations and prosecutions; invitations to the U.N. special rapporteurs on torture, extrajudicial executions, and violence against women; and binding commitments not to compel displaced persons to return to Chechnya until it is safe to do so, to provide decent and humane shelter to those who continue to be displaced, and to allow for international agencies to continue to provide relief for them. They should press for these benchmarks publicly and forcefully, and make clear that political, diplomatic, and financial consequences will follow should improvements not be forthcoming.

The international community can also help the cause of justice by supporting local organizations that help victims of abuse in Chechnya press their claims with the European Court of Human Rights. Once there is momentum on justice, international financial institutions should make clear that they will make the Russian government's compliance with court judgments a condition for future loan and credit disbursements.

Wishing away the human rights crisis in Chechnya will in the long run will not serve the goal of a peaceful resolution to the armed conflict. It is also a disservice to the thousands of people who have suffered human rights abuses and who are left with nowhere to turn for justice. A robust international response to Russia, one that backs words with action, is a critical part of the solution.

Above the Law: Executive Power after September 11 in the United States

By Alison Parker and Jamie Fellner

Justice today, injustice tomorrow. That is not good government.

- Asante proverb, Ghana

Good Government Under Law

In fourteenth century Italy, Ambrogio Lorenzetti painted frescoes in Siena's city hall depicting good and bad government through allegorical figures. Rendered in shades of gold, cobalt blue, red, and ochre, the fresco of good government depicts Justitia twice, reflecting her cardinal importance. In one classic image, she sits balancing the scales held by wisdom. The fresco of bad government presents the enthroned figure of Tyrannia, who sits above a vanquished Justitia, pieces of broken scales at her side. Lorenzetti's message, drawing on a revolution in political thought, was clear: justice is central to good government. In bad government, the ruling power places himself above a defeated and supine Justitia. Justice no longer protects the individual—the executive acts above the law and without restraint.

In Renaissance Siena, as elsewhere in Western Europe, officials who were part and parcel of the ruling power meted out justice. Modern governments have tried to ensure justice by creating an independent and impartial judiciary, capable of holding the government as well as the governed accountable for breaking the law. Certainly, the separation of the courts from the executive branch and the ability of the courts to scrutinize the constitutionality of executive actions has been a crucial feature of the legal framework in the United States. Indeed, it has been the lynchpin for the rule of law and the protection of human rights in that country.

Nevertheless, since taking office, U.S. President George W. Bush has governed as though he had received an overwhelming mandate for policies that emphasize strong executive powers and a distrust—if not outright depreciation—of the role of the judiciary. The Bush administration has frequently taken the position that federal judges too often endorse individual rights at the expense of policies chosen by the executive or legislative branches of government, and it has looked to nominate judges who closely share its political philosophy. But the concern is more fundamental than specific judges or decisions. Rather, the administration seems intent on shielding executive actions deemed to promote national security from any serious judicial scrutiny, demanding instead deference from the courts on even the most cherished of rights, the right to liberty.

Much of the U.S. public's concern about post-September 11 policies has focused on the government's new surveillance powers, including the ability to peruse business records, library files, and other data of individuals against whom there may not even be any specific suspicion of complicity with terrorism. These policies potentially affect far more U.S. citizens than, for example, the designation of "enemy combatants,"

141

or the decision to hold individuals for months in prison on routine visa charges. But the latter efforts to diminish the right to liberty and to curtail or circumvent the courts' protection of that right may be far more dangerous to the U.S. polity as a whole. Critics of the administration's anti-terrorism efforts have raised concerns that civil liberties are being sacrificed for little benefit in national security. But those critiques have generally failed to grapple with more fundamental questions: who should decide how much protection should be afforded individual rights and who should determine what justice requires—the executive or the judiciary? And who should determine how much the public is entitled to know about domestic anti-terrorist policies that infringe on individual rights?

Many of the Bush administration's post-September 11 domestic strategies directly challenge the role of federal and administrative courts in restraining executive action, particularly action that affects basic human rights. Following September 11, the Bush administration detained over one thousand people presumed guilty of links to or to have knowledge of terrorist activities and it impeded meaningful judicial scrutiny of most of those detentions. It has insisted on its right to withhold from the public most of the names of those arrested in connection with its anti-terrorism efforts. It has designated persons arrested in the United States as "enemy combatants" and claims authority to hold them incommunicado in military prisons, without charges or access to counsel. It insists on its sole authority to keep imprisoned indefinitely and virtually incommunicado hundreds of men at its military base at Guantánamo Bay, Cuba, most of whom were taken into custody during the U.S. war in Afghanistan. It has authorized military trials of foreign detainees under rules that eschew a meaningful right of defense and civilian appellate review.

In all of these actions, the Bush administration has put the ancient right to habeas corpus under threat, perhaps unsurprisingly since habeas "has through the ages been jealously maintained by courts of law as a check upon the illegal usurpation of power by the executive."[24] Habeas corpus, foreshadowed in 1215 in the *Magna Carta* and enshrined in the U.S. Constitution after centuries of use in England, guarantees every person deprived of his or her liberty a quick and efficacious check by the courts against "all manner of illegal confinement."[25]

The Bush administration argues that national security—the need to wage an all out "war against terrorism"—justifies its conduct. Of course, there is hardly a government that has not invoked national security as a justification for arbitrary or unlawful arrests and detentions. And there is hardly a government that has not resisted judicial or public scrutiny of such actions. But the administration's actions are particularly troubling and the damage to the rule of law in the United States may be more lasting because it is hard to foresee an endpoint to the terrorist danger that the administration insists warrants its actions. It is unlikely that global terrorism will be defeated in the foreseeable future. Does the U.S. government intend to hold untried detainees for the rest of their

---

[24] *Sec'y of State for Home Affairs v. O'Brien*, 1923 A.C. 603, 609.

[25] Sir William Blackstone, *Commentaries on the Laws of England*, 1765-1769, Book III, Ch. 8, p. 131.

lives? Does it intend to keep the public from knowing who has been arrested until the last terrorist is behind bars?

U.S. anti-terrorism policies not only contradict principles woven into the country's political and legal structure, they also contradict international human rights principles. The diverse governmental obligations provided for in human rights treaties can be understood as obligations to treat people justly. The imperative of justice is most explicitly delineated with regard to rights that are particularly vulnerable to the coercive or penal powers of government, such as the right to liberty of person. Human rights law recognizes that individual freedom should not be left to the unfettered whim of rulers. To ensure restraints on the arbitrary or wrongful use of a state's power to detain, the International Covenant on Civil and Political Rights (ICCPR), to which the United States is a party, requires that the courts—not the executive branch—decide the legality of detention.[26] The ICCPR also establishes specific requirements for court proceedings where a person's liberty is at stake, including that the proceedings be public. Even if there were to be a formally declared state of emergency, restrictions on the right to liberty must be "limited to the extent strictly required by the exigencies of the situation."[27]

---

[26] International Covenant on Civil and Political Rights, G.A. res. 2200A (XXI), 21 U.N. GAOR Supp. (No. 16) at 52, U.N. Doc. A/6316 (1966), 999 U.N.T.S. 171, entered into force Mar. 23, 1976, articles 9 and 14.

[27] The U.N. Human Rights Committee, the body that monitors compliance with the International Covenant on Civil and Political Rights, states in its commentary to article 4 on states of emergency, that limitations to derogation "relates to the duration, geographical coverage and material scope of the state of emergency and any measures of derogation resorted to because of the emergency.... [T]he obligation to limit any derogations to those

Justice cannot exist without respect for human rights. As stated in the
preamble of the Universal Declaration of Human Rights, "recognition
of the inherent dignity and of the equal and inalienable rights of all
members of the human family is the foundation of freedom, justice and
peace in the world." The Bush administration's rhetoric acknowledges
human rights and insists that the fight against terrorism is a fight to
preserve "the non-negotiable demands of human dignity, the rule of law,
limits on the power of the state…and equal justice," as President Bush
told the graduating class of the West Point military academy in June
2002. But the Bush administration's actions contradict such fine words.
Taken together, the Bush administration's anti-terrorism practices
represent a stunning assault on basic principles of justice, government
accountability, and the role of the courts.

It is as yet unclear whether the courts will permit the executive branch to
succeed. Faced with the government's incantation of dangers to
national security if it is not allowed to do as it chooses, a number of
courts have been all too ready to abdicate their obligation to scrutinize
the government's actions and to uphold the right to liberty. During
previous times of national crisis the U.S. courts have also shamefully
failed to protect individual rights—the internment of Japanese
Americans during World War II, which received the Supreme Court's
seal of approval, being one notorious example. As new cases arising
from the government's actions make their way through the judicial

---

strictly required by the exigencies of the situation reflects the principle of proportionality
which is common to derogation and limitation powers." Human Rights Committee, General
Comment 29, States of Emergency (article 4), U.N. Doc. CCPR/C/21/Rev.1/Add.11 (2001),
para. 4.

process, one must hope the courts will recognize the unprecedented dangers for human rights and justice posed by the Bush administration's assertion of unilateral power over the lives and liberty of citizens and non-citizens alike.

Arbitrary Detentions of Visa Violators

In a speech shortly after the September 11 attacks, U.S. Attorney General John Ashcroft said, "Let the terrorists among us be warned. If you overstay your visa, even by one day, we will arrest you. If you violate a local law, you will be put in jail and kept in custody for as long as possible."[28] The Attorney General carried out his threat, using a variety of strategies to secure the detention of more than 1,200 non-citizens in a few months. We do not know how many, if any, terrorists were in fact included among these detainees. Only a handful was charged with terrorism-related crimes. But we do know that the haphazard and indiscriminate process by which the government swept Arabs and Muslims into custody resulted in hundreds of detentions that could not be effectively reviewed or challenged because the executive weakened or ignored the usual checks in the immigration system that guard against arbitrary detention.

The right to liberty circumscribes the ability of a government to detain individuals for purposes of law enforcement—including protection of

---

[28] Attorney General John Ashcroft, *Prepared Remarks to the U.S. Mayors Conference*, Washington, D.C., October 25, 2001.

national security. While the right is not absolute, it is violated by arbitrary detentions, i.e., detentions that are either not in accordance with the procedures established by law or which are manifestly disproportional, unjust, unpredictable, or unreasonable. International and U.S. constitutional law mandate various safeguards to protect individuals from arbitrary detention, including the obligations of authorities to inform detainees promptly of the charges against them; the obligation to permit detainees to be released on bail pending conclusion of legal proceedings absent strong countervailing reasons such as the individual's danger to the community or flight risk; and the obligation to provide a detainee with effective access to a court to review the legality of the detention. In the case of hundreds of post-September 11 detainees in the United States, the government chose as a matter of policy and practice to ignore or weaken these safeguards.

It did so because one of its key post-September 11 strategies domestically was to detain anyone who it guessed might have some connection to past or future terrorist activities, and to keep them incarcerated as long as necessary to complete its investigations into those possible connections. U.S. criminal law prohibits detention solely for the purpose of investigation, i.e., to determine whether the detained individual knows anything about or is involved in criminal activities. The law also prohibits "preventive" detentions, incarceration designed to prevent the possibility of future crimes. Detention must be predicated on probable cause to believe the suspect committed, attempted, or conspired to commit a crime. Judges—not the executive branch—have the ultimate say, based on evidence presented to them, as to whether such probable cause exists. The Bush administration avoided these legal strictures against investigative or preventive detentions through the use of arrests for immigration law violations and "material witness" warrants. At the same time it avoided or limited the ability of detainees to avail themselves of protections against arbitrary detention, including through meaningful judicial review.

Immediately after the September 11 attacks, the Department of Justice began a hit or miss process of questioning thousands of non-citizens, primarily foreign-born Muslim men, who it thought or guessed might have information about or connections to terrorist activity. At least 1,200 non-citizens were subsequently arrested and incarcerated, 752 of whom were charged with immigration violations.[29] These so-called "special interest" immigration detainees were presumed guilty of links to terrorism and incarcerated for months until the government "cleared" them of such connections. By February 2002 the Department of Justice acknowledged that most of the original "special interest" detainees were no longer of interest to its anti-terrorist efforts, and none were indicted for crimes related to the September 11 attacks. Most were deported for visa violations.

In effect, the Department of Justice used administrative proceedings under the immigration law as a proxy to detain and interrogate terrorism suspects without affording them the rights and protections that the U.S. criminal system provides. The safeguards for immigration detainees are

---

[29] Because the government announced the number of persons arrested as "special interest" detainees only in November 2001, the total number eventually held as such has never been made public.

considerably fewer than for criminal suspects, and the Bush administration worked to weaken the safeguards that do exist. Human Rights Watch and other groups have documented the various ways the administration ran roughshod over the rights of these special interest detainees.[30] In June 2003, the Department of Justice's Office of the Inspector General released a comprehensive report on the treatment of the September 11 detainees that confirmed a pattern of abuses and delays for the "detainees, who were denied bond and the opportunity to leave the country.... For many detainees, this resulted in their continued detention in harsh conditions of confinement."[31]

For example, unlike criminal suspects, immigration detainees have no right to court-appointed counsel although they do have a right to seek private counsel at their own expense. But in the case of the September 11 detainees, public officials placed numerous obstacles in the way of obtaining legal representation.[32] Detainees were not informed of their right to counsel or were discouraged from exercising that right. The

---

[30] See U.S. Department of Justice, Office of the Inspector General (OIG), *The September 11 Detainees: A Review of the Treatment of Aliens Held on Immigration Charges in Connection with the Investigation of the September 11 Attacks*, April 2003 (hereinafter OIG 9/11 Report). *See also* Human Rights Watch, *Presumption of Guilt: Human Rights Abuses of Post-September 11 Detainees*, Vol. 14, No. 4 (G), August 2002; Migration Policy Institute, *America's Challenge, Domestic Security, Civil Liberties, and National Unity After September 11*, June 26, 2003.

[31] OIG 9/11 Report, p. 71.

[32] OIG 9/11 Report, p. 130 (stating that "[w]e found that the BOP's [Bureau of Prisons] decision to house September 11 detainees in the most restrictive confinement conditions possible severely limited the detainees' ability to obtain, and communicate with, legal counsel.")

08l .

Immigration and Naturalization Service (INS), a division of the U.S. Department of Justice,[33] failed to inform attorneys where their clients were confined or when hearings were scheduled. Detainees in some facilities were permitted one weekly phone call, even to find or speak to an attorney; a call that did not go through nonetheless counted as the one permissible call. Not having prompt access to lawyers, these "special interest" detainees were unable to protest violations of immigration rules to which they were subjected, including being held for weeks without charges (some detainees were held for months before charges were filed). The government never revealed the alleged links to terrorism that prompted their arrest, leaving them unable to prove their innocence. The government also took advantage of the lack of counsel to conduct interrogations that typically addressed criminal as well as immigration matters (under criminal law, suspects have the right to have an attorney present during custodial interrogations, including free legal counsel if necessary).

In most immigration proceedings where non-citizens have violated the provisions of their visa, their detention is short. They will have a bond

---

[33] Until November 2002, the Immigration and Naturalization Service (INS) was a part of the United States Department of Justice. However, most of the former INS functions since have been divided into the Bureau of Citizenship and Immigration Services (BCIS), handling immigration processing and citizenship services; and the Bureau of Immigration and Customs Enforcement (BICE) of the Directorate of Border and Transportation, handling border control and immigration enforcement. Both Bureaus are under the direction of the Department of Homeland Security (DHS), which is a department of the federal government of the United States, and was created partially in response to the September 11 attacks. The new department was established on November 25, 2002 and officially began operations on January 24, 2003.

hearing relatively quickly after charges have been filed, and unless there is reason to believe the detainee is a danger to the community or will abscond, immigration judges will permit the detainee to be released on bond. With regard to the special interest detainees, however, the Department of Justice adopted several policies and practices to ensure they were denied release until it cleared them of terrorism links. For example, under immigration procedure, immigration judges do not automatically review whether there is probable cause for detention; hearings are not scheduled until after charges have been filed. The government's delay of weeks, and in some cases months, in filing charges had the practical effect of creating long delays in judicial review of the detentions. Additionally, the government urged immigration judges to either set absurdly high bonds that the detainee could never pay or simply to deny bond, arguing that the detainee should remain in custody until the government was able to rule out the possibility of links to or knowledge of the September 11 attacks.

The INS also issued a new rule that permitted it to keep a detainee in custody if the initial bond was more than $10,000, even if an immigration judge ordered him released; since the INS sets the initial bond amount, this rule gave the Department of Justice the means to ensure detainees would be kept in custody. In addition, there were cases in which the Department of Justice refused to release a special interest detainee even if a judge ordered the release because the detainee had not yet been "cleared" of connections to terrorism. Indeed, the INS continued to hold some detainees even after they had been ordered deported because of lack of "clearance" even though the INS is required to remove non-citizens expeditiously, and in any event within 90 days of a deportation order as required by statute. In short, through these and other mechanisms, the immigration process to which the special interest detainees were subjected effectively reversed the presumption of innocence—non-citizens detained for immigration law violations were kept jailed until the government concluded they had no ties to criminal terrorist activities. As a result, special interest detainees remained in detention for an average of eighty days, and in some cases up to eight months, while they waited for the Federal Bureau of Investigation (FBI) to clear them of links to terrorism.

The long delays were endured by non-citizens who were picked up accidentally by the FBI or INS as well as those the government actually had reason to believe might have a link to terrorism. Once a person was labeled of "special interest," there were no procedures by which those who in fact were of no interest could be processed more quickly. As the Office of the Inspector General noted, the lengthy investigations "had enormous ramifications," since detainees "languished" in prison while waiting for their names to be cleared.[34]

Despite the Inspector General's scathing criticism of the government's treatment of the detainees, the Department of Justice was unrepentant, issuing a public statement that it makes "no apologies for finding every legal way possible to protect the American public from further terrorist attacks.... The consequences of not doing so could mean life or

---

[34] OIG 9/11 Report, p.71.

death."[35] As of October 2003, the executive branch had adopted only two of the Inspector General's twenty-one recommendations designed to prevent a repetition of the problems documented.

Secret Arrests and Hearings of Special Interest Detainees

History leaves little doubt that when government deprives persons of their liberty in secret, human rights and justice are threatened. In the United States, detentions for violations of immigration laws are traditionally public. Nevertheless, of the 1,200 people reported arrested in connection with the post-September 11 investigations in the United States, approximately one thousand were detained in secret.[36] The government released the names of some one hundred detained on criminal charges, but it has refused to release the names, location of detention, lawyers' names, and other important information about those held on immigration charges. Even now, it refuses to release the names of men who have long since been deported.

---

[35] Department of Justice, *Statement of Barbara Comstock, Director of Public Affairs, Regarding the Inspector General's Report on 9/11 Detainees*, June 2, 2003.

[36] In November 2001, the U.S. government announced that 1,200 individuals were detained in connection with September 11. Of this number, some one hundred plus had their names revealed when they were criminally charged. Most were charged with relatively minor crimes, such as lying to FBI investigators. Only a handful of the one hundred plus were charged with terrorism-related crimes and none have been charged with involvement in the September 11 attacks. The government provided no further information regarding the number of additional persons detained. Given the public information disclosed on the persons criminally charged, Human Rights Watch estimates that at least one thousand were detained in secret.

The public secrecy surrounding the detentions had a very real and negative impact on detainees' ability to defend themselves. It made it difficult for family members and lawyers to track the location of the detainees—who were frequently moved; it prevented legal services organizations from contacting detainees who might need representation; and it prevented organizations such as Human Rights Watch from getting in touch with detainees directly and talking to them about how they were treated during their arrests and detentions.

On October 29, 2001, Human Rights Watch and other groups sought the names of the detainees, their lawyers' names, and their places of detention under the U.S. Freedom of Information Act (FOIA)—legislation that mandates government disclosure of information subject to certain narrowly defined exceptions. The Department of Justice denied the request. When Human Rights Watch and the other groups went to court to challenge the government's denial, the government insisted that release of the names would threaten national security, speculating about possible scenarios of harm that could flow if the names were public. For example, it asserted that revealing the names would provide terrorists a road map to the government's anti-terrorism efforts. This argument appeared particularly specious since it was unlikely that a sophisticated terrorist organization would fail to know that its members were in the custody of the United States government, especially since detainees were free to contact whomever they wished.

A federal district court rejected the government's arguments for secrecy in August 2002 and ordered the release of the identities of all those detained in connection with the September 11 investigation. The judge called the secret arrests "odious to a democratic society…and profoundly antithetical to the bedrock values that characterize a free and open one such as ours."[37] However, in June 2003 the court of appeals reversed that decision. In a passionate dissent, one appellate judge noted:

> Congress…chose…to require meaningful judicial review
> of all government [FOIA] exemption claims…. For all
> its concern about the separation-of-powers principles at
> issue in this case, the court violates those principles by
> essentially abdicating its responsibility to apply the law
> as Congress wrote it.[38]

In October 2003, Human Rights Watch and twenty-one other organizations asked the U.S. Supreme Court to overturn the appellate decision and to compel the Department of Justice to release the names.

Meanwhile, the Department of Justice imposed blanket secrecy over every minute of 600 immigration hearings involving special interest detainees so that even immediate family members were denied access to the hearings. The policy of secrecy extended even to notice of the

---

[37] *Center for National Security Studies v. U.S. Department of Justice*, 215 F. Supp. 2d 94, 96 (D.C. Dist. 2002) (quoting *Morrow v. District of Columbia*, 417 F.2d 728, 741-742 (D.C. Cir. 1969)).

[38] *Center for National Security Studies, et al v. U.S. Department of Justice*, 331 F.3d 918 (D.C. Cir. 2003) (Tatel, J., dissenting).

hearing itself: courts were ordered not to give out any information about whether a case was on the docket or scheduled for a hearing.[39] The Justice Department has never presented a cogent rationale for this closure policy, particularly since deportation proceedings are typically limited to the simple inquiry of whether the individual is lawfully present or has any legal reason to remain in the United States, an inquiry that should not require disclosure of any classified information. Moreover, if the Justice Department sought to present classified information during a hearing, simply closing those portions of the proceedings where such material was presented could have protected national security.

Newspapers brought two lawsuits challenging the secret hearings, alleging the blanket closure policy violated the public's constitutional right to know "what their government is up to." In one case in August 2002, an appellate court struck down the policy. The court minced no words in explaining just what was threatened by the government's insistence on secrecy, stating that:

> The Executive Branch seeks to uproot people's lives, outside the public eye, and behind a closed door. Democracies die behind closed doors. The First Amendment, through a free press, protects the people's right to know that their government acts fairly, lawfully,

---

[39] *See Memorandum from Chief Immigration Judge Michael Creppy to all Immigration Judges and Court Administrators,* September 21, 2001 (outlining "additional security procedures" to be immediately applied in certain deportation cases designated by the Attorney General as special interest cases).

and accurately in deportation proceedings. When government begins closing doors, it selectively controls information rightfully belonging to the people.[40]

The government declined to appeal this decision to the Supreme Court.

In the second case, a federal appeals court upheld the closures, finding that the need for national security was greater than the right of access to deportation hearings. The Supreme Court declined to review that decision in May 2003. Significantly, in its brief filed in opposition to the Supreme Court hearing the case, the U.S. government distanced itself from the blanket closure policy, stating that it was not conducting any more secret hearings and that its policies relating to secret hearings were under review and would "likely" be changed.

Material Witness Warrants

In addition to immigration charges, the Bush administration has used so-called material witness warrants to subject individuals of interest to its terrorism investigation to "preventive detention" and to minimize judicial scrutiny of these detentions. U.S. law permits detention of a witness when his or her testimony is material to a criminal proceeding, and when the witness presents a risk of absconding before testifying. According to the Department of Justice, the government has used the

---

[40] *Detroit Free Press v. Ashcroft*, 303 F.3d 681, 683 (6th Cir. 2002).

material witness law to secure the detention of less than fifty people (it has refused to release the exact number) in connection with the September 11 investigations.[41]

The U.S. government has obtained judicial arrest warrants for material witnesses by arguing that they have information to present to the grand juries investigating the crimes of September 11. The available information on these cases suggests that the government was misusing the material witness warrants to secure the detention of people it believed might have knowledge about September 11—but who could not be held on immigration charges and against whom there was insufficient evidence to bring criminal charges. In many of the cases, the witnesses were in fact never presented to a grand jury but were detained for weeks or months—under punitive prison conditions— while the government interrogated them and continued its investigations.[42] For example, Eyad Mustafa Alrabah was detained as a material witness for more than two months after he voluntarily went to an FBI office to report that he had briefly met four of the alleged hijackers at his mosque in March 2001. During his detention, he was routinely strip and cavity searched and held in isolation with the light constantly on in his cell. Alrabah, however, never testified in front of a grand jury.

---

[41] *See* Letter from Jamie E. Brown, *Acting Assistant Attorney General, Office of Legislative Affairs, to Rep. F. James Sensenbrenner, Jr., chairman, House Judiciary Committee,* May 13, 2003.

[42] *See* Human Rights Watch, *Presumption of Guilt: Human Rights Abuses of Post-September 11 Detainees,* Vol. 14, No. 4 (G), August 2002

The *Washington Post* reported in November 2002 that of the forty-four men it identified as being detained as material witnesses since September 11, 2001, nearly half had never been called to testify in front of a grand jury. In at least several cases, men originally held as material witnesses were ultimately charged with crimes—strengthening the suspicion that the government was using the material witness designation as a pretext until it had time to accumulate the evidence necessary to bring criminal charges. A number of the witnesses languished in jail for months or were eventually deported based on criminal and immigration charges unrelated to September 11 that were supported by evidence the government gathered while detaining them as material witnesses.

Material witness warrants are supposed to ensure the presentation of testimony in a criminal proceeding where the witness cannot otherwise be subpoenaed to testify and where there is a serious risk that the witness will abscond rather than testify. In September 11 cases, at least some courts have accepted with little scrutiny the government's allegations that these requirements are satisfied. At the insistence of the government, the courts have also agreed to restrict access by the detainees' lawyers to the government's evidence, making it difficult if not impossible for the lawyers to object to the necessity of detention. For example, in some cases lawyers were only able to review the evidence supporting the request for the warrant quickly in court and they were unable to go over the information carefully with their clients before the hearing started. In addition, the government has argued in at least some cases that the mostly male Arab and Muslim witnesses were flight risks simply because they are non-citizens (even though some are lawful permanent residents), and have family abroad. The government's argument amounted to no more than an astonishing assumption that millions of non-citizens living in the United States with family living abroad cannot be counted on to comply with U.S. law and to testify under a subpoena.

The Bush administration has held the material witnesses in jail for extended periods of time, in some cases for months, and subjected them to the same conditions of confinement as given to accused or convicted criminals. Indeed, some have been held in solitary confinement and subjected to security measures typically reserved for extremely dangerous persons.

The Department of Justice has argued that it must keep all information pertaining to material witnesses confidential because "disclosing such specific information would be detrimental to the war on terror and the investigation of the September 11 attacks," and that U.S. law requires that all information related to grand jury proceedings to be kept under seal.[43] It has refused to identify which information must specifically be kept secret because of its relevance to grand jury proceedings and national security interests; instead it has not only kept witnesses' identities secret, but has also refused to reveal the actual number of them, the grounds on which they were detained, and the length and location of their detention. To shroud the circumstances of detention of innocent witnesses in secrecy raises serious concerns. As one court recently stated: "To withhold that information could create public

---

[43] Ibid.

perception that an unindicted member of the community has been arrested and secretly imprisoned by the government."[44]

Presidential Exercise of Wartime Powers

Since September 11 the Bush administration has maintained that the president's wartime power as commander-in-chief enables him to detain indefinitely and without charges anyone he designates as an "enemy combatant" in the "war against terrorism." On this basis the government is currently holding three men incommunicado in military brigs in the United States and some 660 non-citizens at Guantánamo Bay in Cuba. With regard to the three in the United States, the administration has argued strenuously that U.S. courts must defer to its decision to hold them as "enemy combatants." With regard to the Guantánamo detainees, the administration contends that no regular U.S. court has jurisdiction to review their detention. It has also authorized the creation of military tribunals to try non-U.S. citizens alleged to be responsible for acts of terrorism; as proposed, the tribunals evade important fair trial requirements, including a full opportunity to present a defense and the right to independent judicial review. The administration's actions display a perilous belief that, in the fight against terrorism, the executive is above the law.

---

[44] See In Re Grand Jury Material Witness Detention, (U.S. Dist. Ore. Apr. 7, 2003).

Enemy Combatants Held in the United States

President Bush has seized upon his military powers as commander-in-chief during war as a justification for circumventing the requirements of U.S. criminal law. Alleged terrorism suspects need not be treated as criminals, the government argues, because they are enemies in the war against terror. In the months and years since the detention of these suspects in the United States, the executive branch has not sought to bring them to trial. Instead, it claims the authority to subject these suspects to indefinite and potentially lifelong confinement in military brigs based on the president's decision that they are enemy combatants. Although there is no ongoing war in any traditional sense in the United States and the judicial system is fully functioning, the Bush administration claims that the attacks of September 11 render all of the United States a battlefield in which it may exercise its military prerogative to detain enemy combatants.

To date, the U.S. government has designated as enemy combatants in the United States two U.S. citizens and one non-citizen residing in the United States on a student visa. One of the U.S. citizens, Yaser Esam Hamdi, was allegedly captured during the fighting in Afghanistan and was transferred to the United States after the military learned he was a U.S. citizen. The other two, Jose Padilla, who is a U.S. citizen, and Ali Saleh Kahlah al-Marri, a student from Qatar, were arrested in the United States; Padilla was getting off a plane in Chicago after traveling abroad, and al-Marri was sleeping in his home.

The Bush administration initially claimed these enemy combatants had no right to challenge their detention in court, even though they are U.S. citizens and/or reside in the United States. The Department of Justice eventually conceded they had a constitutional right to habeas review, but it has fought strenuously to deny them the ability to confer with counsel to defend themselves in the court proceedings—much less to be present at the hearings—and has insisted that the courts should essentially rubber stamp its declaration that they are enemy combatants not entitled to the protections of the criminal justice system.

In the case of U.S. citizen Jose Padilla,[45] on December 4, 2002, a federal district court upheld the government's authority to order citizens held without trial as enemy combatants. The court also accepted the government's "some evidence" standard for reviewing the president's conclusion that Padilla was "engaged in a mission against the United States on behalf of an enemy with whom the United States is at war." But Padilla's lawyers succeeded in convincing the court that Padilla's right to habeas corpus includes the right to be able to confer with counsel. The government has appealed that decision and the case is pending before the Second Circuit Court of Appeals.

---

[45] Padilla was taken into custody by federal law enforcement agents on May 8, 2002 at an airport in Chicago and held pursuant to a material witness warrant. On June 9, two days before he was to be brought to court for his first scheduled hearing, President Bush designated Padilla as an enemy combatant. He was transferred from the criminal justice system to a naval brig in South Carolina. The government claims he was an al-Qaeda operative involved in a plot to explode a radioactive ("dirty bomb") in the United States.

World Report 2004

Ali Saleh Kahlah al-Marri, a Qatari national who entered the United States on a student visa, was arrested and charged by a federal grand jury for allegedly lying to investigators, credit card fraud, and other fraudulent acts.[46] However, after the indictment, the executive branch decided to re-designate him an enemy combatant and transferred him to a Navy facility in South Carolina on June 23, 2003. The government explained that it determined al-Marri was an enemy combatant because of information gleaned from interrogations of an accused al-Qaeda official.[47] Legal challenges to his detention have so far been held up by a threshold jurisdictional dispute between al-Marri's lawyers and the government over which court can hear his habeas petition.[48]

Two years since the fall of the Taliban government, Yaser Esam Hamdi, a U.S. citizen, remains in military custody without charges. According to

---

[46] Al-Marri was originally arrested on a material witness warrant in December 2001 because of several phone calls that he allegedly made to an individual in the United Arab Emirates who is suspected of sending funds to some of the September 11 hijackers for flight training.

[47] One newspaper account at the time of al-Marri's designation as an enemy combatant alleged that the government's actual reason for the change in status was to pressure him to cooperate. The story quoted an unnamed Department of Justice official as saying, "If the guy says 'Even if you give me 30 years in jail, I'll never help you,'" the official said. "Then you can always threaten him with indefinite custody incommunicado from his family or attorneys." See P. Mitchell Prothero, "New DOJ Tactics in al-Marri Case," United Press International, June 24, 2003.

[48] See, Al-Marri v. Bush, 274 F. Supp. 2d 1003 (C.D. Ill. 2003) (holding that al-Marri could not have his habeas petition heard in Illinois, and implying that he should file in South Carolina since "[h]is immediate custodian is there, and the Court has been assured by the Assistant Solicitor General of the United States and the U.S. Attorney for this district that Commander Marr [in charge of the Navy brig] would obey any court order directed to her for execution.")

the U.S. government, Hamdi was "affiliated" with a Taliban unit in the Afghan war. The unit surrendered to Afghan Northern Alliance forces in November 2001 and Hamdi was then turned over to the U.S. military.[49] In habeas proceedings, a federal district court noted "this case appears to be the first in American jurisprudence where an American citizen has been held incommunicado and subjected to an indefinite detention in the continental United States, without charges, without any findings by a military tribunal, and without access to a lawyer."[50] However, the district court and an appellate court agreed that the president had the constitutional authority to designate persons as enemy combatants. In addition, a district court ruled that Hamdi had a right to confer with his counsel, but an appellate court reversed that decision.[51]

To support its contention that Hamdi was properly designated an enemy combatant, the government submitted a vague nine-paragraph declaration by a U.S. Department of Defense official named Michael Mobbs. The government argued that the "Mobbs declaration" constituted "some evidence" that Hamdi was an enemy combatant, and "some evidence" was enough. After several hearings,[52] an appeals court

---

[49] Hamdi was first sent to Guantánamo Bay, Cuba, until it emerged in April 2002 that he was a U.S. citizen, at which point the government moved him to a Naval Station Brig in Virginia.

[50] *Hamdi v. Rumsfeld*, 243 F. Supp. 2d 527, 528 (E.D. Va. 2002).

[51] See, *Hamdi v. Rumsfeld*, 316 F.3d 450 (4th Cir. 2003).

[52] The declaration was provided by a special adviser to the undersecretary of defense for policy, but the district court judge felt that the declaration was insufficient basis for a ruling and sought more evidence. The government argued that "some evidence" was enough to support the designation. On appeal, the fourth circuit court of appeals accepted the government's view that courts should not closely examine military decisions. It ruled that

accepted the enemy combatant designation since the court lacked a "clear conviction" that Hamdi's detention as an enemy combatant was "in conflict with the Constitution or laws of Congress."[53]

Although the appellate court said that the facts of Hamdi's involvement in the fighting in Afghanistan were uncontested, it did not address how Hamdi could contest those facts if he was never given access to the declaration, nor permitted to confer with his attorney, nor able to speak directly to the court. On October 1, 2003 his lawyers filed briefs seeking Supreme Court review of his case. Before the Supreme Court decided whether they would take the case, on December 3, 2003, Defense Department officials reversed their position again, stating that Hamdi would be allowed to see a lawyer for the first time in two years. But the government took the position that Hamdi would be allowed access to counsel "as a matter of discretion and military policy; such access is not required by domestic or international law and should not be treated as a precedent."[54] While allowing Hamdi access to an attorney resolved one question before the U.S. Supreme Court, several other issues remain.

---

while some scrutiny of the detention of a so-called enemy combatant designation was required because of the right to habeas corpus possessed by all citizens and all non-citizens detained in the United States, such scrutiny was satisfied by the nine paragraphs submitted by government.

[53] *Hamdi v. Rumsfeld*, 316 F.3d 450, 474 (4th Cir. 2003).

[54] U.S. Department of Defense News Release No. 908-03, "DoD Announces Detainee Allowed Access to Lawyer," December 2, 2003.

If the U.S. Supreme Court upholds the "some evidence" standard, the right to habeas review will be seriously weakened. In the Padilla case, for example, the government's Mobbs declaration refers to intelligence reports from confidential sources whose corroboration goes unspecified. Moreover, the declaration even acknowledges grounds for concern about the informants' reliability.

The U.S. government asserts that its treatment of Padilla, Hamdi, and al-Marri is sanctioned by the laws of war (also known as international humanitarian law). During an international armed conflict, the laws of war permit the detention of captured enemy soldiers until the end of the war; it is not necessary to bring charges or hold trials. But the U.S. government is seeking to make the entire world a battlefield in the amorphous, ill-defined and most likely never-ending "war against terrorism." By its logic, any individual believed to be affiliated in any way with terrorists can be imprisoned indefinitely without any showing of evidence, and providing no opportunity to the detainee to argue his or her innocence. The laws of war were never intended to undermine the basic rights of persons, whether combatants or civilians, but the administration's re-reading of the law does just that.

Detainees at Guantánamo

For two years, the U.S. government has imprisoned a total of more than seven hundred individuals, most of whom were captured during or immediately after the war in Afghanistan, at a U.S. naval base at Guantánamo Bay, Cuba. The United States has asserted its authority to

exercise absolute power over the fate of individuals confined in what the
Bush administration has tried to make a legal no man's land.

The detainees were held first in makeshift cages, later in cells in
prefabricated buildings. They have been held virtually incommunicado.
Apart from U.S. government officials as well as embassy and security
officials from detainees' home countries, only the International
Committee of the Red Cross (ICRC) has been allowed to visit the
detainees, but the ICRC's confidential operating methods prevent it
from reporting publicly on conditions of detention. Even so, in
October the ICRC said that it has noted "a worrying deterioration in the
psychological health of a large number" of the detainees attributed to
the uncertainty of their fate. Thirty-two detainees have attempted
suicide.[55] The Bush administration has not allowed family members,
attorneys, or human rights groups, including Human Rights Watch, to
visit the base, much less with the detainees. While allowed to visit the
base and talk to officials, the media have not been allowed to speak with
the detainees and have been kept so far away that they can only see
detainees' dark silhouettes cast by the sun against their cell walls. The
detainees have been able to communicate sporadically with their families
through censored letters.

The Bush administration has claimed all those sent to Guantánamo are
hardened fighters and terrorists, the "worst of the worst." Yet, U.S.
officials have told journalists that at least some of those sent to

---

[55] John Mintz, "Clashes Led to Probe of Cleric," *Washington Post*, October 24, 2003.

Guantánamo had little or no connection to the U.S. war in Afghanistan or against terror. The Guantánamo detainees have included very old men and minors, including three children between thirteen and fifteen who are being held in separate facilities. The U.S. government acknowledges that there are also some sixteen and seventeen-year-olds at the base being detained with adults, but—without explanation—it refuses to say exactly how many of them there are. Some sixty detainees have been released because the United States decided it had no further interest in them.

According to the Bush administration, the detainees at Guantánamo have no right to any judicial review of their detention, including by a military tribunal. The administration insists that the laws of war give it unfettered authority to hold combatants as long as the war continues— and the administration argues that the relevant "war" is that against terrorism, not the long since concluded international armed conflict in Afghanistan during which most of the Guantánamo detainees were picked up.[56]

The Bush administration has ignored the Geneva Conventions and longstanding U.S. military practice which provides that captured combatants be treated as prisoners of war unless and until a "competent tribunal" determines otherwise. Instead of making individual determinations through such tribunals as the Geneva Conventions

---

[56] Under the Geneva Conventions, the ongoing fighting in Afghanistan is considered a non-international armed conflict.

require, the Bush administration made a blanket determination that no person apprehended in Afghanistan was entitled to prisoner-of-war status. The United States is thus improperly holding without charges or trial Taliban soldiers and hapless civilians mistakenly detained, as well as terrorist suspects arrested outside of Afghanistan who should be prosecuted by civilian courts.

The Bush administration, in its determination to carve out a place in the world that is beyond the reach of law, has repeatedly ignored protests from the detainee's governments and intergovernmental institutions such as the Inter-American Commission on Human Rights, the U.N. Special Rapporteur on the independence of judges and lawyers, the U.N. Working Group on Arbitrary Detention, and the U.N. High Commissioner for Human Rights. Without ever laying out a detailed argument as to why its actions are lawful under either the laws of war or international human rights law, the U.S. government has simply insisted that national security permits the indefinite imprisonment of the Guantánamo detainees without charges or judicial review.

Thus far the U.S. government has been able to block judicial oversight of the detentions in Guantánamo. In two cases, federal district and appellate courts have agreed with the Department of Justice that they lack jurisdiction to hear habeas corpus petitions because the detainees are being held outside of U.S. sovereign territory.[57] The ruling that the

---

[57] *See Al Odah v. United States*, 321 F.3d 1134 (D.C. Cir. 2003); *Coalition of Clergy v. Bush*, 310 F.3d 1153 (9th Cir. 2002); *Gherebi v. Bush*, 262 F. Supp. 2d 1064 (C.D. Ca. 2003); *Rasul v. Bush*, 215 F. Supp. 2d 55 (D.C. Dist. 2002).

courts lack jurisdiction is based on a legal fiction that Guantánamo remains under the legal authority of Cuba. The United States has a perpetual lease to the land it occupies in Cuba, which grants it full power and control over the base unless both countries agree to its revocation.

Under international law, a state is legally responsible for the human rights of persons in all areas where it exercises "effective control." Protection of rights requires that persons whose rights are violated have an effective remedy, including adjudication before an appropriate and competent state authority.[58] This makes the Bush administration's efforts to block review by U.S. courts and frustrate press and public scrutiny all the more troubling. No government should be able to create a prison where it can exercise unchecked absolute power over those within the prison's walls.

On November 11, 2003, the Supreme Court decided to review the lower court decisions rejecting jurisdiction over the detainees' habeas petitions. Amicus briefs had been filed by groups of former American prisoners of war, diplomats, federal judges, and military officers, non-governmental organizations, and even Fred Korematsu, a Japanese-American interned by the United States during World War II. Until the court renders its decision in June or July 2004, the detainees will remain in legal limbo, without a court to go to challenge their detention.

---

[58] ICCPR, article 3.

Military Tribunals

Fair trials before impartial and independent courts are indispensable to justice and required by international human rights and humanitarian law. Nevertheless, the U.S. government plans to try at least some persons accused of involvement with terrorism before special military commissions that risk parodying the norms of justice.

Authorized by President Bush in November 2001 for the trial of terrorist suspects who are not U.S. citizens, the military commissions will include certain procedural protections—including the presumption of innocence, ostensibly public proceedings, and the rights to defense counsel and to cross-examine witnesses. However, due process protections have little meaning unless the procedures in their entirety protect a defendant's basic rights. The Pentagon's rules for the military commissions fail miserably in this regard.

Perhaps most disturbing is the absence of any independent judicial review of decisions made by the commissions, including the final verdicts. Any review will be by the executive branch, effectively making the Bush administration the prosecutor, judge, jury and, because of the death penalty, possible executioner. There is no right to appeal to an independent and impartial civilian court, in contrast to the right by the U.S. military justice system to appeal a court-martial verdict to a civilian appellate court and, ultimately, to the Supreme Court. The fairness of the proceedings is also made suspect by Pentagon gag orders that prohibit defense lawyers from speaking publicly about the court proceedings without prior military approval—even to raise due process issues unrelated to security concerns—and that prohibit them from ever commenting on anything to do with any closed portions of the trials.

The right to counsel is compromised because defendants before the commissions will be required to retain a military defense attorney, although they may also hire civilian lawyers at their own expense. The commission rules permit the monitoring of attorney-client conversations by U.S. officials for security or intelligence purposes, destroying the attorney-client privilege of confidentiality that encourages clients to communicate fully and openly with their attorneys in the preparation of their defense.

The commission rules call for the proceedings to be presumptively open, but the commissions will have wide leeway to close the proceedings as they see fit. The commission's presiding officer can close portions or even all of the proceedings when classified information is involved and bar civilian counsel even with the necessary security clearance from access to the protected information, no matter how crucial it is to the accused's case. This would place the defendant and his civilian attorney in the untenable position of having to defend against unexamined and secret evidence.

In July 2003, President Bush designated six Guantánamo detainees as eligible for trial by military commission. The U.S. government has put the prosecutions on hold in three of these cases involving two U.K. nationals and one Australian citizen in response to concerns raised by the British and Australian governments about due process and fair trial in the military commissions. Decisions have been reached that the United States would not subject these three men to the death penalty or listen in on their conversations with their defense lawyers, but the governments continue to negotiate over other issues. There is no indication thus far that the bilateral negotiations address such shortcomings as the lack of independent appellate review. Moreover, the Bush administration has not suggested that any modifications to the procedures for British or Australian detainees would be applied to all detainees at Guantánamo, regardless of nationality. The negotiations thus raise the prospect of some detainees receiving slightly fairer trials, while the rest remain consigned to proceedings in which justice takes a backseat to expediency.

Shock and Awe Tactics

Protecting the nation's security is a primary function of any government. However, the United States has long understood "that in times of distress the shield of military necessity and national security must not be used to protect governmental actions from close scrutiny and accountability . . . . our institutions, legislative, executive and judicial, must be prepared to exercise their authority to protect all citizens from the petty fears and prejudices that are so easily aroused."[59]

Despite this admonition, since September 11 the Bush administration has used the words "national security" as a shock and awe tactic,

---

[59] *Korematsu v. United States*, 584 F. Supp. 1406, 1442 (N.D. Ca 1984).

blunting the public's willingness to question governmental actions. But even those who have asked questions have rarely found an answer. The government has by and large been successful in ensuring little is known publicly about who it has detained and why. It has kept the public in the dark about deportation proceedings against September 11 detainees and the military commission rules certainly leave open the possibility of proceedings that are closed to the public in great part. So long as the secrecy is maintained, doubts about the justice of these policies will remain and any wrongs will be more difficult to right.

The Bush administration's disregard for judicial review, its reliance on executive fiat, and its penchant for secrecy limit its accountability. That loss of accountability harms democratic governance and the legal traditions upon which human rights depend. Scrutiny by the judiciary— as well as Congress and the public at large—are crucial to prevent the executive branch from warping fundamental rights beyond recognition. A few courts have asserted their independence and have closely examined government actions against constitutional requirements. But other courts have abdicated their responsibility to perform as guarantors of justice. Some courts have failed to apply a simple teaching at the heart of the Magna Carta: "in brief. . .that the king is and shall be *below* the law."[60] For its part, Congress is only now beginning to question seriously the legality and necessity of the Bush administration's post-September 11 detentions.

---

[60] *Regina v. Sec'y of State for Foreign and Commonwealth Affairs,* Q.B. 1067, 1095 (2001) (citing Pollock & Maitland, *The History of English Law* (1923) (emphasis added).

Confronted with a difficult and complex battle against international terrorism, the United States must not relinquish its traditions of justice and public accountability. The United States has long held itself up as the embodiment of good government. But it is precisely good governance—and its protection of human rights—that the Bush administration is currently jeopardizing with its post-September 11 anti-terrorist policies.

Drawing the Line: War Rules and Law Enforcement Rules in the Fight against Terrorism

By Kenneth Roth

Where are the proper boundaries of what the Bush administration calls its war on terrorism? The recent wars against the Afghan and Iraqi governments were classic armed conflicts, with organized military forces facing each other. But the administration says its war on terrorism is global, extending far beyond these typical battlefields. On September 29, 2001, U.S. President George W. Bush said, "Our war on terror will be much broader than the battlefields and beachheads of the past. The war will be fought wherever terrorists hide, or run, or plan."

This language stretches the meaning of the word "war." If Washington means "war" metaphorically, as when it speaks of the war on drugs, the rhetoric would be uncontroversial—a mere hortatory device designed to rally support to an important cause. But the administration seems to think of the war on terrorism quite literally—as a real war—and that has worrying implications.

The rules that bind governments are much looser during wartime than in times of peace. The Bush administration has used war rhetoric to give itself the extraordinary powers enjoyed by a wartime government to detain or even kill suspects without trial. Enticing as such enhanced power might be in the face of the unpredictable and often lethal threat posed by terrorism, it threatens basic due process rights and the essential liberty such rights protect.

War and Peace Rules

By literalizing its "war" on terror, the Bush administration has broken down the distinction between what is permissible in times of peace and what can be condoned during a war. In peacetime, governments are bound by strict rules of law enforcement. Police can use lethal force only if necessary to meet an imminent threat of death or serious bodily injury. Once a suspect is detained, he or she must be charged and tried. These requirements—what one can call "law enforcement rules"—are codified in international human rights law.

In times of war, law enforcement rules are supplemented by the more permissive rules of armed conflict, or international humanitarian law. Under these "war rules," an enemy combatant can be shot without warning (unless he is incapacitated, in custody, or trying to surrender), regardless of any imminent threat. If a combatant is captured, he or she can be held in custody until the end of the conflict, without being charged or tried.

These two sets of rules have been well developed over the years, by both tradition and detailed international conventions. There is little law, however, to explain when one set of rules should apply instead of the other. Usually the existence of an armed conflict is obvious, especially when two governments are involved. But in other circumstances, such as the Bush administration's announced war on terrorism as it extends beyond Afghanistan and Iraq, it is less clear.

For example, the Geneva Conventions—the principal codification of war rules—apply to "armed conflict" but do not define the term. However, the International Committee of the Red Cross (ICRC), the official custodian of the conventions, does provide some guidance in its commentary, in distinguishing between civil war and mere riots or disturbances.

One test suggested by the ICRC for determining whether wartime or peacetime rules apply is to examine the intensity of hostilities. The Bush administration, for example, claims that al-Qaeda is at war with the United States because of the magnitude of the September 11, 2001 attacks as well as the pattern of al-Qaeda's alleged bombings including of the U.S. embassies in Kenya and Tanzania, the *U.S.S. Cole* in Yemen, and residential compounds in Saudi Arabia. Each of these attacks was certainly a serious crime warranting prosecution. But technically speaking, was the administration right to say that they add up to war? Is al-Qaeda a ruthless criminal enterprise or a military operation? The ICRC's commentary does not provide a clear answer.

In addition to the intensity of hostilities, the ICRC suggests considering such factors as the regularity of armed clashes and the degree to which opposing forces are organized. Whether a conflict is politically motivated also seems to play an unacknowledged role in deciding whether it is "war" or not. Thus, organized crime or drug trafficking,

179

though methodical and bloody, are generally understood to present problems of law enforcement, whereas armed rebellions, once sufficiently organized and violent, are usually seen as "wars."

The problem with these guidelines, however, is that they were written to address domestic conflicts rather than global terrorism. Thus, they do not make clear whether al-Qaeda should be considered an organized criminal operation (which would trigger law-enforcement rules) or a rebellion (which would trigger war rules). The case is close enough that the debate of competing metaphors does not yield a conclusive answer. Clarification of the law would be useful.

Even in the case of war, another factor in deciding whether law-enforcement rules should apply is the nature of a given suspect's involvement. War rules treat as combatants only those who are taking an active part in hostilities. Typically, that includes members of an armed force who have not laid down their arms as well as others who are directing an attack, fighting or approaching a battle, or defending a position. Under these rules, even civilians who pick up arms and start fighting can be considered combatants and treated accordingly. But this definition is difficult to apply to terrorism, where roles and activities are clandestine, and a person's relationship to specific violent acts is often unclear.

Given this confusion, a more productive approach is to consider the policy consequences of applying wartime or law enforcement rules.

Unfortunately, the Bush administration seems to have ignored such concerns.

Padilla and al-Marri

Consider, for example, the cases of Jose Padilla and Ali Saleh Kahlah al-Marri. Federal officials arrested Padilla, a U.S. citizen, in May 2002 when he arrived from Pakistan at Chicago's O'Hare Airport, allegedly to scout out targets for a radiological or "dirty" bomb. As for al-Marri, a student from Qatar, he was arrested in December 2001 at his home in Peoria, Illinois, for allegedly being a "sleeper," an inactive accomplice who could be activated to help others launch terrorist attacks. If these allegations are true, Padilla and al-Marri should certainly be prosecuted. Instead, after initially holding each man on other grounds, President Bush declared them both to be "enemy combatants" and claimed the right to hold them without charge or trial until the end of the war against terrorism—which, of course, may never come.

But should Padilla and al-Marri, even if they have actually done what the U.S. government claims, really be considered warriors? Aren't they more like ordinary criminals? A simple thought experiment shows how dangerous are the implications of treating them as combatants. The Bush administration has asserted that the two men planned to wage war against the United States and therefore can be considered de facto soldiers. But if that is the case, then under war rules, the two men could have been shot on sight, regardless of any immediate danger they posed. Padilla could have been gunned down as he stepped off his plane at

O'Hare, al-Marri as he left his home in Peoria. That, after all, is what it means to be a combatant in time of war.

Most people, I suspect, would be deeply troubled by that result. The Bush administration has not alleged that either suspect was anywhere near to carrying out his alleged terrorist plan. Neither man, therefore, posed an imminent threat of the sort that might justify the preventive use of lethal force under law enforcement rules. With a sophisticated legal system available to hear their cases, killing these men would have seemed gratuitous and wrong. Of course, the Bush administration has not proposed summarily killing them; it plans to detain them indefinitely. But if Padilla and al-Marri are not enemy combatants for the purpose of being shot, they should not be enemy combatants for the purpose of being detained, either. The one conclusion necessarily implies the other.

Even if they were appropriately treated as combatants, Padilla's and al-Marri's lives might still have been spared under the doctrine of military necessity, which precludes using lethal force when an enemy combatant can be neutralized through lesser means. But from the bombing of urban bridges in northern Serbia during the Kosovo war to the slaughter on the "Highway of Death" during the 1991 Gulf War, the U.S. government has been at best inconsistent in respecting the doctrine of military necessity. Other governments' records are even worse. That terrorist suspects who pose no immediate danger might only sometimes be shot without warning should still trouble us and lead us to question the appropriateness of their classification as combatants in the first place.

Yemen

A similar classification problem, though with an arguably different result, arose in the case of Qaed Salim Sinan al-Harethi. Al-Harethi, who Washington alleges was a senior al-Qaeda official, was killed by a drone-fired missile in November 2002 while driving in a remote tribal area of Yemen. Five of his companions also died in the attack, which was carried out by the CIA. The Bush administration apparently considered al-Harethi an enemy combatant for his alleged involvement in the October 2000 *U.S.S. Cole* bombing, in which seventeen sailors died.

In this instance, the case for applying war rules was stronger than with Padilla or al-Marri, although the Bush administration never bothered to spell it out. Al-Harethi's mere participation in the 2000 attack on the *Cole* would not have made him a combatant in 2002, since in the interim he could have withdrawn from al-Qaeda; war rules permit attacking only current combatants, not past ones. And if al-Harethi were a civilian, not a member of an enemy armed force, he could not be attacked unless he were actively engaged in hostilities at the time. But the administration alleged that al-Harethi was a "top bin Laden operative in Yemen," implying that he was in the process of preparing further attacks. If true, this would have made the use of war rules against him more appropriate. And unlike Padilla and al-Marri, arresting al-Harethi may not have been an option. The Yemeni government has little control over the tribal area where al-Harethi was killed; eighteen Yemeni soldiers had reportedly died in an earlier attempt to arrest him. However, even in this arguably appropriate use of war rules, the Bush administration offered no public justification, apparently unwilling to acknowledge even implicitly any legal constraints on its use of lethal force against alleged terrorists.

Bosnia and Malawi

In other cases outside the United States, the Bush administration's use of war rules has had far less justification. For example, in October 2001, Washington sought the surrender of six Algerian men in Bosnia. At first, the U.S. government followed law enforcement rules and secured the men's arrest. But then, after a three-month investigation, Bosnia's Supreme Court ordered the suspects released for lack of evidence. Instead of providing additional evidence, however, Washington switched to war rules. It pressured the Bosnian government to hand the men over anyway and whisked them out of the country—not to trial, but to indefinite detention at the U.S. naval base at Guantánamo Bay. If the men had indeed been enemy combatants, a trial would have been unnecessary, but there is something troubling about the administration's resort to war rules simply because it did not like the result of following law enforcement rules.

The administration followed a similar pattern in June 2003, when five al-Qaeda suspects were detained in Malawi. Malawi's high court ordered local authorities to follow criminal justice laws and either charge or release the five men, all of whom were foreigners. Ignoring local law, the Bush administration insisted that the men be handed over to U.S. security forces instead. The five men were spirited out of the country to an undisclosed location—not for trial, but for interrogation. The move sparked riots in Malawi. The men were released a month later in Sudan, after questioning by Americans failed to turn up incriminating evidence.

These cases are not anomalies. In the last two-and-a-half years, the U.S. government has taken custody of a series of al-Qaeda suspects in countries such as Pakistan, Thailand, and Indonesia. In many of these cases, the suspects were not captured on a traditional battlefield, and a local criminal justice system was available. Yet instead of allowing the men to be charged with a crime under local law-enforcement rules, Washington had them treated as combatants and delivered to a U.S. detention facility in an undisclosed location.

A Misuse of War Rules?

Is this method of fighting terrorism away from a traditional battlefield an appropriate use of war rules? At least insofar as the target can be shown to be actively involved in ongoing terrorist activity amounting to armed conflict, war rules might be acceptable when there is no reasonable criminal justice option, as in tribal areas of Yemen. But there is something troubling, even dangerous, about using war rules when law enforcement rules reasonably could have been followed.

Errors, common enough in ordinary criminal investigations, are all the more likely when the government relies on the murky intelligence that drives many terrorist investigations. The secrecy of terrorist investigations, with little opportunity for public scrutiny, only compounds the problem. If law enforcement rules are used, a mistaken

185

arrest can be rectified at a public trial. But if war rules apply, the government is never obliged to prove a suspect's guilt. Instead, a supposed terrorist can be held for however long it takes to win the "war" against terrorism—potentially for life—with relatively little public oversight. And the consequences of error are even graver if the supposed combatant is killed, as was al-Harethi. Such mistakes are an inevitable hazard of the traditional battlefield, where quick life-and-death decisions must be made. But when there is no such urgency, prudence and humanity dictate applying law enforcement rules.

Washington must also remember that its conduct sets an example, for better or worse, for many governments around the world. After all, many other states would be all too eager to find an excuse to eliminate their enemies through war rules. Israel, to name one, has used this rationale to justify its assassination of terrorist suspects in Gaza and the West Bank. It is not hard to imagine Russia doing the same to Chechen leaders in Europe, Turkey using a similar pretext against Kurds in Iraq, China against Uighurs in Central Asia, or Egypt against Islamists at home.

There is some indication that the Bush administration may be willing to abide by a preference for law enforcement rules when it comes to using lethal force. President Bush has reportedly signed a secret executive order authorizing the CIA to kill al-Qaeda suspects anywhere in the world but limiting that authority to situations in which other options are unavailable. But when it comes to detention, the administration has been quicker to invoke war rules.

Both the administration's reluctance to kill terrorist suspects and its preference for detention over trial presumably stem in part from its desire to interrogate suspects to learn about potential attacks. Just as a dead suspect cannot talk, a suspect with an attorney may be less willing to cooperate. Moreover, trials risk disclosure of sensitive information, as the administration has discovered in prosecuting Zacarias Moussaoui. These are the costs of using a criminal justice system.

But international human rights law is not indifferent to the needs of a government facing a security crisis. Under a concept known as "derogation," governments are permitted to suspend certain rights temporarily if they can show that it is necessary to meet a "public emergency threatening the life of the nation." The International Covenant on Civil and Political Rights, which the United States has ratified, requires governments invoking derogation to file a declaration justifying the move with the U.N. secretary-general. Among the many governments to have done so are Algeria, Argentina, Chile, Colombia, Peru, Poland, Russia, Sri Lanka, and the United Kingdom. Yet instead of derogating from law enforcement rules, the Bush administration has opted to use war rules.

The difference is more than a technicality. Derogation is a tightly circumscribed exception to ordinary criminal justice guarantees, permitted only to the extent necessary to meet a public emergency and scrutinized by the U.N. Human Rights Committee. Moreover, certain rights—such as the prohibition of torture or arbitrary killing—can never be suspended. The Bush administration, however, has resisted justifying its suspension of law enforcement rules and opposed scrutiny of that decision, whether by international bodies or even by U.S. courts. Instead, it has unilaterally given itself the greater latitude of war rules.

The U.S. Justice Department has defended the Bush administration's use of war rules for suspects apprehended in the United States by citing a U.S. Supreme Court decision from World War II, *Ex Parte Quirin*. In that case, the court ruled that German army saboteurs who landed in the United States could be tried as enemy combatants before military commissions. The court distinguished its ruling in an earlier, Civil War-era case, *Ex Parte Milligan*, which had held that a civilian resident of Indiana could not be tried in military court because local civil courts remained open and operational. Noting that the German saboteurs had entered the United States wearing at least parts of their uniforms, the court in *Quirin* held that the *Milligan* protections applied only to people who are not members of an enemy's armed forces.

But there are several reasons why, even under U.S. law, *Quirin* does not justify the Bush administration's broad use of war rules. First, the saboteurs in *Quirin* were agents of a government with which the United States was obviously at war. The case does not help determine whether, away from traditional battlefields, the United States should be understood as fighting a "war" with al-Qaeda or pursuing a criminal enterprise. Second, although the court in *Quirin* defined a combatant as anyone operating with hostile intent behind military lines, the case has arguably been superseded by the 1949 Geneva Conventions (ratified by the United States), which, as noted, treat as combatants only people who are either members of an enemy's armed force or are taking active part in hostilities. *Quirin* thus does not help determine whether, under current law, people such as Padilla and al-Marri should be considered civilians (who, under *Milligan,* must be brought before civil courts) or combatants (who can face military treatment).

Moreover, *Quirin* establishes only who can be tried before a military tribunal. The Bush administration, however, has asserted that it has the right to hold Padilla, al-Marri, and other detained "combatants" without charge or trial of any kind—in effect, precluding serious independent assessment of the grounds for potentially lifetime detention. The difference is especially significant because in the case of terrorist suspects allegedly working for a shadowy group, error is more likely than it was for the uniformed German saboteurs in *Quirin.*

Finally, whereas the government in *Quirin* was operating under a specific grant of authority from Congress, the Bush administration, in treating suspects as enemy combatants, is operating largely on its own. This lack of congressional guidance means that the difficult judgment calls in drawing the line between war and law enforcement rules are being made behind closed doors, without the popular input that a legislative debate would provide.

A Policy Approach

So, when the "war" on terrorism is being fought away from a traditional battlefield, how should the line be drawn between war and law enforcement rules? No one should lightly give up due process rights, as the Bush administration has done with its "enemy combatants"—

particularly when a mistake could result in death or lengthy detention without charge or trial. Rather, law enforcement rules should presumptively apply to all suspects, and the burden should fall on those who want to invoke war rules to demonstrate that they are necessary and appropriate.

The following three-part test would help assess whether a government has met its burden when it asserts that law enforcement rules do not apply. To invoke war rules, a government should have to prove, first, that an organized group is directing repeated acts of violence against it, its citizens or interests with sufficient intensity that it constitutes an armed conflict; second, that the suspect is an active member of the opposing armed force or an active participant in the violence; and, third, that law enforcement means are unavailable.

Within the United States, the third requirement would be nearly impossible to satisfy—as it should be. Given the ambiguities of investigating terrorism, it is better to be guided more by *Milligan*'s affirmation of the rule of law than by *Quirin*'s exception to it. Outside the United States, Washington should never resort to war rules away from a traditional battlefield if local authorities can and are willing to arrest and deliver a suspect to an independent tribunal—regardless of how the tribunal then rules. War rules should only be used in cases when no law enforcement system exists (and the other conditions of war are present), not when the rule of law happens to produce inconvenient results. Even if military forces are used to make an arrest in such cases, law enforcement rules might still apply; only when attempting an arrest is too dangerous should war rules be countenanced.

This approach would recognize that war rules may have their place in fighting terrorism, but given the way they inherently compromise fundamental rights, they should be used sparingly. Away from a traditional battlefield, they should be used, even against a warlike enemy, as a tool of last resort—when there is no reasonable alternative, not when a functioning criminal justice system is available. Until there are better guidelines on when to apply war and law enforcement rules, this three-part test, drawn from the policy consequences of the decision, offers the best way to balance security and rights. In the meantime, the Bush administration should abandon its excessive use of war rules. In attempting to make Americans safer, it has made all Americans, and everyone else, less free.

Israeli Assassinations

The Israeli-Palestinian conflict provides a useful context to apply this test. Since late 2000, the Israeli government has been deliberately assassinating Palestinians in the West Bank and Gaza Strip whom it claims are involved in attacks against Israelis, particularly Israeli civilians. In many cases, Palestinian civilians died in the course of these assassinations, sometimes because suspects were targeted while in residential buildings or on busy thoroughfares. Even if these attacks might otherwise have been justified, some would violate the international prohibition on attacks that are indiscriminate or cause disproportionate harm to civilians. In other cases, however, the assassinations have hit their mark with little or no harm to others. Can these well-targeted assassinations be justified?

191

Although the level of violence between Israeli and Palestinian forces has varied considerably over time, the violence in certain cases has been intense and sustained enough for the Israeli government reasonably to make the case that in those instances an armed conflict exists.

As for the second prong, the Israeli government would have to show, as noted, that the targeted individual was an active participant in these hostilities, such as by directing an attack, fighting or approaching a battle, or defending a position. The Israeli government used to claim that the Palestinians targeted for assassination were involved in plotting attacks against Israelis, although increasingly the government has not bothered to make that claim. Even when it does so, the summary nature of the claim means that there is nothing to stop Israel from declaring virtually any Palestinian an accomplice in the violent attacks and thus subject to assassination. Given that these assassinations are planned well in advance, Israel should provide evidence of direct involvement in plotting or directing violence before overcoming the legal presumption that all residents of occupied territories are protected civilians. Moreover, because unilateral allegations are so easy to make falsely or mistakenly, and in light of their lethal consequences, these claims should be tested before an independent review mechanism.

As for the third prong, Israel has made no effort to explain why these suspected participants in violent attacks on Israelis could not be arrested and prosecuted rather than summarily killed. Significantly, assassinations are taking place not on a traditional battlefield but in a situation of occupation in which the Fourth Geneva Convention imposes essentially law enforcement responsibilities on the occupier.

These responsibilities do not preclude using war methods in the heat of battle, but the assassinations typically take place when there is no battle raging. In these circumstances, Israel has the burden of explaining why law enforcement means could not be used to arrest a suspect rather than war-like tools to kill him. Theoretically Israel might claim that its forces are unable to enter an area under occupation without triggering armed conflict, but in fact the Israeli military has shown itself capable of operating throughout the West Bank and Gaza with few impediments. In these circumstances, Israel would be hard-pressed to show that a law-enforcement enforcement option is unavailable. It would thus not be justified to resort to the war rules of assassination.

Beyond the Hague: The Challenges of International Justice

By Richard Dicker and Elise Keppler

During the 1990s, the international community took unprecedented steps to limit the impunity all too often associated with mass slaughter, forced dislocation of ethnic groups, torture, and rape as a weapon of war. Along with two genocides and many other widespread crimes, the decade was marked by the creation of international criminal justice mechanisms and the application of universal jurisdiction to hold perpetrators of the most serious crimes to account. Due to inherent difficulties in rendering justice for these crimes, there have been failings, but the new approaches have nonetheless made great strides.

In the last few years, opposition to this nascent "system" of international justice has intensified and today the landscape is less hospitable to the types of advances that took place in the 1990s. In this context, those supporting efforts to hold the world's worst abusers to account need to take a hard look at recent experiences to chart the path forward. The victims who suffer these crimes, their families, and the people in whose names such crimes are committed deserve nothing less. In so doing, it is necessary to emphasize that although international justice mechanisms provide imperfect remedies, they are a vitally necessary alternative to impunity. This essay proposes a perspective of the road ahead in light of both the successes of the recent past and current obstacles to further progress.

A Developing System of International Justice

Soon after the end of the Cold War, with the horrors in the former Yugoslavia and Rwanda and the stark failures of national court systems freshly in mind, the United Nations, a number of governments, and many citizens groups and international nongovernmental organizations (NGOs) worked to create international criminal courts. The Security Council created two ad-hoc international criminal tribunals, the International Criminal Tribunal for the former Yugoslavia (ICTY) in 1993 and the International Criminal Tribunal for Rwanda (ICTR) in 1994, to try alleged perpetrators of genocide, war crimes, crimes against humanity, and other serious violations of international humanitarian law in those particular conflicts.

Affirming the viability of international criminal mechanisms after a fifty-year hiatus, the tribunals held perpetrators of crimes in the former Yugoslavia and Rwanda accountable. Suspects were arrested and tried before these tribunals regardless of their official status, leading to the first indictment of a sitting head of state, namely Slobodan Milosevic by the ICTY, as well as the indictment of the former Prime Minister of Rwanda, Jean Kambanda, by the ICTR. The Rwandan and Yugoslav tribunals revitalized an international criminal jurisprudence that had not developed since the Nuremberg and Tokyo trials.

In response to shortcomings in their performance, described in more detail below, the ICTY and ICTR improved their practice over time. By 2002, between four and six trials were taking place each day in the three courtrooms at the ICTY. Changes were also implemented to improve the functioning of the ICTR where major problems had persisted. In

2002, the capacity of the Rwandan tribunal increased when the Security Council amended the ICTR Statute to permit ad litem judges to serve in trial chambers. After a long delay, two senior posts in the ICTR Office of the Prosecutor were filled and a new president and vice-president were elected. In September 2003, the Security Council separated the ICTY and ICTR prosecutor posts and appointed a separate ICTR prosecutor.

The experience of the ad hoc tribunals revived an idea that first gained currency after World War II: the creation of a standing forum where justice can be rendered for the gravest crimes when national courts are unwilling or unable to do so (the latter limitation on jurisdiction is known as the "complementarity principle"). In 1998, more than 150 countries completed negotiations to establish the International Criminal Court (ICC), a permanent international court charged with prosecuting war crimes, crimes against humanity, and genocide in such circumstances. Reflecting the dynamism of efforts to limit impunity during this period, the necessary sixty states ratified the court's treaty— known as the Rome Statute—to bring it into force in July 2002, less than four years after it had been opened for signature. The establishment of the ICC, a huge step forward for human rights, has the potential to focus international attention on impunity for the "most serious crimes of concern to the international community," as noted in the preamble of the Rome Statute. The court has engendered great expectations.

While the ICC will face many obstacles in bringing justice, the most immediate threat to its effectiveness comes from the ideologically motivated hostility of the Bush administration. The U.S. government's campaign against the court, while both shameful and damaging, has nevertheless failed to derail the considerable momentum behind the ICC's establishment. To date, ninety-two states have ratified the Rome Statute and nearly fifty more have signed it.

In the brief period since the Rome Statute's entry into force, the ICC has moved from an institution on paper to a permanent court staffed with highly qualified judges and an experienced prosecutor and registrar. ICC officials familiar with the experience of the two ad hoc tribunals consciously drew on the lessons of those mechanisms to create a more efficient court. In July 2003, one month after taking office, the prosecutor announced he was following closely the situation in Ituri province of the Democratic Republic of Congo (DRC). Since there is incontrovertible evidence that the DRC currently lacks capacity to adjudicate cases involving serious human rights crimes, the situation there is precisely one of the scenarios the ICC was intended to address.

Over the past decade, several European states also began to meet their obligations to prosecute those found on their territory accused of atrocities. Using domestic universal jurisdiction laws in domestic courts, Switzerland, Denmark, Belgium, Germany and other states have tried such individuals far from the countries where the crimes were committed.

In October 1998, the United Kingdom arrested former President Augusto Pinochet on a Spanish warrant charging the former dictator with human rights crimes committed in Chile during his seventeen-year rule. As a result, four states, Belgium, France, Spain, and Switzerland, litigated the right of their courts to try Pinochet. The arrest of Pinochet sparked litigation before the United Kingdom's highest court, the House of Lords, that resulted in the landmark decision that Pinochet, as a former head of state, could face prosecution for acts of torture in relation to crimes committed after 1988, when the United Kingdom became a party to the U.N. Convention against Torture.

A synergy developed between efforts to bring justice at the international level and access to national courts where the crimes occurred. There was a profoundly important "spillover" effect: national courts began to take on litigation of previously barred cases. The Pinochet litigation prompted an opening of the domestic courts in Chile to victims who had been denied access to remedies. In August 2003, trials of military officers responsible for gross violations of human rights during Argentina's "dirty war" were reopened in Buenos Aires. A Spanish judge prompted this development when he issued warrants for the extradition of forty-five former military officers and a civilian accused of torture and "disappearances" in Argentina so that they could stand trial in Spain.

The spillover effect has been particularly pronounced in countries that have undergone a thorough transition from authoritarian rule to democracy, such as in Chile and Argentina. But also in Chad, victims were emboldened by international efforts to indict former dictator Hissène Habré, leading them to bring cases before their national court against former Habré associates.

These different developments taken together have formed the components of a new, fragile, yet unprecedented system of international justice consisting of ad hoc tribunals, the permanent ICC, and various other international mechanisms. These institutions promise an end to the impunity that perpetrators of some of the world's worst crimes have long enjoyed.

A Changing Landscape

By 2001, steps to enhance international justice began to encounter broadening political opposition. Electoral changes on both sides of the Atlantic brought in political leaders less supportive of these courts. The Bush administration's unilateralist policies were hostile to international institutions. The election of several new governments in Europe reduced the willingness of the European Union to stand up to such hostility. The attacks of September 11, 2001 further contributed to a shift away from support for international justice, with efforts to combat terrorism taking precedence over international law.

In May 2002, the Bush administration launched a worldwide campaign to undermine and marginalize the ICC. After repudiating the U.S. signature of the Rome Statute, the Bush administration threatened to veto all U.N. peacekeeping operations unless Security Council members passed a resolution exempting citizens of non-ICC states parties involved in U.N. operations, such as the United States, from the reach of the ICC. The Bush administration also played hardball to pressure individual ICC states parties to sign bilateral immunity agreements exempting U.S. citizens—and foreign nationals working under contract with the U.S. government—from ICC jurisdiction. These agreements put states parties in violation of their treaty obligations to the court. The actions of the United States—in effect threatening economically vulnerable states with sanctions for supporting the rule of law through the ICC—marked a perverse low point in U.S. human rights policy.

Washington's efforts to undermine the ICC coincided with a rising level of disenchantment among some powerful Security Council members towards the ad hoc tribunals it had created due to their cost and slow-moving procedures. As entirely new entities with only the Nuremberg and Tokyo tribunals as institutional precedents, the ad hoc tribunals for the former Yugoslavia and Rwanda, not surprisingly, had their share of difficulties. With Security Council members increasingly skeptical of the utility of the tribunals and concerned with rising costs, political and financial support waned. This culminated in pressure to adopt a "completion strategy" with a 2010 deadline regardless of whether this date allows the tribunals to fulfill their mandates.

Imposing increased political and financial constraints, the U.N. Security Council then made efforts to bring international expertise to bear on questions of justice in ways that were less politically controversial and costly. These factors prompted the emergence of a diverse "second generation" of international criminal justice mechanisms: "hybrid" national/international tribunals that utilized varying degrees of international involvement.

A U.N. International Commission of Inquiry on East Timor recommended that an international tribunal be created to try those responsible for atrocities committed by the Indonesian army and Timorese militias backed by Indonesia at the time of the vote for independence in 1999. However, Indonesia promised to prosecute individuals responsible for these crimes. As a result, Secretary-General Kofi Annan did not endorse and the Security Council did not implement the Commission's recommendation. In August 2001, an Ad Hoc Human Rights Court on East Timor was established in Indonesia. To try alleged perpetrators who remained in East Timor, the U.N. transitional administration appointed international judges to the newly created Dili District courts. Even after East Timorese independence on May 20, 2002, panels comprised of one East Timorese and two international judges, known as the Special Panels for Serious Crimes, adjudicate these cases.

The U.N. Mission in Kosovo took a similar approach to try serious crimes committed during the armed conflict in 1999. The ICTY lacked the resources and the mandate to act as the main venue to bring justice for these crimes. Although a justice system was reestablished in Kosovo following the conflict, underfunding, poor organization, and political manipulation plagued the newly ethnic-Albanian-dominated system. The new U.N. administration initially appointed a limited number of international judges to sit on panels with a majority of Kosovar judges without restrictions on the cases that these panels could adjudicate. Subsequently, the U.N. administration provided, pursuant to Regulation 2000/64, for panels comprised of at least two international judges and one Kosovar judge to adjudicate cases where "necessary to ensure the independence and impartiality of the judiciary or the proper administration of justice." These panels are known as Regulation 64 Panels after the regulation that created them. They generally adjudicate cases involving serious crimes committed during the conflict. As discussed in the following section, the hybrid mechanisms in East Timor and Kosovo have faced serious difficulties in administering justice in such cases.

In 2002, taking a different "hybrid" approach, the United Nations signed an agreement with the government of Sierra Leone to create the Special Court for Sierra Leone. The Special Court was mandated to bring to justice those "most responsible" for atrocities committed during the country's internal armed conflict. Like the two ad hoc international tribunals, the Special Court has its own statute and rules of procedure. It does not operate as part of the national courts of Sierra Leone. Unlike the Rwandan and Yugoslav tribunals, the court is situated in Sierra Leone, has jurisdiction over some crimes under Sierra Leonean law, and has judicial panels composed of international and Sierra Leonean judges. The court is expected to try between fifteen and twenty alleged perpetrators of the horrific crimes of the conflict.

Due to Herculean efforts by the staff of the Registry and Office of the Prosecutor, the Special Court was established in war-ravaged Freetown, Sierra Leone, in the space of a few months in 2002 and 2003. To date, the prosecutor has issued nine indictments. While the Special Court aroused great expectations, including strong support from the United States due to its low cost and enhanced national character, it too has encountered disenchantment among some Security Council members and the U.N. Secretariat. These attitudes congealed as the cost of the court's operations began to rise beyond initial budget projections. The reservations took a qualitative leap when the prosecutor unsealed an indictment against former Liberian President Charles Taylor while the latter was attending peace talks in Ghana in June 2003. The appropriateness of unsealing the indictment during peace talks generated considerable objections, although no one denies that Taylor's long awaited departure took place soon thereafter. At this writing, the Special Court was facing serious budgetary problems due to the voluntary nature of its financial support.

In Cambodia, efforts to create a stand-alone "hybrid" court to bring members of the Khmer Rouge to justice have been less successful. The United States, France, Japan, and others pressured the United Nations to conclude an agreement with Cambodia to establish a Khmer Rouge Tribunal that lacked fundamental protections to ensure that the tribunal would be independent and impartial. The proposed tribunal would have a majority of Cambodian judges and a minority of international judges, working alongside Cambodian and international co-prosecutors. Cambodia's judiciary has been widely condemned by the United Nations and many of its member states for lack of independence, low levels of competence, and corruption. There are serious concerns about this mechanism.

There are other post-conflict situations where the permanent members of the Security Council have yet to address impunity. These include Afghanistan, Liberia, Côte d'Ivoire, as well as the Democratic Republic of the Congo. In Afghanistan, a national human rights commission, rather than an international commission of inquiry, was given the task of addressing past abuses committed during two decades of war despite its very limited capacity. This was largely due to resistance by the newly established Afghan government, the U.S. government, and the U.N. Assistance Mission in Afghanistan to a serious accountability process that might upset the political transition. To date, the national human rights commission has not made meaningful progress to address past crimes, a result of inadequate training, resources, and equipment, and threats against commission members.

The accountability process in Iraq marks another missed opportunity for the international community. The Iraqi Governing Council has drafted a law to establish a domestic war crimes tribunal to prosecute the former Iraqi leadership for crimes including genocide, crimes against humanity, war crimes, torture, "disappearances," and summary and arbitrary executions committed during Ba`th Party rule. The United States has backed such an "Iraqi-led" tribunal to try these crimes and many Iraqis have expressed support for this approach. However, Iraqi jurists have not had experience in complex criminal trials applying international standards. In the face of very limited United Nations involvement in post-war Iraq, the Security Council, for its part, even shied away from a proposal to establish an expert group comprised of Iraqi and international experts to assess how to best bring justice for Iraq. There is real concern that the projected trials in Baghdad could end up as highly politicized proceedings, undercutting the fairness and legitimacy of the process.

In the last several years, although some states continued to meet their obligation to prosecute the most serious international crimes through their national courts, the application of universal jurisdiction laws also has been scaled back somewhat. While there are a number of pending cases involving mid-level officials before national courts in Europe, there has been no increase in prosecutions of senior officials.

In the so-called Yerodia case of February 2002, the International Court of Justice (ICJ) held that a sitting foreign minister was immune from prosecution in another country's court system regardless of the seriousness of the crimes with which he was charged. Although the ICJ noted that such officials would not be immune to prosecution before international criminal courts where these courts have jurisdiction, its decision went against recent trends to deny immunity for serious human rights crimes.

In 2003, Belgium was forced to revise its universal jurisdiction law in response to intense economic and diplomatic threats by the Bush administration. This included the Bush administration raising the possibility of moving NATO headquarters elsewhere unless Belgium capitulated to its demands. The Belgian law had a particularly expansive reach: the absence of a jurisdictional "presence" requirement in the law together with a provision allowing private individuals, known as "parties civiles," to file complaints directly with an investigating judge resulted in the indiscriminate filing of a spate of cases against high profile officials from around the world. This attracted enormous media attention and opposition even though the investigative judge had the power to, and undoubtedly would have, ultimately dismissed patently unfounded complaints. The revised law restricts the reach of universal jurisdiction to cases where either the accused or victim has ties to Belgium, making it similar to or more restrictive than the laws of most countries that recognize universal jurisdiction.

A Way Forward

The backlash against the developing international justice system, while dismaying, is hardly surprising given the extent to which the significant advances of the past decade have begun to constrain the prerogatives of abusive state officials. The challenge now is to work effectively in a more difficult international environment while many national courts remain unable and unwilling to prosecute the most serious human rights crimes. The gains engendered by international justice institutions need to be preserved and the international system strengthened until many more national courts assume their front-line role in combating impunity.

We see three critical steps: make a sober assessment of the challenges facing international justice today; analyze and draw lessons from experience to date; and take strategic, measured steps forward. This essay concludes with separate descriptions of each of these steps, including specific recommendations on how to implement them to maximize the effectiveness of existing institutions.

Assessing the Challenges Facing International Justice Today

The system of international justice has made several singular advances. At the same time, as described below, the ad hoc international tribunals have not been as effective or as efficient as envisioned. The achievements of the courts in Kosovo and East Timor have been similarly mixed. Grasping the combination of the inherent institutional limitations and the objective difficulties to international justice is crucial in evaluating the performance of these tribunals and continuing efforts to more fully assure justice for atrocities.

Prosecuting senior officials for serious human rights crimes where there are a large number of victims is a complex and expensive process regardless of whether the cases are tried before national or international courts. These prosecutions tend to involve massive amounts of evidence that must be analyzed and classified by crime scene, type of crime, and alleged perpetrator. Such cases require a sophisticated prosecution strategy. Trials must comply with international human rights standards to ensure their legitimacy and credibility. Ensuring the fairness of these trials—including their compliance with human rights standards—often results in a slow process.

Cases brought before international criminal tribunals or in national courts (based on universal jurisdiction) are often tried far away from the crime scene and thus are less accessible to victims and those in whose name the crimes were committed. These trials sometimes lack the visibility in the country where the crimes occurred that a local trial would have. The state where the crimes occurred, whose government may include accused war criminals or their confederates, may oppose the prosecutions, resisting cooperation and making it difficult to obtain custody of the defendants or obtain evidence. Gathering evidence for crimes that occurred hundreds or thousands of miles away makes it more difficult to meet the level of proof required for a conviction and for the accused to develop a comprehensive defense. Another downside to distance includes a lack of familiarity with the cultural and historical context in which the crimes occurred. The need for translation services also slows the pace of trials and makes them more costly.

International criminal tribunals, as global institutions, also face their own unique institutional challenges. Bringing together judges, prosecutors, and other court personnel from different backgrounds and legal cultures creates obstacles to efficient trials. Reconciling the civil and common law traditions to establish and implement rules of procedure and evidence is time-consuming and costly.

The Yugoslav and Rwandan tribunals are illustrative of some of these problems. After approximately seven years of work, the ICTR has completed only fifteen trials. This is due to a variety of factors including an overly ambitious prosecution strategy that pursued too many suspects; poor coordination between investigators and prosecutors; and failure to fill some long vacant posts. The slow pace of trials has resulted in unusually long pre-trial detentions that raise human rights concerns. Although significantly more efficient, cases at the ICTY have also progressed slowly, in some part due to indictments overloaded with numerous counts. The cost of the tribunals has been extraordinarily high, reaching U.S. $100 million a year.

At the ICTR, there have also been ongoing problems with witness and victim protection. Witnesses and victims have described being treated with a lack of sensitivity due in part to lack of communication with victims and witnesses and inadequate follow-up. Major indicted war criminals of both tribunals remain at-large due to a failure of cooperation and assistance by the states where they are located and other states with the capacity to arrest them.

The national component of the hybrid mechanisms offers the potential advantage that the trials will leave a more lasting legacy in the countries where the crimes occurred. In theory, the existence of national staff working alongside internationals with expertise in adjudicating complex criminal trials could over time enhance the capacity of national courts. The proximity of the court to the site of the crimes could make the trials more accessible to victims and those in whose name the crimes were committed. However, the local component of these mechanisms also presents particular challenges. Security risks may be increased, local staff hired to work on these cases may be linked to past abuses, thereby re-traumatizing victims and witnesses, and national staff may be subject to political interference or lack the expertise to ensure that cases are tried fairly and effectively.

The work of the hybrid mechanisms in East Timor and Kosovo up to this point has been far from ideal. Representing "justice on the cheap," they have been seriously under funded by the international community. In both situations, cases have progressed slowly and the administration of justice has suffered from a range of problems including: lack of qualified staff to investigate, prosecute, and adjudicate cases; arbitrary or lengthy pre-trial detention and ineffective defense counsel; lack of effective translation services and support staff; and allegations of political interference or intimidation.

As the Special Court for Sierra Leone has yet to begin trials, it is too soon to evaluate its success as an accountability model. However, it appears so far to be operating efficiently.

In establishing the Yugoslav and Rwandan tribunals, the international community faced specific challenges that resulted from their *sui generis* nature. The only models from which they had to work were the Nuremberg and Tokyo tribunals, courts conducted by the victors of World War II, fifty years ago, and in which trials and sentences were quickly carried out. While not absent, fair trial safeguards in these prosecutions would probably not pass muster under today's standards. Most strikingly, there was no right to appeal. The establishment of the Yugoslav and Rwandan tribunals thus occurred without any pre-existing adequate model and high start-up costs could have been expected.

Objective institutional problems have also been aggravated by a tendency to misunderstand the immediate impact of the Nuremberg trials. The short-term effect of Nuremberg has, unfortunately, been inflated over the years. At the time the trials were conducted, they were enormously controversial among Germans. While illuminating to the international audience, the German people initially dismissed the proceedings as political show trials. The International Military Tribunal (IMT) that conducted the Nuremberg trials did not significantly enable Germans to come to grips with the horrific crimes that were committed by the Nazi government. This reckoning only occurred decades later when a new generation began to ask questions about individual responsibility during the Third Reich. At that time, the IMT's record provided an invaluable and incontrovertible reference point of past crimes. Nevertheless, conventional wisdom about the Nuremberg trials is that they quickly enabled the population of Germany to confront what had happened under the Nazi Party. This idealized view has led to unrealistic expectations for war crimes trials. We need to better calibrate our expectations given the experience of the last half-century.

The international community, moreover, is only beginning to reap the benefits of its investment in the Yugoslav and Rwandan tribunals. It has drawn on the lessons of the two tribunals in establishing the ICC and hybrid mechanisms, and can also be expected to benefit from this experience in structuring future justice mechanisms.

Learning from Experience

National courts are not about to become uniformly capable or willing to bring justice for atrocities in the immediate future. This is particularly true in post-conflict situations where justice systems have been either partially or completely destroyed. As a result, international justice will remain a crucial last resort that must continue to be fortified against efforts to undermine it.

The achievements and failings of the ICTY and ICTR need to be thoroughly assessed. While it may be unrealistic to expect that full-scale ad hoc international tribunals will be created in the current environment, the lessons of these tribunals can help inform other efforts, including the development of hybrid justice mechanisms. Similarly, the record of existing hybrid mechanisms must be evaluated so that the benefits of national participation can be fully realized while better achieving fair and effective trials. The effects of differences between existing hybrid courts, including the extent to which they operate more as national courts, as do the Regulation 64 Panels in Kosovo, or as international courts, as does the Special Court for Sierra Leone, should receive particular scrutiny. Hybrid mechanisms should not be established simply because they are an inexpensive alternative if an international mechanism would be more appropriate.

In addition, we need to evaluate situations in which international mechanisms are rejected notwithstanding serious concerns about national capacity and willingness to pursue justice, as in Indonesia for crimes in East Timor and as is likely to be the case in Iraq. The consequences of failing to address impunity at all, as appears likely in Afghanistan, must also be documented. Such efforts will help build support for international justice.

More countries should be encouraged to adopt and implement universal jurisdiction laws. This could be accomplished as part of their adoption of ICC implementing legislation. Politicized use of universal jurisdiction against high profile figures, however, will only weaken the credibility of international justice efforts and should be avoided. In general, prosecutors and investigating judges should initiate cases against lower-rank defendants found on their territories. This will allow the jurisprudence and practice to be built from the bottom up. This could lead over time to the successful application of extra-territorial jurisdiction against more prominent figures. However, where a strong legal basis exists, cases against more prominent figures must also be pursued.

The United Nations must play a more central and systematic role in post-conflict situations. Although the United Nations has often been pivotal in forging the international response to serious human rights crimes in such settings, the "justice gap" in countries such as Liberia, the Democratic Republic of Congo, and Côte d'Ivoire underscores the need for more systematic U.N. efforts. Over the last decade, the Security Council, the secretary-general, and the General Assembly have convened several commissions of experts to assess evidence of serious human rights crimes and recommend appropriate mechanisms. Such commissions were created for the former Yugoslavia, Rwanda, East Timor, and Cambodia. The U.N. Secretariat should create a permanent post or entity charged with analyzing the work of such commissions, identifying successes and failures, and advising future commissions. Creation of such commissions should become a regular part of the Security Council's response to post-conflict situations.

Taking Strategic Steps Forward

The ICC will only realize its potential with the concerted assistance of states, intergovernmental organizations, and NGOs. States parties need to strengthen and defend the integrity of the ICC statute. They should find ways to diffuse attacks on the court by the Bush administration, and continue to provide additional financial and diplomatic support for the court. States parties must also adopt strong legislation implementing the provisions of the Rome Statute into national law.

There likely will be intense scrutiny of the ICC's performance in the first cases it adjudicates. It will be difficult work to do well and there will be shortcomings. However, the ICC should make every effort to conduct the most fair, impartial, effective, and efficient trials possible so that the court gains legitimacy and credibility.

Even if the ICC achieves its full potential, it realistically will not be able to address all situations in which national courts are unwilling or unable to prosecute perpetrators. Among other factors, there are temporal and other jurisdictional limitations on what cases the ICC can hear. The ICC's jurisdiction is also restricted to cases in which the state where the crimes occurred is a party to the Rome Statute, the state of the nationality of the accused is a party to the Rome Statute, or the Security Council refers the situation. Even where these requirements are satisfied, the ICC will be able to prosecute only a small percentage of the highest-level alleged perpetrators. Cases of mid-level perpetrators and cases where there are numerous perpetrators bearing significant responsibility, as in many post-conflict situations, are unlikely to be fully addressed by the ICC.

In light of the constraints on the ICC and other international justice mechanisms, efforts to strengthen weak but politically willing national courts are all the more important. The ICC's operations must leverage the complementarity provisions of the Rome Statute to create a synergy between its work and prosecutions for serious human rights crimes by national courts. The ICC should strive to focus international attention on situations where serious human rights crimes have occurred, both where it is pursuing cases and not pursuing cases. Where it is pursuing cases, such attention could help garner support to enhance the capacity of national courts to prosecute mid-level and lower-level perpetrators effectively and in accordance with fair trial standards. Where it is unable to pursue cases involving serious crimes due to jurisdictional limitations or some other obstacle, such attention could help garner support to enhance the capacity of national courts to prosecute the highest-level perpetrators. This will maximize the ICC's catalytic effect on international support for fair and effective prosecutions at the national level.

Hybrid mechanisms, universal jurisdiction, and other solutions will be essential to filling justice gaps where the ICC and national courts are unable to address serious crimes. The international community should apply the lessons learned from existing hybrid mechanisms to develop new models that are able to bring justice more fairly, effectively, and efficiently. Universal jurisdiction should be applied where appropriate.

The work of the ICTY and ICTR should effectively draw on the lessons of experience to date to complete their work. Given the emphasis the Security Council has placed on a completion strategy for these tribunals to cease operations by 2010, states and intergovernmental organizations should work assiduously to arrest key suspects and prosecute them. The tribunals should continue to amend their rules and improve courtroom management to increase efficiency and effectiveness. Some cases are likely to be referred back to the national courts of the former Yugoslavia and Rwanda as part of the completion strategy. The lessons of the tribunals should be used to increase the capacity of the national courts to adjudicate these cases fairly and effectively by conditioning referral on national courts' compliance with international fair trial and human rights standards.

Conclusion

The development of a system of international justice to limit impunity for serious human rights crimes has struck at outmoded notions of national sovereignty and the absolute prerogative of states. It would have been unrealistic to expect that progress would occur in a straight line. To address today's more difficult environment, recent achievements must be secured and the system must be refined so that perpetrators of the most serious crimes are increasingly held to account.

Children as Weapons of War
By Jo Becker

Over the last five years, the global campaign to stop the use of child soldiers has garnered an impressive series of successes, including new international legal standards, action by the UN Security Council and regional bodies, and pledges from various armed groups and governments to end the use of child soldiers. Despite gains in awareness and better understanding of practical policies that can help reduce the use of children in war, the practice persists in at least twenty countries, and globally, the number of child soldiers—about 300,000—is believed to have remained fairly constant.

As the end of wars in Sierra Leone, Angola, and elsewhere freed thousands of former child soldiers from active armed conflict, new conflicts in Liberia and Côte d'Ivoire drew in thousands of new child recruits, including former child soldiers from neighboring countries. In some continuing armed conflicts, child recruitment increased alarmingly. In Northern Uganda, abduction rates reached record levels in late 2002 and 2003 as over 8,000 boys and girls were forced by the Lord's Resistance Army to become soldiers, laborers, and sexual slaves. In the neighboring Democratic Republic of Congo (DRC), where all parties to the armed conflict recruit and use children, some as young as seven, the forced recruitment of children increased so dramatically in late 2002 and early 2003 that observers described the fighting forces as "armies of children."

In many conflicts, commanders see children as cheap, compliant, and effective fighters. They may be unlikely to stop recruiting child soldiers or demobilize their young fighters unless they perceive that the benefits of doing so outweigh the military advantage the children provide, or that the costs of continuing to use child soldiers are unacceptably high.

In theory, the benefits of ending child soldier use can include an enhanced reputation and legitimacy within the international community, and practical support for rehabilitation of former child soldiers, including educational and vocational opportunities. Possible negative consequences of continued child soldier use can include "shaming" in international fora and the media, restrictions on military and other assistance, exclusion from governance structures or amnesty agreements, and prosecution by the International Criminal Court or other justice mechanisms.

In practice, however, the use of child soldiers all too often fails to elicit action by the international community at all, apart from general statements of condemnation. Human Rights Watch is aware of no examples of military aid being cut off or other sanctions imposed on a government or armed group for its use of child soldiers. Conversely, when armed forces or groups do improve their practices, benefits also frequently fail to materialize. Although governments and armed groups receive public attention for commitments to end use of child soldiers, concrete support for demobilization and rehabilitation efforts often does not follow.

If the international community is serious about ending the use of child soldiers, it needs to build on the successes of the past five years, but with a sober eye for the obstacles that have stymied further progress. This essay gives an overview of developments over that period, both positive and negative, and offers suggestions on the way forward.

Renewed progress will depend on clearly and publicly identifying the responsible parties; providing financial and other assistance for demobilization and rehabilitation; and, most importantly, ensuring that violators pay a price should they continue to recruit and deploy child soldiers. Some concrete suggestions on how these remedies should be pursued, including the critical role that the U.N. Security Council is poised to play, are described in the concluding section of the essay.

New Visibility and the Emergence of New Legal Norms

In a span of just two years, but following years of campaigning, three important new treaties were adopted that significantly strengthened legal norms regarding the use of child soldiers. In July 1998, 120 governments adopted the Rome Statute for the International Criminal Court, defining the conscription, enlistment, or use in hostilities of children under the age of fifteen as a war crime. Less than a year later, in June of 1999, the member states of the International Labor Organization (ILO) acted to prohibit the forced recruitment of children under age eighteen for use in armed conflict as part of the Worst Forms of Child Labor Convention (Convention 182). And in May 2000, the U.N. adopted the Optional Protocol to the Convention on the Rights of the Child, establishing eighteen as the minimum age for participation in armed conflict, for compulsory or forced recruitment, and for any recruitment by nongovernmental armed groups.

The treaties were embraced rapidly. The Worst Forms of Child Labor Convention quickly became the most rapidly ratified labor convention in history, with 147 states parties by November 2003. In April 2002, the Rome Statute reached the threshold of sixty ratifications needed to bring the International Criminal Court into being, and by November 2003, sixty-six nations had ratified the Optional Protocol.

Intensive lobbying by nongovernmental organizations, (NGOs) notably the Coalition to Stop the Use of Child Soldiers and the coalition's national partners, helped build a global consensus against the use of child soldiers, and brought new attention to the issue. The coalition spearheaded the campaign for the adoption, ratification, and implementation of the Optional Protocol, holding a series of high-profile regional conferences, documenting child recruitment policies and practices worldwide, lobbying the Security Council and other international actors, and supporting regional networks working to end the use of child soldiers. The coalition's national partners launched public awareness campaigns, lobbied for changes in national policy and practice, and in many countries, helped drive forward the ratification and implementation of the optional protocol.

Attention to child soldiers has emerged in numerous other fora, including the Organization for Security and Cooperation in Europe, the European Parliament, the Organization of American States, the

European Union-African, Caribbean and Pacific group (E.U.-ACP), and the Economic Community of West African States (ECOWAS), resulting in resolutions, joint strategies to address children and armed conflict, and the establishment of regional child protection mechanisms.

Government Forces and Child Soldiers

While some governments have taken concrete steps to end child soldier use, others flout the new norms by continuing to use children in conflict. Between 1999 and 2001, South Africa, Portugal, Denmark, and Finland each adopted new national legislation, raising the minimum age for voluntary recruitment to eighteen. In early 2003, the National Security Council of Afghanistan established a new minimum recruitment age of twenty-two.

Some governments raised their recruitment age even in the midst of conflict. In May of 2000, the government of Sierra Leone announced government policy setting eighteen as the minimum age for bearing arms. Previously, military law had set the age at seventeen. The government of Colombia, engaged in a thirty-year civil war, adopted legislation in December 1999 prohibiting all recruitment of children under the age of eighteen, and discharged over 600 children from the army and more than 200 from other government forces.

The ratification of the optional protocol has brought additional changes by other governments. Until 2002, the United States routinely recruited seventeen-year-olds on a volunteer basis, and deployed them into conflict situations. Seventeen-year-old U.S. soldiers served in U.S. operations in Somalia, Bosnia, and the 1991 Gulf War. Once the U.S. ratified the Optional Protocol in December 2002, it changed its deployment practices to exclude seventeen-year-old troops from combat positions.

The United Kingdom recruits at age sixteen—one of the lowest official voluntary recruitment ages of any country—and has been the only European country to send under-eighteens routinely into battle. When ratifying the optional protocol in early 2003, the U.K. made a declaration stating that it would continue to deploy under-eighteens in situations of "genuine military need" when withdrawing them is deemed "impractical." The Coalition to Stop the Use of Child Soldiers and other human rights advocates sharply criticized the declaration, stating that it was contrary to the object and purpose of the protocol, and that the U.K.'s declaration should be considered null and void. A change in practice became evident when the U.K. government announced that it would not deploy under-eighteens in the U.S.-led military operation against Saddam Hussein's forces in Iraq, and removed under-age soldiers from ships being sent to the region. In contrast, over 200 British under-eighteens participated in the 1991 Gulf War, two of whom died during the war.

Other governments have continued to recruit and use children in armed conflict, including Burma, Burundi, the DRC, Liberia, Sudan, and Uganda. Burma's national army alone includes an estimated 70,000 child soldiers (nearly one-quarter of the world's total) and routinely sends children as young as twelve into battle against armed ethnic opposition groups. Both Uganda and the DRC have ratified the optional protocol, but flout their obligations by using child soldiers. The Ugandan People's Defense Force has recruited children who escaped or were captured from the rebel Lord's Resistance Army, and has trained and deployed children recruited into local defense units. The government of DRC maintains children in its ranks despite a 2000 presidential decree calling for the demobilization of child soldiers.

Paramilitaries or civil defense forces that are linked to the government frequently recruit children as well. As many as 20,000 children may serve in militias supported by the government of Sudan. In Colombia, the paramilitary United Self-Defense Forces of Colombia (Autodefensas Unidas de Colombia, AUC) receive support from some army units, and often work in close collaboration with the Colombian military, which prohibits the recruitment of children. The AUC includes over 2,000 children, including many girls and children as young as age seven. In other countries, including the DRC and Rwanda, child recruitment by government-linked militias is also common.

Child Soldiers and Opposition Forces

Child soldier use is endemic among non-state armed groups. In nearly every conflict where government forces use child soldiers, opposition forces do as well. But even when governments do not recruit children, as in Nepal, the Philippines, or Sri Lanka, use of child soldiers by opposition forces may be routine. The use of child soldiers by nongovernmental armed groups is perceived as a more intractable problem than such use by states, due to the more limited range of pressure points available to the international community when dealing with non-state actors.

Many armed groups are sensitive to world opinion, however, and heightened attention to the issue of child soldiers has prompted a growing number of non-governmental armed groups to make public commitments to end the use of child soldiers. Among these are the Rassemblement Congolais pour la Démocratie-Goma (RCD-Goma) in the DRC, Revolutionary Armed Forces of Colombia-People's Army (Fuerzas Armadas Revolucionarias de Colombia-Ejército del Pueblo, FARC-EP) in Colombia, the Liberation Tigers of Tamil Eelam (LTTE) in Sri Lanka, Liberians United for Reconciliation and Democracy (LURD) in Liberia, the Sudan People's Liberation Army (SPLA) in Sudan, and several ethnic armed opposition groups in Burma (Myanmar).

One of the most recent commitments by non-state actors was contained in a statement by the Liberians United for Reconciliation and Democracy (LURD) on June 30, 2003. The LURD statement instructed all military commanders to refrain from the "unwholesome" act of recruiting children under the age of eighteen for active combat, and to release all children under the age of eighteen to LURD headquarters for demobilization and social reintegration. Several factors may have precipitated the announcement. Human rights advocates had raised the child soldiers issue with LURD's political leadership, suggesting that the LURD demobilize child soldiers not only for principled reasons, but also pointing out the indictment of then-president of Liberia Charles Taylor by the Sierra Leone special court for crimes including the use of child soldiers. The advocates suggested that the LURD would not want similar charges hanging over their heads should they eventually take power. Members of the U.N. Security Council delegation led by Sir Jeremy Greenstock of the U.K. also urged an end to the use of child soldiers during meetings with parties to the Liberian peace talks in Accra in late June 2003. Like many other parties to armed conflict that have made similar pledges, however, the LURD has not implemented its commitment, and has continued its use of child soldiers

The U.N. secretary-general's special representative on children and armed conflict, Olara Otunnu, has secured a number of high-profile commitments from non-state armed groups. Although highly touted, few of these commitments have been kept in practice. During a June 1999 visit to Colombia by the special representative, the FARC agreed not to recruit children under the age of fifteen. However, the FARC's recruitment practices remained unchanged, and Human Rights Watch estimates that over 7,400 children (including those in urban-based militias) serve in its ranks, including many under the age of fifteen. Of seventy-two former child soldiers from the FARC interviewed by Human Rights Watch in 2002, fifty-seven (nearly 80 percent) were recruited before the age of fifteen.

In May of 1998, Otunnu traveled to Sri Lanka and received a commitment from the LTTE to end its use of children under eighteen in combat, and not to recruit children below the age of seventeen. In 2001, UNICEF reported that child recruitment had actually increased in the interim. The LTTE reaffirmed its commitment during a February 2001 visit by UNICEF's deputy director, but child recruitment by the

LTTE continued unabated, including the kidnapping of school children traveling home from school. In June 2003, the government and LTTE agreed on an action plan for children affected by war, including mechanisms for the release and reintegration of former child soldiers, primarily the establishment of transit centers co-managed by the Tamils Rehabilitation Organization and UNICEF. At this writing, child recruitment by the LTTE was continuing, and it was unclear whether the agreement would prompt significant progress.

The continuing pressure by the U.N. to induce the LTTE to fulfill its commitment is more the exception than the rule. The special representative has not made follow-up visits to either Sri Lanka or Colombia, and a UNICEF representative told Human Rights Watch that the commitments are "not systematically monitored." The representative cited a general lack of coordination between the special representative and UNICEF in following up the commitments.

Another underlying problem is that armed groups perceive a public relations benefit from making public commitments not to recruit child soldiers, but often lack the political will or resources to actually demobilize children from their ranks. Commanders who are concerned with maintaining military strength may be reluctant to release young soldiers, particularly when alternatives for the children, including school or vocational training, are not available.

In many cases, assistance in creating educational and vocational alternatives for child soldiers is critical in ensuring compliance by armed groups with their commitments. Top-ranking commanders in the Karenni Army, one of Burma's armed ethnic opposition groups, admit that 20 percent of the group's ranks are children despite policies prohibiting the recruitment of children under the age of eighteen. A Karenni Army general told Human Rights Watch that he was aware of international standards and would prefer to exclude children from his forces, but that many of the children who seek to join are displaced or refugee children with no access to school. He said that if viable educational or vocational alternatives were available to young volunteers, it would be easier to comply with international standards:

> "We have some ideas for projects for some of our young boys in the army, but we can't get any support from outside organizations. . . . No resources means no skills. . . . The only option for child soldiers is if we can have a special school for them, not only for reading and writing but also for vocational skills like carpentry or auto mechanics. We can't send fourteen and fifteen-year-olds to ordinary kindergarten. The most important thing for these young people is education."

In eastern DRC, complementary efforts by the U.N. and NGOs resulted in the demobilization of more than 1,200 children from RCD-Goma and other armed groups in North and South Kivu from 1999 to early 2003. Following a massive recruitment drive by the RCD-Goma in 2000, Save the Children U.K. sought the agreement of RCD-Goma commanders to hold a series of workshops for military personnel on international law related to child soldiers, and the demobilization and rehabilitation programs operated by Save the Children. Seven workshops were held in 2001, prompting a noticeable increase in the number of children demobilized. During the same period, UNICEF held a series of meetings with the RCD-Goma political leadership, culminating in a formal plan of action for the demobilization of child soldiers that was agreed in December of 2001. In April of 2002, RCD-Goma formally demobilized 104 children from a military training camp near Goma. However, thousands of additional child soldiers remain in RCD-Goma's ranks.

Transitioning Children Out of War

By late 2003, demobilization and rehabilitation programs for former child soldiers were operating in a half-dozen countries, including Colombia, the DRC, Rwanda, Sierra Leone, Somalia, Sudan, and Uganda, and new programs were beginning in Afghanistan, Burundi, Liberia, and Sri Lanka. However, with few exceptions, these programs were available to only a small percentage of the children who needed them, and in some countries, including Myanmar, Nepal, and the Philippines, such programs were practically nonexistent.

Rehabilitation assistance for child soldiers is often delayed. In Afghanistan, parties to conflict regularly used child soldiers during more than two decades of civil war, and one survey of over 3000 Afghans found that up to 30 percent had participated in military activities as children. However, it was nearly two years after the Afghan conflict had officially ended before a UNICEF program for the rehabilitation and reintegration of former child soldiers was established. In Angola, a peace agreement was reached in April of 2002, but child soldiers were excluded from formal demobilization programs and, at this writing, no special rehabilitation services had been set up for an estimated 7,000-11,000 children who served with UNITA or government forces. In the DRC, the government issued a decree in June of 2000 to demobilize child soldiers from government forces. It subsequently developed a plan for demobilization, rehabilitation, and reintegration, but complained that it was unable to implement the plan because donors had not provided sufficient resources. Between July 2001 and November 2002, only 280 child soldiers were reportedly released from the government's forces.

Not surprisingly, the most significant reductions in child soldier use have accompanied the end of conflicts themselves. From May 2001 through January 2002, the U.N. mission in Sierra Leone disarmed and demobilized close to 48,000 combatants from rebel forces and government-allied militias, including 6,845 child soldiers. Most former child soldiers were reunited with their families, and about half were either enrolled in educational support or skills training programs

A significant weakness of the Sierra Leone program and many others is the exclusion of girls from demobilization, rehabilitation, and reintegration processes. In Sierra Leone, hundreds of girls were left out of the demobilization program and remained with their rebel captors. In the DRC, thousands of girls are thought to be involved in armed groups, but the demobilization of over 1000 children in North and South Kivu by Save the Children and other partners since 1999 included only nine girls. The exclusion of girls is due to multiple factors. Girls who do not serve in visible combatant roles are often overlooked. Some may be reluctant to participate in demobilization programs because of the stigma of being associated with military forces, particularly when sexual abuse is common. In other cases, programs are not designed with girls or their particular needs in mind, despite the significant numbers of girls involved in many armed conflicts.

Demobilization of children during an active armed conflict is particularly challenging. Southern Sudan is one of the few examples of such efforts. In 2000, the SPLA made a commitment to UNICEF executive director Carol Bellamy to end its use of child soldiers. The following year, the SPLA cooperated with UNICEF and other organizations in the demobilization of over 3,500 children from its forces and their reunification with their families. By 2003, however, the process of demobilization had stagnated. UNICEF estimates that 7,000-8,000 children remain with the SPLA, and that some recruitment continues, including re-recruitment of children who had been previously demobilized.

Re-recruitment of some former child soldiers occurs in nearly all cases where demobilization of children is attempted during a continuing armed conflict. In Northern Uganda, where the Lord's Resistance Army has abducted an estimated 20,000 children for use as slaves and soldiers, programs operated by World Vision and Gulu Save Our Children Organization (GUSCO) provide rehabilitation support for many former child soldiers who manage to escape or are released. However, the World Vision center reports that since 2000, at least eighteen children who had passed through the center were reabducted and escaped for a second time. GUSCO reported that ten children from their program were reabducted between September and December 2002. For many former child soldiers, fear of reabduction prevents them from returning to their homes, making social reintegration and the resumption of civilian life very difficult.

Re-recruitment of previously demobilized children has also been reported in the Democratic Republic of Congo, Sierra Leone, and Sudan. In early 2001, 163 Congolese children were demobilized and returned to Eastern DRC by UNICEF after being discovered in a military training camp in Uganda. However, by mid-2003, local NGOs reported that the majority had been recruited again by an opposition group, the Union of Congolese Patriots (UPC), and that some had been killed during fighting.

The risk of re-recruitment underlines the need for adequate security in areas where forced recruitment takes place, support mechanisms in the child's community to facilitate their reintegration, and advocacy networks to follow up any cases of re-recruitment.

The Role of the U.N. Security Council

Beginning in 1998, the U.N. Security Council began a series of annual debates and resolutions on children and armed conflict, and more broadly on the protection of civilians and human security. On the issue of child soldiers in particular, the Council has taken progressively stronger measures. The Council's first resolutions on the issue (in 1999 and 2000) simply urged U.N. member states and parties to armed conflict to abide by international standards on the issue and support rehabilitation efforts for former child soldiers. However, in November 2001, the Council took the unusual step of asking the secretary-general to compile and publish a list of specific parties to armed conflict that were recruiting or using child soldiers in violation of their international obligations. This "name and shame" initiative was the first time that the Council had specifically named abusive parties, and was intended to hold violators accountable for their actions. In addressing the Council, the secretary-general said of the list, "By exposing those who violate standards for the protection of children to the light of public scrutiny, we are serving notice that the international community is finally willing to back expressions of concern with action."

The list of violators produced by the secretary-general in November of 2002 included twenty-three parties in five countries—Liberia, Somalia, Democratic Republic of Congo, Afghanistan and Burundi. Because the list was confined to the situations on the Security Council's agenda, it excluded some of the countries with the most severe child soldier problems, including Colombia, Burma, and Sri Lanka. However, the text of the secretary-general's report raised concerns about child recruitment and use in nine additional countries not on the Security Council's agenda, including the three just mentioned.

Following the receipt of the report, the Council took several additional steps. First, it indicated its intention to enter into dialogue with parties using child soldiers in order to develop action plans to end the practice. Secondly, it requested specific information from the parties named on steps taken to end their use of child soldiers. Third, it requested a progress report on the parties named in the secretary-general's report (including parties in situations not on the Security Council's agenda) by October 31, 2003. Finally, it indicated its intention to consider additional steps (which could include sanctions) against parties that demonstrated "insufficient progress" in ending their use of child soldiers.

In two missions to Africa in 2003, Security Council members raised concerns about the use of child soldiers. In June, members traveled to Central Africa, where the delegation raised the recruitment and use of child soldiers with parties to the conflict in the DRC. Shortly afterwards, in late June and early July, another Security Council delegation raised similar concerns with parties to conflicts in Côte d'Ivoire and Liberia. On that mission, the council also urged parties to those conflicts to arrest and prosecute anyone responsible for recruitment of child soldiers.

The council's "name and shame" strategy, however, has yet to yield concrete results. From late 2002 to mid-2003, the list of violators actually expanded with the addition of both governmental and opposition forces in Côte d'Ivoire, and additional parties to the conflicts in Burundi, DRC, and Liberia. In addition, several of the parties included in the secretary-general's list or report significantly escalated their use of child soldiers during 2003. These include both government and opposition forces in Liberia, the UPC and other armed groups in the DRC, and the Lord's Resistance Army in Northern Uganda.

The limited impact of the list to date is rooted in several factors. According to U.N. workers, the list has not been used extensively as an advocacy tool at the field level, where its potential may not be understood, or it may be seen as irrelevant to the local situation. The limited scope of the 2002 list—covering only countries on the Security Council's agenda, and excluding others with extensive child soldier problems—has caused some to question its validity (although this concern was largely addressed with the publication of two lists in late 2003, one encompassing situations on the Security Council's agenda and the other covering all other situations). Most importantly, at this writing, the council has not yet demonstrated its willingness to take concrete action against parties on the list that show no improvement.

The Way Forward

Ending the use of child soldiers demands strategic and sustained efforts by national, regional and international actors, utilizing and strengthening the tools and norms that have developed over the past few years.

The U.N. Security Council

The recent initiatives taken by the Security Council hold promise for prompting positive change. However, these initiatives require systematic application and follow-through. To be more effective, the U.N. must ensure that all parties that are "named" by the Security Council for recruiting or using child soldiers in violation of their obligations are promptly and officially notified of the fact, and should pursue systematic dialogue with all such parties regarding the creation of action plans and concrete steps to end child recruitment and demobilize child soldiers.

The council should commit to systematic monitoring, and annual reviews of progress (or backsliding) by parties named. Most importantly, it must be clear to governments and armed groups that continued recruitment and use of child soldiers will result in decisive and negative consequences.

At a minimum, the council should impose strict bans on the supply of arms or any military assistance to any party recruiting or using child soldiers in violation of international obligations, for as long as such recruitment and use continues. Other targeted measures should also be employed, including financial restrictions (such as the freezing of assets), travel restrictions on leaders of government or armed groups, and their exclusion from any governance structures or amnesty provisions. Demobilization and rehabilitation assistance should be assured for governments and groups that effectively end new recruitment and demonstrate a clear willingness to demobilize children from their forces.

Third-party Governments

The actions of third party governments are also critical. For example, arms-supplying countries bear a measure of responsibility for the abuses carried out with the weapons they furnish and, as a matter of principle, countries should commit to and stop weapons transfers to parties known to use child soldiers. Countries such as Ukraine, Yugoslavia, the

Russian Federation, and China have provided arms or other military equipment to Burma, despite that government's widespread recruitment of children. Since 1999, Angola (which used child soldiers against UNITA during the country's civil war) received arms from Belarus, Bulgaria, the Czech Republic, Kazakhstan, Slovakia, Russia, and Ukraine. The U.K. approved licenses for exports of military equipment to Angola during the same period.

Bilateral agreements regarding other military assistance should be conditioned on recruitment practices that exclude children. One positive example of such engagement is that of the U.K. and Sierra Leone. In early 1999, the U.K. reached an agreement with the government of Sierra Leone to provide a £10 million package of assistance to promote stability and reconciliation in the country. Among the conditions for the program, the U.K. government sought and secured an assurance from President Kabbah that children would not be used by the Sierra Leone Armed Forces or the Civil Defense Forces. Later in 1999, and again in 2000, Human Rights Watch provided the U.K. government with information regarding child recruitment by civil defense forces. In both instances, the U.K. government raised the issue with Kabbah. There are currently no indications of child soldier use by government armed forces.

Another positive example is the Belgian Parliament, which adopted legislation in March 2003 barring arms transfers to forces that use child soldiers. The new law entered into force in July 2003. Belgium's law and the U.K.'s agreement with the Sierra Leone government, though unfortunately all too rare examples of governments conditioning assistance on performance related to child soldiers, provide a model for future initiatives.

Other tools exist, but are not well-utilized. For example, the U.S. Congress has adopted legislation (the Trade and Development Act of 2000) that conditions trade benefits to developing countries on implementation of their commitments to eliminate the worst forms of child labor, including the forced recruitment of children for use in armed conflict. The U.S. Department of Labor publishes an annual report describing the child labor laws, policies, and practices of nearly 150 beneficiary countries, including the use of child soldiers. To date, however, this has not consistently led to negative consequences for countries found to have used child soldiers. The 2002 report, for example, listed both DRC and Burundi as beneficiaries of U.S. trade benefits, even though both governments had been cited by the U.N. for child soldier use during the same year. To date, only one country— Pakistan—has had its trade benefits partially suspended because of a failure to address child labor issues adequately. No country has had its trade preferences revoked by the U.S. government because of failure to end the use of child soldiers.

National-level Initiatives

At the national level, greater investments must be made in both preventing recruitment of children and rehabilitating former child soldiers. For either to succeed, alternatives to military service are essential. Without access to quality education, or vocational training that can support a viable livelihood, children are much more likely to join armies or armed groups. Keeping families together and reunifying separated children with family members also reduces recruitment risks and facilitates social reintegration of former child soldiers.

Effective prevention also includes sensitizing children, their families, and community leaders to international norms and the negative impact of child soldiering, and engaging local communities in identifying local risk factors for recruitment. At the national level, birth registration, to ensure that children can produce proof of age, and close monitoring of recruitment practices are key. In areas where abduction or forced recruitment of children takes place, increased security at and near schools is needed to ensure that children can pursue their education in safety.

Significant improvements are possible when civil society and national authorities take responsibility for addressing child recruitment. In Paraguay, forced recruitment of children between ages twelve and seventeen was common in the late 1990's, despite legal prohibitions against any recruitment of children below age eighteen. A local non-governmental organization estimated in 2000 that 80 percent of conscripts (more than 10,000 people) were under age eighteen. Between 1996 and 2000, a total of fifty-six under-age soldiers died during military service, often due to training accidents and ill treatment. Local NGOs organized a national campaign, documenting and publicizing cases of under-age recruitment, and filing cases with the Inter-American Commission on Human Rights. In response, the Senate formed an investigatory commission (including both governmental and nongovernmental representatives) to monitor conditions in military barracks. The commission visited sixty-five military barracks in 2001 and 2002, identifying the presence of nearly 200 children. By 2003, local organizations reported that under-age recruitment had essentially stopped. For the first time, official recruitment documents now clearly stipulate the eighteen-year minimum age.

Justice

Finally, stronger efforts must be made to address impunity. In countries where child soldier use is routine, recruiters are rarely, if ever, held to account for recruiting children under the age prescribed by law or policy. In Burma, government law sets the recruitment age at eighteen and recruiters are subject to imprisonment for up to seven years for recruiting children under age. However, not only are these laws routinely flouted, but recruiters receive incentives in the form of cash and bags of rice for every recruit—regardless of age—that they deliver to recruitment centers. In response to requests, the government could provide Human Rights Watch with no information regarding any individuals who had been sanctioned for child recruitment.

This pattern of impunity fuels the cycle of child recruitment. Without a credible threat of criminal or disciplinary action, many recruiters will continue to seek out children, who are easily intimidated by threats, and easily lured by promises.

Impunity can be challenged through national courts, ad hoc tribunals, the International Criminal Court (ICC), and other justice mechanisms.

To date, the most active pursuit of child recruitment cases has come through the Special Court for Sierra Leone, which has one investigator—a specialist in child rights issues—dedicated to investigating these crimes. Investigating crimes related to the use of child soldiers was included in the investigative and prosecutorial strategy from the very inception of operations at the court. The use of child soldiers is included in each of the court's thirteen indictments against defendants linked to abuses by the Civil Defense Forces or the Armed Forces Revolutionary Council/Revolutionary United Front, including, as noted above, former Liberian President Charles Taylor. If convicted, these defendants will likely face lengthy prison terms.

The ICC has great potential for pursuing high profile cases against those responsible for child recruitment. The ICC prosecutor has identified the DRC as a likely source of first cases for the court. Child recruitment has been a hallmark of the war in the DRC, and the country is probably second only to Burma in numbers of child soldiers. Prosecuting the top leadership of RCD-Goma, the UPC, the MLC, and other armed groups for their recruitment and use of children would send a powerful message to others who seek children for their forces.

National justice mechanisms must also hold recruiters to account. Laws on the books are not enough. Colombian law, for example, punishes the recruitment of children under age eighteen by armed groups with a six to ten-year prison sentence for those responsible. Yet the government has failed to enforce the law energetically.

The persistent recruitment and use of child soldiers presents the international community with a formidable, but not insurmountable challenge. The efforts of the past five years have established strong new norms and developed promising new avenues for addressing the problem. But these efforts are clearly not sufficient. Stronger, more concerted pressure is needed to persuade governments and armed groups to abandon their use of children as weapons of war. Success will depend on continued monitoring and advocacy, practical assistance for demobilization and rehabilitation, effective use of political and military leverage by international actors, and an uncompromising commitment by local, national, and international authorities to hold perpetrators accountable.

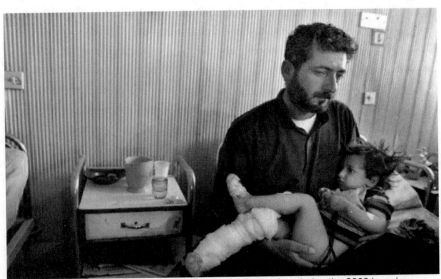
A father holds his son who was wounded and lost his right foot during the 2003 invasion into Iraq by coalition forces. © 2003 Bruno Stevens

Cluster Munitions: Toward a Global Solution

By Steve Goose[61]

On March 31, 2003, a United States cluster munition attack on al-Hilla in central Iraq killed at least thirty-three civilians and injured 109. While an egregious incident, this was not an anomaly in the conflict in Iraq, or in Afghanistan in 2001 and 2002, or in Yugoslavia in 1999. In all of these recent conflicts, and others as well, cluster munition strikes caused significant civilian casualties—casualties that could have been avoided had greater care been taken. Worse still, the vast number of explosive "duds" these weapons left behind have continued to kill and maim civilians long after the attacks, and the conflicts, have ended.

In the past decade the international community has banned two weapons—antipersonnel landmines and blinding lasers—on humanitarian grounds.[62] Cluster munitions now stand out as the weapon category most in need of stronger national and international regulation in order to protect civilians during armed conflict. The

---

[61] The author gratefully acknowledges significant contributions from Bonnie Docherty and Mark Hiznay to the writing of this essay.

[62] Human Rights Watch was at the forefront of both these efforts, which resulted in the 1997 Convention on the Prohibition of the Use, Stockpiling, Production and Transfer of Anti-personnel Mines and Their Destruction (also known as the Mine Ban Treaty), and the 1995 Protocol on Blinding Laser Weapons (Protocol IV) to the Convention on Prohibitions or Restrictions on the Use of Certain Conventional Weapons Which May Be Deemed to Be Excessively Injurious or to Have Indiscriminate Effects (also known as the Convention on Conventional Weapons, or CCW).

immediate danger that cluster munitions pose to civilians during attacks due to their inaccuracy and wide dispersal pattern, the long-term danger they pose after conflict due to the high number of landmine-like submunition duds, and the potential future dangers of widespread proliferation demand urgent action to bring the threat of cluster munitions under control.

Governments and civil society have an opportunity to deal with cluster munitions before they become a global crisis that could easily exceed that posed by antipersonnel landmines. Thus far, cluster munitions have been used in about sixteen countries. But nearly sixty countries have stockpiles of cluster munitions, and the numbers in stockpiles are staggering. The United States alone has cluster munitions containing more than one billion submunitions. Russia and China are likely to have similar quantities. Most of the submunitions now in stockpiles are not sophisticated weapons, but rather those that are known to be highly inaccurate and to have high failure rates, thus producing many hazardous duds.

It is imperative to deal effectively with cluster munitions before they wreak further havoc throughout the world. There is hope for a timely solution because there is already a keen awareness of the problems posed by cluster munitions among governments and nongovernmental organizations (NGOs), and some efforts to resolve the problems are already underway. Most notably, more than eighty NGOs, including Human Rights Watch, on November 13, 2003, launched a new Cluster Munition Coalition to stop the use of these weapons. Moreover, governments have been considering submunitions—if somewhat obliquely—as part of negotiations during the past year on new international law dealing with "explosive remnants of war" (ERW). There is also reason for optimism because humanitarian and military interests largely coincide in the desire to eliminate, or at least decrease dramatically, the indiscriminate effects of the weapon.

What Are Cluster Munitions?

Cluster munitions are large weapons that open in mid-air and scatter widely smaller submunitions, which usually number in the dozens or hundreds.[63] Cluster munitions can be launched from the air by a variety of aircraft, including fighters, bombers, and helicopters. On the ground, cluster munitions can by shot out of artillery, rockets, and missile systems. Air-dropped cluster bombs release submunitions most often called "bomblets," while surface-delivered cluster weapons release submunitions most often called "grenades."

The military values cluster munitions because of their wide dispersal and versatile submunitions. These munitions are "area" weapons that spread their contents over a large field, or "footprint." They can destroy broad

---

[63] "Cluster bombs" is a more common term, but "cluster munitions" is preferable because it encompasses both air- and ground-delivered cluster weapons. For a more in-depth discussion of cluster munitions, see Human Rights Watch, *Off Target: The Conduct of the War and Civilian Casualties in Iraq* (New York: Human Rights Watch, November 2003), and Human Rights Watch, "Fatally Flawed: Cluster Bombs and Their Use by the United States in Afghanistan," *A Human Rights Watch Report*, vol. 14, no. 7 (G), December 2002. For a complete list of Human Rights Watch documents on cluster munitions, see http://www.hrw.org/arms/clusterbombs.htm.

targets like airfields and surface-to-air missile sites. They are also effective against targets that move or do not have precise locations, such as enemy troops or vehicles; the submunitions themselves often have both anti-armor and antipersonnel effects.

The submunitions are designed to explode on impact, which differentiates them from antipersonnel mines, which are designed to be activated by the victim. However, when submunitions fail to explode as expected, the "duds" usually remain hazardous and will explode when touched or disturbed in some manner, thus becoming *de facto* antipersonnel mines. While all weapons have a dud rate, also called the initial failure rate, cluster munitions are more dangerous for a number of reasons. First and foremost is the large numbers of submunitions that are released. Nearly every cluster munition will leave behind significant amounts of hazardous unexploded ordnance. Certain types of submunition duds are considered even more volatile and difficult to clear and destroy than most antipersonnel mines. Submunition duds are more lethal than antipersonnel mines; incidents involving submunition duds are much more likely to cause death than injury.

Most models, whether air-dropped or ground-launched, are unguided, and even the few with guidance mechanisms are not precision-guided. Unguided cluster munitions can miss their mark and hit nearby civilian objects. The numerous submunitions are also unguided and disperse over an area that is not always predictable.[64] Although other types of unguided bombs can miss their target, the humanitarian effects of a cluster attack are often more serious because of the number of submunitions and their wide dispersal. Even if a cluster munition hits its target, the submunitions may kill civilians within the footprint. The inherent risks to civilian life and property increase when these weapons are used in or near populated areas. If cluster munitions are used in an area where combatants and civilians commingle, civilian casualties are almost assured.

Scope of the Problem: Use, Stockpiling, Production, and Trade of Cluster Munitions

Cluster munitions have been used in at least sixteen countries by at least eleven nations.[65] The affected countries include Afghanistan, Albania, Bosnia and Herzegovina, Cambodia, Chad, Eritrea, Ethiopia, Iraq, Kuwait, Laos, Lebanon, Russia (Chechnya), Saudi Arabia, Serbia and Montenegro (including Kosovo), Sudan, and Vietnam. Cluster munitions were also used in the Falklands/Malvinas conflict. In

---

[64] There are exceptions to this. In the Iraq conflict in 2003, the United States for the first time employed cluster munitions containing submunitions that have sensors to guide them, the air-delivered Sensor Fuzed Weapon and the SADARM ("search and destroy armor") artillery projectile.

[65] The information in this section is drawn primarily from: Human Rights Watch, "Cluster Munitions: Measures to Prevent ERW and to Protect Civilian Populations," Memorandum to Delegates to the Convention on Conventional Weapons Group of Governmental Experts on Explosive Remnants of War, Geneva, March 10-14, 2003. See also Human Rights Watch, "A Global Overview of Explosive Submunitions," Memorandum to CCW Delegates, Geneva, May 21-24, 2002.

addition, unconfirmed reports cite use of cluster munitions in Colombia, Morocco (Western Sahara), Sierra Leone, and Turkey.

Nations known to have used cluster munitions include Eritrea, Ethiopia, France, Israel, the Netherlands, Russia, Saudi Arabia, the former Yugoslavia, Sudan, the United Kingdom, and the United States.

At least fifty-seven countries stockpile cluster munitions. Broken down regionally, these countries include:

- Five in Africa—Eritrea, Ethiopia, Nigeria, South Africa, and Sudan;

- Five in the Americas—Argentina, Brazil, Canada, Chile, and the United States;

- Seven in Asia—China, India, Japan, North Korea, South Korea, Pakistan, and Singapore;

- Twenty-two in Europe—Belgium, Bosnia and Herzegovina, Bulgaria, Croatia, Czech Republic, Denmark, Finland, France, Germany, Greece, Italy, the Netherlands, Norway, Poland, Romania, Serbia and Montenegro, Slovakia, Spain, Sweden, Switzerland, Turkey, and the United Kingdom;

- Seven in the Former Soviet Union region—Belarus, Kazakhstan, Moldova, Russia, Turkmenistan, Ukraine, and Uzbekistan;

- Eleven in the Middle East/North Africa—Algeria, Bahrain, Egypt, Iran, Iraq, Israel, Jordan, Kuwait, Oman, Saudi Arabia, and United Arab Emirates.

The United States alone has more than one billion submunitions in stockpiles. Other nations are likely to have billions more. While cluster munitions are often thought of as sophisticated weapons for advanced armed forces, the vast majority of the world's stockpiles consist of weapons based on decades-old technology that did not take concerns about accuracy and failure rate very much into account. Indeed, because cluster munitions are by nature wide-area weapons, accuracy was not seen as a particularly important attribute. Moreover, until very recently the trend was not to spend money to improve the reliability of submunitions, but rather to put more of the high-failure-rate submunitions into each cluster weapon in order to assure a successful strike.

The large stocks of unreliable early generation cluster munitions in the successor states of the Soviet Union and countries of the former Warsaw Pact are of particular concern. The effects of prolonged storage could contribute to extremely high failure rates, and thus high numbers of hazardous duds, if these weapons are used.

Thirty-three countries have produced at least 208 different types of cluster munitions that contain a wide variety of submunitions. The largest producers are likely to be the United States, Russia, and China. Outside of NATO and former Warsaw Pact nations, producers have included Argentina, Brazil, Chile, Egypt, India, Iran, Iraq, Israel, North Korea, South Korea, Pakistan, Singapore, and South Africa.

The full scope of the global trade in cluster munitions is not known. At least nine countries have transferred thirty different types of cluster munitions to at least forty-six other countries. The nine known exporters are Brazil, Chile, Egypt, Germany, Israel, Russia, the former Yugoslavia, the United Kingdom, and the United States. It appears that some older cluster munitions (and their delivery systems) have been transferred as surplus weapons from more to less technologically advanced armed forces. This could be a dangerous trend in the future.

Impact on Civilians

While the number of conflicts in which cluster munitions have been used is still relatively limited, the harm to the civilian population is striking in nearly every case. The attacks have caused civilian deaths and injuries that could have been avoided with better targeting and weapon choices. In most cases, large numbers of explosive submunition duds have taken even more civilian lives and limbs after the cluster munition strikes than during the attacks. The impact can go beyond needless civilian casualties, as extensive submunition contamination can have far-reaching socio-economic ramifications, hindering post-conflict reconstruction and development.

The long-term devastation that cluster munitions can cause is most evident in Southeast Asia, as Laos, Cambodia, and Vietnam still struggle to cope with the threat posed by cluster munitions dropped by the United States from 1964 to 1973. The International Committee of the Red Cross estimates that in Laos alone, nine to twenty-seven million unexploded submunitions remain, and some 11,000 people have been killed or injured, of which more than 30 percent have been children.[66]

Human Rights Watch conducted field investigations into use of cluster munitions in the conflicts in the Gulf War in 1991, Yugoslavia in 1999, Afghanistan in 2001 and 2002, and Iraq in 2003. Short summaries follow:

Gulf War 1991

In more recent years, the most widespread use of cluster munitions was in the Gulf War of 1991.[67] Between January 17 and February 28, 1991, the United States and its allies dropped 61,000 cluster bombs containing some twenty million submunitions. Cluster bombs accounted for about one-quarter of the bombs dropped on Iraq and Kuwait. A significant number of surface-delivered cluster munitions were also used. The number of civilian casualties caused by the cluster strikes is not known.

---

[66] International Committee of the Red Cross, "Explosive Remnants of War: The Lethal Legacy of Modern Armed Conflict," June 2003, p. 6.

[67] Most of the information in this section was first published in Human Rights Watch, "U.S. Cluster Bombs for Turkey?," *A Human Rights Watch Report*, vol. 6, no. 19, December 1994, pp. 15-19.

A U.S. Air Force post-war study cited an "excessively high dud rate" due to the high altitude from which cluster bombs were dropped and the sand and water on which they landed.[68] Even using a conservative 5 percent dud rate, more than one million unexploded submunitions were left behind by cluster bombs, and a similar number by ground cluster systems. By February 2003, these had killed 1,600 civilians, and injured more than 2,500 in Iraq and Kuwait. Despite one of the most extensive and expensive clearance operations in history following the war, there were still 2,400 cluster munition duds detected and destroyed in Kuwait in 2002, and a similar number in 2001.

Cluster bombs were used extensively in urban areas, particularly in southern Iraq. The plethora of unexploded bomblets on major roads put both refugees and foreign relief groups at risk. The bomblets particularly endangered children; 60 percent of the victims were under the age of fifteen. Unexploded bomblets slowed economic recovery because industrial plants, communication facilities, and neighborhoods had to be cleared before they could be restored. Iraqi authorities said that they removed tens of thousands of bomblets from such areas. Submunitions also needed to be cleared before people could extinguish the oil fires in Kuwait.

---

[68] U.S. Air Force, "Gulf War Air Power Survey," vol. II, pt. I (1993), p. 261.

Yugoslavia and Kosovo 1999

In Yugoslavia, the United States, the United Kingdom, and the Netherlands dropped 1,765 cluster bombs, containing about 295,000 bomblets, from March to June 1999.[69] Human Rights Watch documented that cluster strikes killed ninety to 150 civilians and injured many more. This constituted 18 to 30 percent of the total civilian deaths in the conflict, even though cluster bombs amounted to just 7 percent of the total number of bombs dropped. The most notable case of civilian deaths occurred in Nis on May 7, 1999, when bomblets mistakenly fell on an urban area, killing fourteen and wounding twenty-eight civilians. The incident led President Clinton to suspend temporarily U.S. use of cluster bombs in the campaign.

The U.N. Mine Action Coordination Center estimated that a dud rate between 7 percent and 11 percent, depending on bomb model, left more than 20,000 unexploded bomblets threatening civilians. Some bomblets penetrated up to twenty inches deep, making clearance slow and difficult. In the year after the war's end, bomblets killed at least fifty civilians and injured 101, with children being frequent victims. Bomblets also interfered with the return of refugees and slowed agricultural and economic recovery.

---

[69] The information in this section is drawn primarily from Human Rights Watch, "Civilian Deaths in the NATO Air Campaign," *A Human Rights Watch Report*, vol. 12, no. 1 (D), February 2000, and Human Rights Watch, "Ticking Time Bombs: NATO's Use of Cluster Munitions in Yugoslavia," *A Human Rights Watch Report*, vol. 11, no. 6 (D), May 1999.

Afghanistan 2001-2002

The United States dropped about 1,228 cluster bombs containing 248,056 bomblets in Afghanistan between October 2001 and March 2002.[70] Cluster bombs represented about 5 percent of the U.S. bombs dropped during that time period. In a limited sampling of the country, Human Rights Watch confirmed that at least twenty-five civilians died and many more were injured during cluster strikes in or near populated areas. These casualty figures do not represent the total for the country because some deaths and injuries go unreported and because Human Rights Watch did not attempt to identify every civilian casualty due to cluster bombs. The United States learned some targeting lessons from its experience in the Gulf War and Yugoslavia, but it continued to make costly cluster bomb strikes on populated areas. The thirteen deaths from an errant cluster bomb in Qala Shater were reminiscent of the fourteen deaths from a stray bomb in Nis, Serbia. While Afghan villages are smaller than Yugoslavian cities, such targets accounted for most, if not all, civilian casualties during cluster bomb strikes in Afghanistan.

Using a conservative estimate of a 5 percent dud rate, the cluster bombs dropped by the United States likely left more than 12,400 explosive duds. From October 2001 to November 2002, at least 127 civilians as well as two deminers were killed or injured by these cluster duds. Common post-strike victims in Afghanistan have included shepherds grazing their flocks, farmers plowing their fields, and children gathering

---

[70] The information in this section is drawn primarily from Human Rights Watch, "Fatally Flawed": Cluster Bombs and Their Use by the United States in Afghanistan," December 2002.

wood. Duds have also interfered with the economic recovery of the country, as they litter farmland, orchards, and grazing areas, which provide Afghans sustenance.

Iraq 2003

The United States and the United Kingdom dropped nearly 13,000 cluster munitions, containing an estimated 1.8 to 2 million submunitions, in the three weeks of major combat in March and April 2003.[71] While only air-dropped cluster bombs were used in Yugoslavia and Afghanistan, far more surface-delivered than air-dropped cluster munitions were used in Iraq. A total of at least 1,276 air-dropped cluster munitions were used, containing more than 245,000 submunitions. A total of some 11,600 surface-delivered cluster munitions were used, containing at least 1.6 million submunitions. Human Rights Watch's field investigation concluded that cluster munition strikes, particularly ground attacks on populated areas, were a major cause of civilian casualties; hospital records show cluster strikes caused hundreds of civilians deaths and injuries in Baghdad, al-Hilla, al-Najaf, Basra, and elsewhere.

The United States and the United Kingdom have not revealed full details about the cluster munitions they used, especially with respect to U.S. artillery projectile cluster munitions. However, based on available

---

[71] The information in this section is drawn primarily from Human Rights Watch, *Off Target: The Conduct of the War and Civilian Casualties in Iraq* (New York: Human Rights Watch, November 2003).

information on numbers, types, and reported failure rates, it is clear that Coalition cluster strikes have left many tens of thousands, and perhaps 200,000 or more, submunition duds. While the United States and the United Kingdom both used new types of more technologically advanced cluster munitions in Iraq, they also continued to use older types known to be inaccurate and to have high failure rates. Again, hospital records in a handful of cities indicated that by the end of May, submunition duds had already caused hundreds of civilian casualties.

Toward a Global Solution

The immediate effect and long-term impact of the use of cluster munitions over the past forty years have demonstrated that cluster munitions pose unacceptable risks to civilians. This is particularly evident from their increased use around the globe in the past thirteen years, with the two conflicts in Iraq as bookends. Having reached that conclusion, the question becomes, what can be done? Governments and NGOs—at long last—have been attempting to address that question in recent years, taking a number of different approaches to the issue.

A small number of NGOs have called for a complete ban on all cluster munitions, most notably the Mennonite Central Committee. While support for a ban has grown, particularly in the wake of the Iraq conflict, most NGOs have not advocated for a total prohibition.

Human Rights Watch has been raising concerns about cluster munitions since the early 1990s, and in 1999 it was the first NGO to call for a global moratorium on use of cluster weapons.[72] Although Human Rights Watch has not called for a permanent ban on cluster munitions, believing that a blanket prohibition is not justified under existing international humanitarian law, it strongly urges a moratorium based on the humanitarian impact of the weapons. In conflict after conflict, the cost to civilians of cluster munition use has been and continues to be unacceptably high. Human Rights Watch has called for no further use of cluster munitions until their humanitarian problems have been resolved.

The new global Cluster Munition Coalition launched on November 12, 2003, and endorsed by more than eighty NGOs has taken a position similar to that of Human Rights Watch.[73] (See below for additional details). It is a loose and diverse coalition, and different members of the coalition have different ideas about how the humanitarian problems can and should be addressed; some believe that they will not and cannot be resolved.

---

[72] Human Rights Watch called for a halt to the use of cluster munitions by allied forces during the Kosovo conflict and later that year formally called for a global moratorium. Human Rights Watch, "Cluster Bombs: Memorandum for Convention on Conventional Weapons (CCW) Delegates," Geneva, December 16, 1999.

[73] Human Rights Watch was one of the leading NGOs in bringing about the new coalition and sits on its initial steering committee.

Indeed, the solution to the cluster munition problem will likely require pursuing many different avenues simultaneously. Any solution will have to have both international and national components. A legally binding international agreement is a desirable, and necessary, future objective. But in the short term, development of model policies, practices, and regulations at the national level is essential. Any solution will have to address both the technical problems associated with cluster munitions, most notably the failure rate and high number of duds, and the targeting and use issues, most notably use in or near populated areas. It will have to address both air- and ground-delivered cluster munitions. It may require the flexibility to take different approaches to different types of cluster munitions, including the notion of a ban on the "worst offenders"—those cluster munitions known to have especially high failure rates, to produce large numbers of hazardous duds, or to be very inaccurate.

Cluster Munitions and International Humanitarian Law

In many if not most cases the use of cluster munitions raises concerns under international humanitarian law (IHL). This body of law, which governs conduct during armed conflict, requires belligerents to distinguish between combatants and non-combatants and prohibits as "indiscriminate" any attacks that fail to do so. Human Rights Watch has not called for a prohibition on all cluster munitions under international humanitarian law because, unlike antipersonnel mines, cluster munitions are not inherently indiscriminate; they can be used in such a way as to respect the legal distinction between military targets and civilians.

However, some uses of cluster munitions consistently rise to the level of being indiscriminate. Particularly troublesome are strikes in or near populated areas, which regularly cause civilian casualties both during strikes, due to the difficulty in precisely targeting cluster submunitions, and after strikes, due to the large number of explosive duds inevitably left behind. An attack is disproportionate, and therefore prohibited, if it "may be expected to cause incidental loss of civilian life, injury to civilians, damage to civilian objects, or a combination thereof, which would be excessive in relation to the concrete and direct military advantage anticipated."[74] Based on research in Iraq, Afghanistan, and Yugoslavia, Human Rights Watch believes that when cluster munitions are used in any type of populated area, there should be a strong, if rebuttable, presumption that an attack is disproportionate. Furthermore, given the foreseeable dangers of using cluster munitions in certain circumstances, an attacker could be judged to have failed to "take all feasible precautions" to avoid civilian harm as required under international humanitarian law.[75]

Convention on Conventional Weapons

Given the devastation already caused by cluster munitions, and the potential for much more far-reaching harm, it seems clear that the

---

[74] Protocol Additional to the Geneva Conventions of 12 August 1949, and Relating to the Protection of Victims of International Armed Conflicts (Protocol I) of 8 June 1977, article 51(5)(b). Protocol I codified and in some measure expanded upon existing law, particularly relating to the conduct of hostilities. Today, many, if not most, of its provisions are considered reflective of customary international law.

[75] Protocol I, art. 57(2)(a)(ii).

international community should formally regulate cluster munitions as it has other problematic weapons, such as anti-vehicle landmines and incendiary weapons. Specific new international law could clarify and strengthen the IHL restrictions noted above relevant to cluster munitions.

The logical venue for dealing with cluster munitions is the 1980 Convention on Conventional Weapons (CCW), which has four protocols addressing different weapons. In December 2001, the Second Review Conference of the CCW agreed to evaluate ways to deal with explosive remnants of war (ERW).[76] In December 2002, the CCW States Parties decided to draft a new instrument, and on November 28, 2003, they reached agreement on Protocol V on Explosive Remnants of War.

Human Rights Watch welcomed the new protocol, though lamenting the weakness of much of the language. The protocol makes a state responsible for clearance of all ERW in territory under its control; it is also to provide warnings and education and take other measures to protect the civilian population. The user of weapons that leave explosive remnants is to provide assistance for clearance of such ERW in territory not under its control.

---

[76] Explosive remnants of war include cluster munition duds and all other types of explosive ordnance (such as bombs, rockets, mortars, grenades, and ammunition) that have been used in an armed conflict but failed to explode as intended, thereby posing ongoing dangers. ERW also include abandoned explosive ordnance that has been left behind or dumped by a party to an armed conflict.

Regrettably, the protocol covers only post-conflict measures. Delegates opted not to negotiate on "preventive measures," such as technical improvements or use restrictions, or specific weapons systems, such as cluster munitions. Instead of making these the subject of negotiations, governments agreed only to discuss possible technical improvements for submunitions and whether or not existing international humanitarian law is sufficient to address issues related to submunitions. While the discussions on the latter topic were limited, most states seemed content with the conclusion that the rules of IHL are adequate and that the main challenge is finding way to improve observance and implementation of the rules. Some states, most notably Norway, questioned this conclusion, noting that IHL is ever evolving, and called for further examination of the way IHL has been applied thus far to the use of cluster munitions.

What seems most telling in this regard is the "ground truth" from recent conflicts. Nations such as the United States, the United Kingdom, and the Netherlands that consider themselves to have among the most sophisticated militaries in the world, with a great understanding of and respect for international humanitarian law, have used cluster munitions and done so in a fashion that has caused extensive civilian casualties and other civilian harm. This calls into question the adequacy of existing international humanitarian law and points to the need to strengthen existing rules or create new rules in order to offer adequate protections to civilians from the effects of cluster munitions.

As the negotiations on ERW progressed, a number of countries stressed the need to tackle more directly the issue of submunitions. In June

2003, Switzerland called for the establishment of a mandate as soon as possible to negotiate a new protocol on submunitions. Supportive countries included Austria, Belgium, Canada, Denmark, France, Ireland, Mexico, the Netherlands, New Zealand, Norway, and Sweden. Those opposed to further work on submunitions included China, Pakistan, Russia, and the United States. In the end, when concluding Protocol V, CCW States Parties agreed only to continue discussions on preventive measures and specific weapons.[77]

It is not difficult to envision key elements of any future instrument on cluster munitions. It should address both technical and targeting issues. It should contain a prohibition on use in or near populated areas. It should have requirements regarding accuracy and circumstances of use. It should require a very high reliability rate, one that should be determined by military and humanitarian experts, perhaps with 99 percent as a starting point. It should require that old stocks that do not meet the new standards be retrofitted or destroyed. It should prohibit the transfer of cluster munitions that do not meet new standards. It should require detailed transparency reporting on existing types and technical characteristics of cluster munitions, (for example, number of submunitions, fuze type, estimated footprint, and known failure rate).

---

[77] In the compromise language, States Parties agree: "To continue to consider the implementation of existing principles of international humanitarian law and to further study, on an open-ended basis and initially with particular emphasis on meetings of military and technical experts, possible preventative measures aimed at improving the design of certain types of munitions, including submunitions, with a view to minimizing the humanitarian risk of these munitions becoming ERW. Exchange of information, assistance and cooperation would be part of this work." CCW document , "Recommendation of the Working Group on Explosive Remnants of War," CCW/MSP/2003/CRP.1, November 27, 2003.

Technological Approaches

Among many militaries, there is an increasing willingness to attempt to deal with cluster munition problems through technological improvements that lower the failure rate and increase accuracy. As noted, an explicit part of the mandate of the CCW Group of Governmental Experts working on explosive remnants of war was to discuss preventive measures to decrease failure rates. Commonly cited were self-destruct mechanisms (those will cause the submunition to explode after a certain period of time if it fails to explode on contact) or other secondary fuzes that serve as a back-up to ensure detonation.

The new CCW Protocol V on Explosive Remnants of War in Article 9 encourages States Parties "to take generic preventive measures, aimed at minimising the occurrence of explosive remnants of war, including, but not limited to, those referred to in part 3 of the technical annex." The annex, which contains "suggested best practice" to be implemented on a voluntary basis, states that, among other measures, "A State should examine ways and means of improving the reliability of explosive ordnance that it intends to produce or procure, with a view to achieving the highest possible reliability." An earlier draft called for a reliability rate of 99 percent. During the CCW ERW process, Switzerland led the way in pushing for agreement on a reliability standard for submunitions.

In 2001, then-U.S. Secretary of Defense William Cohen issued a policy decision that all future submunitions must have a dud rate of less than 1 percent. In August 2003, General Richard Myers, chairman of the Joint Chiefs of Staff, said the U.S. Army planned to produce self-destruct fuzes for submunitions in some ground-launched cluster munitions

(Dual Purpose Improved Conventional Munitions, DPICMs) in 2005.[78] In Iraq, the United States used for the first time air-dropped CBU-105 Sensor Fuzed Weapons and surface-launched M898 SADARM artillery projectiles, both of which contained submunitions with self-destruct features. Likewise, the United Kingdom introduced the L20A1 artillery projectile with an Israeli-designed self-destructing submunition. Other countries that are reported to have developed or deployed cluster munitions with a self-destruct or self-neutralizing capability include France, Germany, Italy, Romania, Russia, Singapore, and Slovakia.

In Iraq, the United States also made greater use of the Wind Corrected Munitions Dispenser, first seen in Afghanistan, in order to increase the accuracy of air-dropped cluster bombs. In perhaps the greatest technological advance, the submunitions in the CBU-105 and SADARM Sensor Fuzed Weapon are capable of independently sensing and attacking specific targets like armored vehicles. Thus, these weapons are designed to address the multiple problems associated with cluster munitions: the inaccuracy of both the munition and the submunition, and the large number of persistent duds.

---

[78] Letter from General Richard B. Myers, chairman, Joint Chiefs of Staff, to Sen. Patrick Leahy, August 11, 2003. Myers said the U.S. Army plans to add a self-destruct fuze to the 155mm extended-range DPICM in 2005. It "is also developing a self-destruct fuze to reduce the dud rate to below 1 percent for its cluster munitions in rocket and other cannon artillery systems. This new fuze may be available for future production of Army cluster munitions as soon as 2005."

While each of these technological developments needs to be further studied and assessed in order to determine their effectiveness and the degree to which they improve protections for civilian populations, the trend is encouraging and should be continued.

At the same time that nations continue efforts to improve the reliability and accuracy of cluster munitions, they should also consider if weapons with fewer humanitarian side effects can replace them. For example, air-dropped cluster bombs appear to be of diminishing importance to the U.S. military, given the prevalence of less expensive precision-guided munitions and the existing and emerging alternatives to cluster munitions.

While technological improvements present one avenue to help remedy the cluster munition problem, there is also reason to question whether a technical "fix" is truly feasible, and whether it is a valid approach on a global scale. There is reason to question whether even the most advanced military will be able to lower the dud rate sufficiently to offset the dangers posed by the release of hundreds, or even thousands, of submunitions at a time. There is reason to question whether low reliability rates that may be achieved in testing will ever be duplicated under battle conditions or in environments that may increase failure rates (such as sand, soft ground, trees, high winds, etc.). There is reason to question how accurate a weapon can be that is designed to cover a broad area.

Apart from technical feasibility, there is very much reason to doubt that a technological solution will ever be pursued by the less advanced and less wealthy militaries, who may not have the know-how or money to do so. Countries with major armed forces such as Russia and China have said they could not afford such an approach for all submunitions. Finally, there is the question of the fate of existing stocks. While the United States introduced new technologically improved cluster munitions in Iraq, it also continued to use large quantities of old, unreliable, inaccurate cluster munitions. The new U.S. standard for reliability applies only to future (post-2005) submunition production, and permits use of all the "legacy" submunitions in stock—those that have already proven to be of great danger to civilian populations.

Targeting and Use Issues

While lowering the failure rate could mitigate the negative impact of cluster munitions following a strike, it would not address the danger posed to civilians during cluster attacks. There is also a need for regulations on the circumstances in which cluster munitions are used. Human Rights Watch field investigations in Yugoslavia, Afghanistan, and Iraq have shown that use of cluster munitions in or near populated areas almost inevitably leads to civilian casualties. If an armed force chooses to use cluster munitions, the most important operational constraint should be no use in or near populated areas.

Like Human Rights Watch and other NGOs, the International Committee of the Red Cross has formally called for a prohibition on the use of submunitions against any military object located in or near civilian areas. However, this proposal has received the support of only a few governments. It remains under discussion within the CCW. In June 2003, Norway submitted a paper to CCW delegates suggesting appropriate measures for the use and targeting of cluster munitions and posing a set of questions on submunition use and targeting to be considered by other governments.

In addition to the prohibition on use in populated areas, there should also be a requirement to record and report information regarding cluster munition strikes, in order to facilitate risk education and rapid clearance. Such information should include location of the strike, number, and type of munitions and submunitions, and technical information to ensure safe clearance operations.

Governments should also assess the feasibility and effectiveness of other potential restrictions on use aimed at avoiding civilian harm, including restrictions related to delivery parameters (such as excessively high or low altitude delivery) and use in environments prone to increase the failure rate of submunitions.

"Worst Offenders"

While Human Rights Watch has not called for a comprehensive prohibition on cluster munitions, it believes that the vast majority of cluster munitions in existing stockpiles of nearly sixty nations should never be used. These weapons are so inaccurate and/or so unreliable as to pose unacceptable risks to civilians, either during strikes, post-conflict or both. A number of NGOs, including Human Rights Watch, are working to develop a list of "worst offenders"—those cluster munitions that are especially dangerous for civilian populations and thus should either be modified or withdrawn from military service and destroyed.

While a good deal of research still needs to be done to identify the worst offenders, prior to the 2003 Iraq conflict Human Rights Watch called on the United States not to use four types of cluster munitions because of the foreseeable dangers to civilians: CBU-99/CBU-100 Rockeye cluster bombs, CBU-87 Combined Effects Munitions (cluster bombs), Multiple Launch Rocket Systems (MLRS) with M77 submunitions, and 155mm artillery projectiles with M42 and M46 Dual Purpose Improved Conventional Munition submunitions.[79] It is important to note that, except for the Vietnam-era Rockeye, these are relatively new types of cluster munitions, first used extensively in the 1991 Gulf War. Most of the world's cluster munitions would pose even more dangers to civilians than these that Human Rights Watch has already put on a "no use" list.

Some nations might invest the funds to improve the reliability and accuracy of their old cluster munitions. As noted above, the United States is retrofitting some of its ground-delivered submunitions with self-destruct devices. However, it is likely that most nations will find this step too expensive, or not cost-effective compared to purchase of other weapons that could accomplish the same military objective.

---

[79] Human Rights Watch Briefing Paper, "Cluster Munitions a Foreseeable Hazard in Iraq," March 2003.

Air- vs. Ground-Delivered Cluster Munitions

Because the only cluster munitions used by allied forces in the Kosovo
and Afghanistan conflicts were air-dropped, international attention
(both government and NGO) has been focused on cluster bombs rather
than surface-delivered cluster weapons. The 2003 war in Iraq has
changed that. Far more ground submunitions (at least 1.6 million) were
used than air (about 245,000), and the great preponderance of civilian
casualties caused by cluster munitions were due to ground systems.

While the sheer number of ground-delivered cluster submunitions is
daunting, the fact that they were used extensively in populated areas is
equally disturbing. It appears that in Iraq, the U.S. and U.K. air forces
learned a lesson from previous conflicts and largely heeded the call of
Human Rights Watch, the ICRC, and others in greatly restricting the use
of cluster munitions in or near populated areas. There were only a few
known instances of civilian casualties due to air cluster attacks, notably
in al-Hilla. The air forces for the most part avoided civilian
concentrations and in some instances used more accurate and reliable
cluster bombs.

It seems the same rules did not apply to ground forces. While a vetting
process to determine the legality and appropriateness of cluster strikes
was in place for both the United States and the United Kingdom, it did
not prevent widespread attacks in Baghdad, al-Hilla, al-Najaf, Basra, and
elsewhere that killed and injured hundreds of civilians. In the case of
the United States, cluster strikes in populated areas were often made
using radar to remotely hone in on targets, without any visual
confirmation whether civilians were present in the target area. U.S.

combatants told Human Rights Watch that cluster munition warheads were often the only weapon choice available, particularly in the case of the MLRS, and that it was often a choice they did not like. U.S. after-action reports have highlighted the need for non-submunition alternatives.

Sensitivity to the dangers to civilians must extend to ground forces using cluster munitions as well as air forces. Uniform standards should apply, particularly with respect to no use in populated areas. Armed forces should develop a vetting process for cluster munition strikes, particularly for surface-launched cluster munitions, that successfully reduces the harm to civilians. Ground forces need to catch up to air forces when it comes to cluster munition targeting and technology.

Intersection of Humanitarian Concerns and Military Interests

The effort to reduce the risk to civilians posed by cluster munitions may significantly benefit from recent concerns in some military circles about the weapons. The armed forces of some nations are increasingly seeing a military advantage to addressing the problems of reliability and accuracy.

Reports after the Gulf War, Kosovo, Afghanistan, and Iraq have all cited the negative impact of cluster munition duds on U.S. and allied forces, as well as peacekeepers: the duds have killed and injured numerous military personnel and have directly affected military operations. The presence of duds can decrease the mobility of one's own troops. Concerns about such dangers and impediments have compelled some coalition forces in Iraq to join those who question use of the weapon. In particular, U.S. and U.K. combat experiences with artillery and MLRS submunitions led some soldiers and Marines to call for an alternative weapon with fewer deadly side effects. A post-conflict "lessons learned" presentation by the U.S. Third Infantry Division echoed the concerns of its field officers. The division described dud-producing submunitions, particularly the DPICM, as among the "losers" of the war. "Is DPICM munition a Cold War relic?" the presentation asked. The dud rate of the DPICM, which represented more than half of the available arsenal, was higher than expected, especially when not used on roads. Commanders were "hesitant to use it . . . but had to." The presentation specifically noted that these weapons are "not for use in urban areas."[80]

It is essential that NGOs and international organizations seeking solutions to the cluster munition problem engage directly and extensively with armed forces and take advantage of this space where military necessity and humanitarian concern coincide.

---

[80] Third Infantry Division, "Fires in the Close Fight: OIF [Operation Iraqi Freedom] Lessons Learned." http://sill-www.army.mil/Fa/Lessons_Learned/3d%20ID%20Lessons%20Learned.pdf (accessed November 10, 2003).

National, Regional and International Steps

It is likely that before an international instrument can be seriously contemplated, there will need to be some model positions, policies, and practices established at the national level that will show the way for others. To date, not a single government that possesses cluster munitions has yet formally endorsed the call for a moratorium on use until the humanitarian problems are resolved. However, as noted above, there has been some positive momentum in the past several years—momentum reflected in part by the efforts by the United States and others to improve the reliability and accuracy of cluster weapons, and in part by the activity at the CCW.

In addition, there have been a number of steps taken at the national level deserving mention. Norway has foresworn the use of air-dropped cluster munitions in international conflicts (and prohibited their use in Afghanistan). Belgium has reportedly destroyed all of its obsolescent BL-755 cluster bombs (a type used by the United Kingdom in Iraq). Sweden has reportedly removed from service obsolescent Rockeye cluster bombs (a type used by the United States in Iraq). Australia said in April 2003 that it does not use cluster munitions; and in October 2003, the Australian Senate passed a motion calling for a moratorium on use.

Regional and international bodies have expressed opposition to cluster munitions. During the Afghanistan conflict, the European Parliament passed a resolution calling for an "immediate moratorium" on use of cluster bombs until an international agreement addressing the weapon was reached. On the final day of the CCW negotiations in November, the United Nations agencies issued a statement calling for a freeze on use of cluster munitions until humanitarian concerns are addressed.

A key challenge for NGOs is to promote a core group of governments that can provide leadership on this issue, for that is sorely lacking at this time.

Cluster Munition Coalition

On November 13, 2003, nongovernmental organizations came together to launch the Cluster Munition Coalition (CMC) in the Hague, the Netherlands. At its birth, the CMC was endorsed by eighty-five NGOs from forty-two countries. The coalition was formed as a global response to cluster munitions and to the humanitarian crisis caused by explosive remnants of war more generally.

The Cluster Munition Coalition calls for:

- No use, production, or trade of cluster munitions until their humanitarian problems have been resolved.

- Increased resources for assistance to communities and individuals affected by unexploded cluster munitions and all other explosive remnants of war.

- Users of cluster munitions and other munitions that become ERW to accept special responsibility for clearance, warnings, risk education, provision of information, and victim assistance.

Human Rights Watch and a handful of other NGOs took the lead in forming the coalition not just out of concern for the negative humanitarian effects of cluster munitions and ERW, but out of recognition that nongovernmental organizations needed to be more active and more organized to have an impact. The Cluster Munition Coalition has many challenges before it, but its very existence has put governments on notice that this is not an issue that will be ignored, or only lamented with the next war; an ongoing and ever-growing effort is underway to ensure that cluster munitions do not create their own global crisis.

It is abundantly clear that dealing with cluster munitions effectively will require much greater effort on the part of governments, international organizations, and NGOs. Thus far, few, if any, have devoted the time, energy, and passion to the cluster munition issue that was brought to bear, for example, on the antipersonnel mine issue. Now is the time for those with vision to seize the moment.

A young boy killed in the shelling of Liberia's capital in July 2003. Arms inflows to Liberia, in spite of a U.N. arms embargo, facilitated atrocities. © 2003, Private

Weapons and War Crimes: The Complicity of Arms Suppliers

By Lisa Misol

Introduction

From Rwanda's genocide to massacres by paramilitaries and rebels in Colombia, the provision of arms, ammunition, and other forms of military support to known human rights abusers has enabled them to carry out atrocities against civilians. The perpetrators of war crimes, crimes against humanity, and genocide are on notice that they may be hauled before a national or international criminal tribunal to face charges. Yet the individuals and states who provide the weapons used in massive human rights abuses have so far been let off the hook for their central role in facilitating these crimes.

Individual arms traffickers and the states who use their services reject out of hand the idea that they bear some responsibility for fueling abuses. Human rights organizations and their allies in the humanitarian, public health, development, conflict prevention, and disarmament communities have set out to prove otherwise. These activists have long worked to develop strong norms to prevent arms transfers in certain circumstances, including transfers that would facilitate the commission of human rights abuses and war crimes, the concern here. Increasingly, they are turning to the obligations of states and individuals under international law, especially concepts akin to complicity, to establish a norm against arms supplies to abusers that has teeth.

279

Arms and Human Rights Abuses

In the early hours of January 6, 1999, rebels of the Revolutionary United Front (RUF) launched an offensive against the Sierra Leonean capital, Freetown. As the rebels took control of the city, they turned their weapons on the civilian population. The rebels gunned down civilians within their houses, rounded them up and massacred them on the streets, hacked off the hands of children and adults, burned people alive in their houses and cars, and systematically sexually assaulted women and girls. Before withdrawing from the city later that month, the rebels set fire to neighborhoods, leaving entire city blocks in ashes and over 51,000 people homeless. On their way back to the hills, the RUF took with them thousands of abductees, mostly children and young women. All told, several thousands of civilians were killed in Freetown by the end of January.

The RUF was heavily backed by the government of Charles Taylor in Liberia, which provided arms, troops, and other support in exchange for diamonds and other riches that were under the RUF's control in Sierra Leone. Never mind that both Liberia and the RUF were subject to mandatory United Nations arms embargoes. All Taylor needed were regional allies such as Burkina Faso willing to provide false cover for weapons deliveries, arms suppliers such as Ukraine willing to sell weapons with no questions asked, and the vast networks provided by private traffickers such as Victor Bout to acquire and move the goods from Point A to Point B, falsifying the paperwork along the way. The private actors involved and the governments they worked with were exposed, including in detailed reports by U.N. investigators. But in spite of about a dozen U.N. investigative reports on violations of arms embargoes imposed on gross abusers—in Angola, Liberia, Rwanda, Sierra Leone, and Somalia—not one of the persons named in the reports has been convicted in national courts for having breached these embargoes and thus having facilitated horrific abuses.

Against this backdrop of impunity, the indictment of Liberia's Charles Taylor by the U.N.-backed Special Court for Sierra Leone represents a watershed. It helps illustrate the concept of responsibility for atrocities committed by abusive forces whom one has supported by furnishing weapons or through other means. The indictment charges Taylor with "individual criminal responsibility" for crimes against humanity, war crimes, and other serious violations of international humanitarian law committed in Sierra Leone by the RUF and allied forces. His responsibility, as detailed in the indictment, is based in part on his role in providing "financial support, military training, personnel, arms, ammunition and other support and encouragement" to these notoriously brutal rebels. By pointing to legal responsibility under international criminal law, the indictment is emblematic of an important approach. Arms campaigners are increasingly turning to human rights and humanitarian law as a basis to assert the responsibilities of both states and individuals.

Arms Transfers and the Responsibility of States

Recognition of states' responsibility to control arms transfers has evolved over time. Affected communities, activists, and progressive governments have moved the debate toward a greater recognition of the human rights consequences of weapons flows and greater consideration of the obligations this imposes on suppliers. This suggests important opportunities to strengthen the emerging norm against arms supplies to abusers.

Building Norms From the Bottom Up

For many years, ethical arguments have been a backbone of efforts to prevent arms from getting into the wrong hands. Nongovernmental organizations (NGOs) have long called for an end to government-authorized military assistance to gross abusers and decried the lack of control on private traffickers. Research has helped spotlight the problem. Groundbreaking investigative reports by Human Rights Watch and Amnesty International in the mid-1990s exposed the role of France, South Africa, Israel, Albania, Bulgaria, and others in arms supplies to Rwanda before and immediately after the 1994 genocide. As events in Rwanda tragically unfolded, the U.N. arms embargo imposed in the midst of the genocide went unheeded. Responding to such concerns, the U.N. Security Council in 1995 formed a commission of inquiry, known as UNICOI, to investigate violations of the Rwanda arms embargo. The Security Council largely buried the work of this commission, however, as its findings were deemed to be too politically sensitive. Little will existed to embarrass states, let alone hold anyone accountable.

Awareness of the human cost of uncontrolled transfers grew throughout the 1990s, as civil wars were spread in many parts of the world. Civilians have been caught in the crossfire or directly targeted by armed attackers. Journalists, humanitarian workers, and peacekeepers have witnessed this violence and often themselves been victims of it. Spurred by such atrocities and by continued civil society research and campaigning, states progressively adopted minimum arms-transfer criteria at the national, regional, and international level. For example, as a new spirit of ethics in foreign policy took hold—in principle if considerably less firmly in practice—in South Africa in 1994 and in the United Kingdom in 1997, these states pledged to halt arms transfers to human rights abusers. By the late 1990s, growing pressure helped lead to a number of voluntary regional and sub-regional measures that built on such national-level commitments. For example, in 1998 the European Union adopted a Code of Conduct on Arms Exports. That same year, the Economic Community of West African States adopted a three-year moratorium, since extended, on the import, export, and manufacture of small arms and light weapons. These and other measures have marked progress, but have fallen woefully short of the mark. A key weakness is that they are not binding and are thus often disregarded in practice.

Much attention has focused on the widespread availability and devastating misuse of one category of conventional weapon: small arms and light weapons, which are personal weapons such as pistols, assault rifles, and rocket-propelled grenade launchers. Some of this attention has been directed to ensuring that minimum arms transfer criteria are in place to keep such weapons out of the hands of abusers. But there also has been resistance to the idea of the responsibility of states with regard to authorized transfers—so called "legal" transfers—and many governments have insisted on discussing small arms only with respect to their illicit traffic—i.e., in cases where there is no state authorization. In July 2001, the U.N. hosted the first-ever international conference on

small arms. It drew needed attention to this global scourge and helped
motivate states to begin to tackle it. The conference resulted in a
"Program of Action" document specifying actions that should be taken
at the national, regional, and international level. Unfortunately, this was
a watered-down consensus document focused on preventing and
combating illicit small arms transfers, and it largely leaves aside the issue
of government-authorized arms deals.

Since 2001, states in some regions have been able to find common
ground and have agreed on measures to restrain authorized arms
transfers. An ever-growing number of states have promised not to
approve arms transfers where there is reason to believe these will
contribute to human rights abuses and violations of international law.
Such commitments are in keeping with the duty of states to respect and
ensure respect for international human rights and humanitarian law.

Toward Legally Binding Measures

Despite pledges to the contrary, weapons continue to find their way all
too readily to areas—from the Democratic Republic of Congo to Sri
Lanka—where they are used to commit serious human rights abuses and
violations of international humanitarian law. There have been many
calls from civil society to give binding legal status to existing
commitments. State practice is slowly developing in this area, in part in
response to scandals. In 2002, for example, Belgium—in contravention
of the E.U. Code of Conduct—approved an arms transfer to Nepal, a
country in conflict whose government had been implicated in a pattern
of serious human rights abuses involving abduction, torture, and

summary executions. The Nepal arms affair led a Belgian government minister to resign and prompted the federal parliament to pass a landmark law making national arms export criteria binding. These criteria are largely based on the E.U. Code of Conduct—and include a requirement that recipients of arms must comply with human rights and international humanitarian law.

Another important trend has been greater, if still uneven, attention to the enforcement of arms embargoes on gross human rights abusers. The efforts of UNICOI in the mid-1990s to document arms supplies to the forces that committed genocide in Rwanda were downplayed at the time. But the UNICOI experience helped open the door to a series of hard-hitting U.N. investigations that garnered greater public attention. Beginning with a March 2000 report on violations of an embargo then in place against Angolan rebels, various U.N. investigations by panels of experts have given new legitimacy and a name—"naming and shaming"—to efforts to hold arms suppliers and traffickers responsible for their behavior. These investigations have largely focused on the private traffickers who are a crucial link in the sanctions-busting chain. But the panels also have named governments, including heads of governments. For example, the president of Burkina Faso was accused of directly facilitating Liberia's arms-for-diamonds trade, to the benefit of the RUF in Sierra Leone.

U.N. arms embargoes are binding on states, but in reality this means little if there are no consequences for their violation. Beginning with the first Angola panel report, the U.N. has considered imposing secondary sanctions on governments found to have breached the embargoes. This was done once, in the case of Liberia, which was subjected to a strengthened arms embargo as well as a travel ban, diamond sanctions, and later timber sanctions, in response to its support for rebels in Sierra Leone in violation of the U.N. embargo.

International Law and the Role of States in Arms Transfers

Beyond respecting arms embargoes, states have other international legal responsibilities they should consider when weighing weapons transfer decisions. For example, the 2001 U.N. Program of Action on small arms included an important reference to states' obligations. It acknowledged that national arms export controls must be "consistent with existing obligations of states under relevant international law." It offered no further elaboration. Arms campaigners have called on states to affirm that those obligations encompass international human rights and humanitarian law. In these and other ways, states have been forced to consider their responsibility under international law for the consequences of their arms transfers.

States involved in arms transfers bear a measure of responsibility for the abuses carried out with the weapons they furnish. This is true of arms-supplying states that approve arms deals where they have reason to believe the weapons may be misused. Exporting states in particular—as well as those that serve as transshipment points or as bases for arms brokering, transport, and financing—also must share in the responsibility for abuses when they fail to exercise adequate control over private traffickers who make weapons available to anyone who can pay.

The notion that one state can bear legal responsibility for helping another state breach international law has been recognized by a leading international body that promotes and codifies developments in international law. The International Law Commission, in its Articles on Responsibility of States for Internationally Wrongful Acts, adopted in 2001, concluded that: "A State which aids or assists another State in the commission of an internationally wrongful act by the latter is internationally responsible for doing so if: (a) That State does so with knowledge of the circumstances of the internationally wrongful act; and (b) The act would be internationally wrongful if committed by that State." In its commentary to the articles, the ILC applied this legal concept to the question of arms transfers: "[A] State may incur responsibility if it assists another State to circumvent [U.N.] sanctions ...or provides material aid to a State that uses the aid to commit human rights violations. In this respect, the United Nations General Assembly has called on Member States in a number of cases to refrain from supplying arms and other military assistance to countries found to be committing serious human rights violations. Where the allegation is that the assistance of a State has facilitated human rights abuses by another State, the particular circumstances of each case must be carefully examined to determine whether the aiding State was aware of and intended to facilitate the commission of the internationally wrongful conduct."

The question of the "secondary responsibility" of governments for armed atrocities has recently been examined by a special rapporteur on human rights and small arms with the U.N. Sub-Commission on the Protection and Promotion of Human Rights. In a May 2002 working

287

paper, she highlighted that: "States are prohibited from aiding another State in the commission of internationally wrongful acts. That prohibition could be invoked in situations where a transferring State supplies small arms to another State with knowledge that those arms are likely to be used in a violation of human rights or humanitarian law ... States do have important obligations under international human rights and humanitarian law that could be interpreted to prohibit them from transferring small arms knowing they will be used to violate human rights." Her work has stressed, as noted in her June 2003 preliminary report, that "[t]o prevent transfer of small arms into situations where they will be used to commit serious violations of international human rights and humanitarian law, the international community should ... further articulate principles regarding State responsibility in the transfer of small arms."

This approach is at the core of a proposed international Arms Trade Treaty, which would be a binding instrument containing strong human rights and international humanitarian law criteria to govern the arms transfer decisions of states. The Arms Trade Treaty grew out of an earlier initiative by Nobel Peace Laureates, led by former Costa Rican president Oscar Arias, to promote international standards on arms transfers. The draft treaty addresses the existing obligations of states under international law and applies them to decisions to authorize arms transfers. Its central provisions would prohibit arms transfers where the authorizing government knows or ought reasonably to know that the weapons will be used to commit genocide, crimes against humanity, serious human rights abuses, or serious violations of international humanitarian law.

In October 2003, Amnesty International, Oxfam, and the International Action Network on Small Arms—consisting of more than 500 organizations, including Human Rights Watch—launched the "Control Arms" campaign in some seventy countries. The centerpiece of this effort is a push to promote negotiation of an Arms Trade Treaty by 2006, when the U.N. will host a follow-up to the 2001 small arms conference. The proposed Arms Trade Treaty is intended to cover all conventional arms and would apply to all manner of arms transfers, including transshipment and re-exports, not only direct exports. Some states have begun to step forward to champion the treaty idea, with Mali and Costa Rica taking an early lead. Negotiating such a binding international instrument on arms transfers would represent a major step forward in defining state responsibility for the human rights consequences of arms transfers.

Arms Transfers and Individual Responsibility

Just as there is a major push to hold states responsible for authorizing transfers of arms used to commit violations of human rights and international humanitarian law, there is also an impetus towards holding individuals accountable for their involvement in such arms transfers under international criminal law. Private arms trafficking to gross human rights abusers is in part an issue of state responsibility, in that such transfers often can be traced to governments that fail to implement and enforce adequate controls on private traffickers. In some cases, governments knowingly take part in illicit arms trafficking, as when officials provide false cover for arms shipments they know are destined elsewhere. But arms traffickers often do not work on behalf of specific states and instead have multiple clients, sometimes arming opposing sides in a given conflict. As arms traffickers establish transnational criminal enterprises, they seek to avoid the reach of national law. To address this widespread problem, nongovernmental groups have pressed for states to impose controls on arms brokers, licensing their activities using strict human rights criteria, and to move forward to negotiate binding international treaties on arms brokering and marking and tracing of weapons.

There is also scope to consider the individual responsibility of arms traffickers under international law. A review of the recent practice of international criminal tribunals suggests how this could come about. Under international criminal law, there are various ways in which a person may incur individual criminal responsibility. The most obvious way is as perpetrator, the person who directly commits the crime, as in the case of an individual soldier who slaughters civilians. A second possibility involves a person who holds a position of superior authority. Under the principle of "command responsibility," this person can be held responsible for crimes committed by a subordinate, where the superior knew or had reason to know of the subordinate's intended or actual crimes and failed to take the necessary and reasonable measures to prevent the crime or to punish the perpetrator. Neither of these two theories is likely to cover the activities of the arms trafficker who supplies the weapons used by the perpetrators.

The legal concept of complicity may be relevant in such cases. In lay terms, complicity relates to knowingly helping someone commit a crime without necessarily sharing the intent of the perpetrator. The Special Court in Sierra Leone drew on this legal concept in its indictment of

Charles Taylor. Among other things, Taylor stands indicted for having "aided and abetted" abuses perpetrated by Sierra Leonean rebels—including acts that terrorized the civilian population, unlawful killings, widespread sexual violence, extensive physical violence, the use of child soldiers, abductions and forced labor, looting and burning, and attacks on peacekeepers and humanitarian workers—through the provision of financing, training, weapons, and other support and encouragement to the rebels. Taylor is also accused of more direct involvement in crimes in Sierra Leone and so it is not clear to what extent the Special Court will examine complicity theory even if Taylor is apprehended and tried, but the indictment itself is nonetheless an intriguing development for those looking for new ways to hold arms suppliers accountable.

Relevant Case Law

An examination of case law from other international criminal tribunals illuminates the potential for prosecuting arms suppliers for providing weapons to known abusers.

The concept of individual criminal responsibility for assisting in the commission of a crime without directly committing that crime is a general principle of criminal law. Indeed, one can be prosecuted for aiding many types of crimes recognized under international law. The International Criminal Tribunal for the Former Yugoslavia (ICTY) has elaborated this point in the context of cases involving accessories to war crimes and crimes against humanity. "Aiding" in international criminal law entails providing practical assistance that has a substantial effect on the commission of the crime.[81] According to the ICTY, an "aider" must intentionally provide assistance to the perpetrator with knowledge of the perpetrator's intent to commit a crime, but need not himself or herself support the aim of the perpetrator.[82] Moreover, the ICTY has stated that a person may be liable as an accessory whether the assistance is provided before, during, or after the specific crime in question is committed.[83]

In the case of the crimes of genocide and torture, international conventions outlawing those acts explicitly state that acts of complicity in those crimes are punishable.[84] The International Criminal Tribunal for Rwanda (ICTR) has further outlined what the specific crime of complicity in genocide entails. As elaborated by the ICTR, there are three elements of complicity in genocide: complicity by procuring means to commit genocide, by knowingly aiding and abetting genocide, or by

---

[81] See, for example, *Prosecutor v. Furundzija,* Case No. IT-95-17/1 (Trial Chamber), December 10, 1998, para. 234-5, 249; *Prosecutor v. Vasiljevic,* Case No. IT-98-32-T (Trial Chamber), November 29, 2002, para. 70; and *Prosecutor v. Blaskic,* Case No. IT-95-14 (Trial Chamber), March 3, 2000, para. 285.

[82] See, for example, *Blaskic,* (Trial Chamber), March 3, 2000, para. 286; *Furundzija,* (Trial Chamber), December 10, 1998, para. 246; and *Furundzija,* (Trial Chamber), December 10, 1998, para. 245, 249.

[83] See, for example, *Vasiljevic,* (Trial Chamber), November 29, 2002, para. 70; and *Blaskic,* (Trial Chamber), March 3, 2000, para. 285.

[84] Convention on the Prevention and Punishment of the Crime of Genocide, December 9, 1948, Article 3 (e); and Convention Against Torture and Other Cruel, Inhuman or Degrading Treatment or Punishment, December 10, 1984, Article 4 (1).

instigating genocide.[85] The first element is the one most likely to apply in relation to arms transfers, though the second could conceivably apply as well in some circumstances.

The ICTR trial chamber explicitly linked weapons to genocide, by stating that one may be complicit in genocide "by procuring means, such as weapons, instruments or any other means, used to commit genocide, with the accomplice knowing that such means would be used for such a purpose."[86] Thus, a person who knowingly provides weapons to a group that he or she was aware was carrying out a genocidal campaign could in principle be tried as an accomplice to acts of genocide. This could be true of someone who distributed the weapons in Rwanda, as has been alleged in several cases brought before the ICTR. An arms trafficker based outside a country in which genocide takes place could also in principle be prosecuted as an accomplice to genocide for making weapons available to genocidal forces.

The Potential to Prosecute: Illustrative Examples

The statutes of neither the ICTR nor ICTY specifically identify the provision of weapons or other concrete military assistance as constituting practical assistance for the purposes of establishing criminal

---

[85] *Prosecutor v. Akayesu,* Case No. ICTR-96-4-T (Trial Chamber), September 2, 1998, para. 533-537. See also, for example, *Prosecutor v. Semanza,* Case No. ICTR-97-20 (Trial Chamber), May 15, 2003, para. 393, 395.

[86] *Akayesu,* (Trial Chamber), September 2, 1998, para. 533-537. The Chamber defined complicity "per the Rwandan Penal Code."

liability for "aiding" in the commission of a crime, yet the case law cited above suggests it is reasonable to interpret them as such. It would be interesting to push this approach further and explore the possibilities of prosecuting an arms supplier under this theory. Persons involved in arms supply networks, by providing such assistance, may in some circumstances make a contribution to the crimes committed with those weapons. Where there is also evidence that these persons were aware of the intent of their clients to commit certain crimes, then they too might be held legally responsible.

In the case of the crime of complicity in genocide, to date no international prosecution has been attempted against an arms trafficker outside the country for making weapons available to genocidal forces. One illustrative example, however, suggests some of the elements a prosecution along those lines might entail. The case is that of Mil-Tec, a British company that delivered weapons to the Rwandan armed forces, including in air deliveries after the genocide was underway.[87] The government that led the Rwandan genocide took power following the April 6, 1994, killing of then President Juvenal Habyarimana. One of the first acts of the new interim government was to make contact with Mil-Tec to place an urgent order for U.S.$854,000 worth of arms and ammunition. Ultimately, Rwandan records show, Mil-Tec provided a total U.S.$5.5 million worth of ammunition and grenades in five separate deliveries on April 18, April 25, May 5, May 9, and May 20. The last of these violated a mandatory U.N. arms embargo imposed on May 17,

---

[87] See, for example, Human Rights Watch, *Leave None to Tell the Story: Genocide in Rwanda* (New York: Human Rights Watch, 1999), pp. 649-53.

1994.[88] The genocide was underway during the time of the arms deliveries—and was widely reported—so one could try to establish that arms traffickers supplying the interim Rwandan government knew how the weapons would be used.

One might also be able to prosecute individuals who supply arms to forces known to be responsible for crimes other than genocide, namely war crimes and crimes against humanity. Here the example of Victor Bout, described by one expert as "the McDonald's of arms trafficking – the brand name" is perhaps apt as an illustration. A string of U.N. reports have accused Bout, a Russian citizen, of playing a key role in illicit weapons deliveries to Angola, Sierra Leone, and Liberia, and of involvement in military transport and the illegal plunder of natural resources in the DRC. In order to establish criminal liability under a complicity theory, one would also need to show that Bout was aware of the circumstances in the recipient countries, the human rights records of the parties he supplied, and their intent to commit more crimes. Bout, who denies being involved in sanctions-busting, is currently in Moscow, successfully avoiding arrest under an international arrest warrant issued by Belgium.

---

[88] Mil-Tec was registered in the Isle of Man, which at the time was not covered in the U.K. legislation codifying the U.N. arms embargo into British law. Due to another loophole, the company also escaped scrutiny under U.K. arms export controls. Thus the activities of Mil-Tec were technically legal and could not be the basis for a prosecution under national law. See, for example, "Human Rights Watch Calls on Britain to Crack Down on Violators of International Arms Embargoes," Press Release, November 25, 1996.

Legal Theories in Action

The indictment of Charles Taylor by the Sierra Leone Special Court (SCSL) explicitly treats the cross-border provision of weapons and other military support to known violators as a prosecutable offense. The case against Charles Taylor rests on much more than the transfer of weapons, and a trial against him would be important in many respects. But to the extent that he is found criminally responsible for providing material support to the RUF, it could serve as an important precedent and wake-up call to arms traffickers the world over.

The Taylor indictment is not the only opportunity to send that message. The SCSL has ongoing investigations related to the arming of the RUF. The Court is actively investigating cases involving those who orchestrated arms shipments. Consistent with its mandate, it is focused on those who thus bear the "greatest responsibility" for the atrocities committed in Sierra Leone, meaning in this case those who played a central role in the provision of arms. As confirmed to Human Rights Watch by the SCSL's Chief of Investigations, Alan White: "If a person is the principal supplier of arms and knows that and also knows that the weapons will be misused, then this person certainly would have individual criminal responsibility and would be prosecuted [by the Court]." The statute of the SCSL specifically provides for prosecution of "a person who planned, instigated, ordered, committed or otherwise aided and abetted" the crimes it sets forth.

While the Special Court is focused on the masterminds of the atrocities in Sierra Leone and their main backers, a Truth and Reconciliation Commission also is examining who took part in gross abuses in Sierra

Leone and who assisted them in the commission of those crimes. To the extent that it looks at the role of arms traffickers, the work of this commission also would help ensure greater accountability for their actions.

The International Criminal Court provides a key possible venue for holding individuals responsible for "the most serious crimes of concern to the international community." The statute of the International Criminal Court explicitly asserts the responsibility of someone who "[f]or the purpose of facilitating the commission of such a crime, aids, abets or otherwise assists in its commission or its attempted commission, including providing the means for its commission."

The chief prosecutor of the International Criminal Court, Luis Moreno-Ocampo, has expressed interest in the role of private actors in fueling war crimes and crimes against humanity, with special reference to the illegal exploitation of resources in the Democratic Republic of Congo. If and when the Court prosecutes persons who have been complicit in or conspired in the commission of gross abuses, it will help further elaborate the legal basis to hold individuals criminally responsible for fanning the flames of armed conflict and associated abuses.

Another possibility, as yet unexplored by the international community, would be to allow international courts to prosecute arms traffickers for violating arms embargoes. Such action would address only those human rights crises that are covered by an arms embargo, but would be an important complement to other efforts. It could be accomplished if an international or hybrid court created to prosecute atrocities in a country subject to a U.N. arms embargo, such as Liberia, were to include violations of that embargo in the list of crimes in its statute. Foreseeing such a possibility, the Security Council could note in its resolutions that violations by governments and individuals of the embargoes it imposes might be prosecuted before international criminal courts with jurisdiction.

Conclusion

Examination and possibly further development of existing legal theories may shed some light on the responsibilities of both states and individuals with respect to the transfer of weapons to gross abusers. Progress to date has been slow, however, and there is a need to push these concepts further to secure change. The governments and private traffickers who dismiss the very notion that they might be held responsible for supplying weapons to known abusers need to learn that they are wrong: they can and should be held accountable for their role in facilitating atrocities.

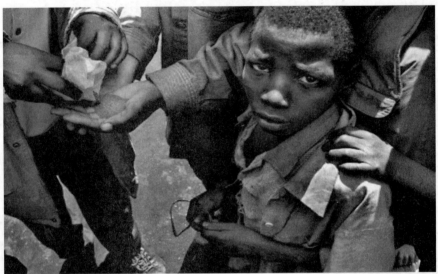

At the Rubaya Sunday market miners sell a highly lucrative powder called coltan, which is used by U.S., European, and Canadian manufacturers of chips for cellular phones and computers. Kivu region, Democratic Republic of Congo. © 2003 Alex Majoli/Magnum Photos

Engine of War: Resources, Greed, and the Predatory State

By Arvind Ganesan and Alex Vines

Internal armed conflict in resource-rich countries is a major cause of human rights violations around the world. An influential World Bank thesis states that the availability of portable, high-value resources is an important reason that rebel groups form and civil wars break out, and that to end the abuses one needs to target rebel group financing. The focus is on rebel groups, and the thesis is that greed, rather than grievance alone, impels peoples toward internal armed conflict.

Although examination of the nexus between resources, revenues, and civil war is critically important, the picture as presented in the just-described "greed vs. grievance" theory is distorted by an overemphasis on the impact of resources on rebel group behavior and insufficient attention to how government mismanagement of resources and revenues fuels conflict and human rights abuses. As argued here, if the international community is serious about curbing conflict and related rights abuses in resource-rich countries, it should insist on greater transparency in government revenues and expenditures and more rigorous enforcement of punitive measures against governments that seek to profit from conflict.

The "Greed vs. Grievance" Theory

Civil wars and conflict have taken a horrific toll on civilians throughout the world. Killings, maiming, forced conscription, the use of child soldiers, sexual abuse, and other atrocities characterize numerous past and ongoing conflicts. The level of violence has prompted increased scrutiny of the causes of such wars. In this context, the financing of conflict through natural resource exploitation has received increased scrutiny over the last few years.

One theory influential in World Bank circles is that countries with abundant natural resources are more prone to violent conflict than those without, and that insurgent groups are more likely motivated by control over resources than by actual political differences with government authorities, ethnic divisions, or other factors typically viewed as root causes of civil war. Paul Collier, formerly the head of the World Bank's development research group, now a professor at Oxford University and one of the strongest proponents of this theory, says, "[e]thnic tensions and ancient political feuds are not starting civil wars around the world...economic forces such as entrenched poverty and the trade in natural resources are the true culprits. The solution? Curb rebel financing, jump-start economic growth in vulnerable regions, and provide a robust military presence in nations emerging from conflict."

The civil wars in Angola, Colombia, Democratic Republic of Congo (DRC), Liberia, and Sierra Leone are often cited as examples of this dynamic. In Angola, the National Union for the Total Independence of Angola (União Nacional para a Independência Total de Angola, UNITA) financed its war largely through the taxation and encouragement of the illicit trade in diamonds from the mid-1990s until the war ended in 2002. The Revolutionary United Front (RUF) in Sierra Leone also financed itself by trading in illicit diamonds. In the DRC, control of diamonds, coltan, and timber has been a powerful incentive to prolong the country's vicious civil war. Collier has also classified the illegal drug trade and kidnapping for profit—predominantly by rebel groups in Colombia—as part of this equation. It is undeniable that non-state actors have financed warfare through trade in resources. Successive U.N. investigative panels monitoring UNITA's sanctions-busting in Angola, for example, reported that UNITA earned approximately U.S.$300 million a year from illicit diamond sales between 1999 and 2002.

The greed vs. grievance theory is provocative and compelling to a point. Even on its own terms, however, there are weaknesses. First, there is evidence that greed is often not the determinative motive for rebel group behavior. El Salvador and Sri Lanka, for example, have endured brutal civil wars where resources were not a factor. Cynical exploitation of ethnicity has been a driving force behind conflicts in Rwanda and Côte d'Ivoire. Colombia's civil war existed long before the cocaine boom in the late 1970s and kidnapping in the 1990s, and even the civil war in resource-rich Angola began some twenty years before UNITA started to finance itself with illicit diamond sales in the mid-1990s. Indeed, UNITA agreed to a ceasefire roughly two months after the death of Jonas Savimbi in February 2002, even though U.N. investigators estimated that UNITA was still able to earn as much as U.S. $1 million per day from illicit diamond sales. Had greed been the primary motive of the rebels, they could have continued to fight for much longer to the detriment of the country and civilians caught in the

303

middle of the conflict. This suggests that funding from commodities was secondary to Savimbi's larger goal of defeating the Angolan government, and was not much of a factor in UNITA's choice to end the war after Savimbi's death.

Another aspect of the problem is that many of the actions and aims of armed groups engaged in combat with a government are by definition illegal, and so such groups are naturally prone to seek extralegal financing for their activities. Absent an international patron state willing to finance weapons purchases and the like (as was common during the Cold War), they tap into illicit sources of financing in much the same way as organized criminal and terrorist networks smuggle and trade in contraband. UNITA's leader Jonas Savimbi only in 1994 authorized significant centralized investment in diamond mining, following a complete cessation of U.S. and South African overt and covert aid that had been given to the rebels since the mid-1970s.

A missing element in this greed vs. grievance theory, however, is the role that governments of resource-rich states play. Too often, government control of important resources and the revenues that flow from those resources goes hand-in-hand with endemic corruption, a culture of impunity, weak rule of law, and inequitable distribution of public resources. These factors often lead to governments with unaccountable power that routinely commit human rights abuses; they can also make prolonged armed conflict more likely. The remainder of this essay examines three different aspects of this dynamic.

First, control over resources gives such governments a strong incentive to maintain power, even at the expense of public welfare and the rights of the population. In many resource-rich countries, governments are abusive, unaccountable, and corrupt, and they grossly mismanage the economy. Rather than representing the citizenry, the government becomes predatory, committing abuses to maintain power and controlling the resources of the state for the benefit of a few. Researchers at the World Bank sometimes refer to these governments as "Predatory Autocracies," where:

> [S]tate power faces few constraints and the exploitation of public and private resources for the gain of elite interests is embedded in institutionalized practices with greater continuity of individual leaders. Such regimes are nontransparent and corrupt...little financial and human capital flows into productive occupations, whose returns are depressed by a dysfunctional environment.

The government of Angola, largely dependent on oil during the latter years of its war with UNITA, is one example of such an unaccountable, predatory state. The roots of the Angolan civil war were political, influenced by the dynamics of the Cold War and divisions among the former nationalist movements. The Angolan government enjoyed significant military assistance from the Soviet Union and Cuba and conducted a semi-conventional war against UNITA, which in turn was supported by its apartheid South Africa backers and encouraged by the West. However, this conflict had been transformed into a low intensity conflict by the end of 1998, and the government of Angola increasingly took on the attributes of a predatory state. During the last years of the war, huge sums of money simply unaccountably disappeared from government coffers, and the population grew ever more impoverished.

Second, unaccountable governments with large revenue streams at their disposal have multiple opportunities to divert funds for illegal purposes. When such a government is involved in armed conflict, the resulting rights abuses can be horrific. The example of the Liberian government under Charles Taylor, as explained below, is a case in point. Relying on off-budget accounts, the Taylor government funded both illegal arms purchases and illegal supplies of arms to rebels in neighboring Sierra Leone, who at the time were subject to a U.N. arms embargo. It took stringent international enforcement of the embargo to put an end to the Liberian government's illegal activities.

Third, armed conflict can be exacerbated by the actions of third-party governments seeking to profit from resource-rich neighbors. A prime example, detailed below, is the way in which both Ugandan and Rwandan governments have intervened in the conflict in DRC, a conflict that itself has been impelled by competition for lucrative resources. (The involvement of Charles Taylor's forces in Sierra Leone's conflict and in western Côte d'Ivoire from September 2002 to mid-2003 was also driven in part by a desire to obtain control of such resources. The incursion into Côte d'Ivoire also fostered individual greed: Taylor's forces resorted to looting in lieu of pay.)

The international community has an important role to play in combating such abuse. Because the problem of abusive, resource-rich states has both economic and political dimensions, a solution requires action by international financial institutions, governments, and corporations to ensure greater transparency and accountability, and, during active conflict, to strengthen enforcement of arms embargoes and sanctions regimes that target known abusers—governments and non-state actors alike.

Angola: Lack of Transparency and Accountability

The Angolan government is notorious for having long mismanaged its substantial oil revenues, especially during the final years of its long conflict with UNITA, when oil was the main source of government funding. In 1999, for example, at a time of a renewed offensives, about 88 percent of the government's total revenue came from oil—more than U.S.$4 billion. In addition to the substantial revenues that went into the war effort, some U.S.$1.1 billion, nearly 20 percent of the country's Gross Domestic Product (GDP), simply disappeared from government coffers in the same year, much of it likely siphoned off through corruption. In its *Country Reports on Human Rights Practices* for 1999, the U.S. State Department noted, "[t]he country's wealth continued to be concentrated in the hands of a small elite whose members used government positions for massive personal enrichment, and corruption continued to be a common practice at all levels."

Despite the substantial revenue inflows, the government in these last years did little for the Angolan population during these years and

307

showed little respect for human rights. Living conditions for millions of Angolans were dismal, and the government made little effort to win over civilians through any type of hearts-and-minds tactics. Government forces routinely resorted to arbitrary arrests and detentions; restricted freedom of expression, assembly, association, and movement; committed extrajudicial killings; "disappeared" people; and engaged in torture and rape.

Essential services and institutions also suffered. The country ranked 160th out of 174 countries in the United Nations Development Programme's Human Development Index (HDI). Some one million people were internally displaced. In 1999 alone, some 3.7 million people, including internally displaced persons, required U.N. or NGO humanitarian assistance, as government assistance was woefully inadequate. Few courts actually functioned. As recently as 2003, the International Bar Association found that only twenty-three municipal courts physically functioned out of the 168 that were supposed to exist. The government even routinely failed to pay salaries of many of its security forces and allowed security personnel to extort the civilian population with virtual impunity.

In recent years, funds lost to corruption or otherwise unaccounted for far exceeded the amount spent on the population. For example, if one combines all government social spending in 1999 with funds spent under the U.N. Interagency Appeal (which funded U.N. programs in the country and most NGO humanitarian programs), the total comes to approximately U.S.$320 million. That is about U.S.$780 million less than the amount of money that disappeared in 1999. The lives of millions of

Angolans could have been improved if at least some of those funds had been used for humanitarian purposes, to reconstitute the judiciary, or pay salaries of security forces. The diversion of funds on such a scale violated the government's commitments under the International Covenant on Economic, Social, and Cultural Rights to "progressively realize" the population's rights to health and education. Throughout the conflict, moreover, it was difficult if not impossible for Angolans to exercise any control over the government's use of public funds because freedom of expression was restricted and basic information simply was not made available.

Although the war with UNITA has ended, a conflict in Cabinda province continues. A major concern is that if Angolans do not see the benefits of their sizable natural wealth, the country may not slide into war, but into lawlessness. Angola has a great potential for improvements in human rights and social development, but if the status quo persists, then that squandered potential could lead to future grievances and prevent the resolution of current ones.

Liberia: Misuse of Resource Revenues for Sanctions-Busting

Unaccountable governments with large revenue streams at their disposal have multiple opportunities to divert funds for illegal purposes. Relying on off-budget accounts, the Taylor government in Liberia fomented national and regional instability by providing arms and other support to a vicious rebel group, the Revolutionary United Front (RUF), in neighboring Sierra Leone and rebel groups in western Côte D'Ivoire, as well as to fund its own war within Liberia. Meanwhile, Liberia remained one of the poorest countries in the world.

Despite international arms embargoes, the Taylor government spent millions for his own wars and to supply the RUF, using revenue from government-controlled diamond and timber sales, and from monies diverted from Liberia's lucrative maritime registry. An arms embargo was placed on all parties to the civil war in Liberia in 1992 after the Economic Community of West African States intervened militarily in large part to prevent Taylor, at the time leader of rebel forces known as the National Patriotic Front for Liberia, from taking power. The sanctions remained in effect when Taylor subsequently was elected president of Liberia in 1997 but were largely ineffective because they were poorly enforced. It was only after the U.N. Security Council introduced a new expanded package of sanctions in May 2001, this time accompanied by a serious international enforcement effort, that Taylor's predatory behavior was checked.

For years, Taylor used illicit funds to pay for the illegal weapons. Liberia's weapons purchases from 1999 to 2003, for example, were mainly financed by off-budget spending by the Liberian government. Taylor favored maintaining major off-budget agencies—the Bureau of Maritime Affairs (BMA), the Forestry Development Authority (FDA) and the Liberia Petroleum Refining Company — headed by his close associates. While neither the BMA nor FDA published its financial accounts or provided financial information, the IMF estimated that, in 2002, off-budget revenues from shipping and timber totaled about

U.S.$26 million, some 36 percent of the government's total revenue and almost six times what the government spent on education and health.

Taylor was able to secretly divert these funds until U.N. investigative panels were constituted to monitor sanctions-busting by the government. In March 2001, the U.N. Security Council decided to approve new sanctions on Liberia to start in May 2001. The sanctions were in response to a report presented by the Panel of Experts on Liberia established to monitor sanctions applied to the RUF and other forces operating in Sierra Leone. The basis for these sanctions was President Taylor's support for the RUF in Sierra Leone in violation of the existing sanctions. Security Council Resolution 1343, passed in March 2001, reauthorized the arms embargo on Liberia; imposed a travel ban on key officials, their spouses, and business associates; called on U.N. member states to freeze all financial assets of the RUF; and called for the expulsion of RUF members from Liberia. An embargo was also imposed on all of Liberia's diamond exports, and in July 2003 a timber embargo was added.

The panel examined the Taylor government's misuse of maritime revenues in order to violate sanctions. Liberia today has the second-largest maritime fleet in the world, and in 2002, maritime revenue constituted about 18 percent of government revenue—about U.S.$13 million. The U.S.-based Liberian International Shipping and Corporate Registry used off-budget accounts to pay U.S.$925,000 for illegal arms and other prohibited items at the request of the government in 2000, a period when Liberia was still deeply involved in supporting the RUF and had also launched incursions into neighboring Guinea. Nathanial

Barnes, finance minister from September 1999 to July 2002, admitted, "revenue was largely diverted," for the "war effort. But there was no kind of accountability." At least U.S.$1.6 million of maritime revenue was used for sanctions-busting from 2000 through 2001.

Timber revenue was also problematic. The U.N. Liberia panel of experts was able to document how Taylor used these resources to violate sanctions. In one case, the panel documented nine payment instructions for a total of U.S.$7.5 million from 1999 to 2001 to nine different bank accounts. These were all off-budget expenditures from the timber industry. Two of these were used as payments for defense-related expenditure.

On May 6, 2002, prior to the introduction of timber sanctions in July 2003, the U.N. Security Council passed Resolution 1408 (2002). That resolution included a requirement to audit revenues derived from the shipping registry and the Liberian timber industry in order to ensure that the revenue is used for "legitimate social, humanitarian and development purposes." It represents the first time that the Security Council has insisted upon an audit. The Security Council formally linked misuse of government revenues and sanctions busting to reducing human rights abuses and spending more resources on social programs by calling for an audit.

The Liberian government did very little in response to the resolution. It commissioned a systems and management audit, one that avoided any financial analysis. There remains an important opportunity to ensure that the timber revenues are appropriately audited and managed. The international community should encourage and provide technical assistance for a full audit and the creation of a system to ensure appropriate use of this revenue.

The Role of Uganda and Burundi in the DRC

An overlooked aspect of resources and conflict is the role of foreign governments who provide political, material, financial, or military support to rebel groups and governments in furtherance of their own economic interests. The presence of natural resources, particularly strategically important resources such as oil, colors the way foreign governments deal with resource-rich states and rebel groups. They may downplay human rights abuses or poor governance in order to maintaining cordial relations with a commodity provider. In some cases, they may engage in the conflict directly or through proxies in order to secure resources. This is nothing new; it was a mainstay of colonial and Cold War politics. For example, in a 1975 National Security Council meeting during the Nixon presidency, senior U.S. officials discussed which of the various factions in Angola to support, either directly or through allies such as Zaire's dictator Mobutu Sese Seko, once the Portuguese withdrew from the country. In considering options, Secretary of Defense James Schlesinger suggested, "[w]e might wish to encourage the disintegration of Angola. Cabinda in the clutches of Mobutu would mean far greater security of the petroleum resources." The enclave Cabinda was and remains Angola's largest area of oil production.

While Mobutu did not end up with Cabinda, his plunder of state resources in Zaire (now the Democratic Republic of Congo) helped create the conditions that led to the country's civil war. The cycle continues. In the DRC today, warring factions backed by neighboring Uganda and Rwanda, among other governments, have ruthlessly exploited the country's natural resources and in some cases, repatriated them. More than three million people have died directly or indirectly as a consequence of war since 1998, and all parties to this complex conflict have been implicated in gross and systematic abuses.

Uganda has benefited from the DRC's gold and diamonds. According to the U.N. Panel of Experts on the Illegal Exploitation of Natural Resources and Other Forms of Wealth in the DRC, Uganda has no diamonds but became a diamond exporter after it had occupied diamond-rich areas in the DRC. Similarly, the panel reported that Uganda's gold exports dramatically increased after its involvement in the conflict. Uganda also backed insurgents in the eastern Ituri region and played a direct role in combat there. Ituri is rich in gold reserves, and the dispute in part involved control of those resources. The Ugandan economy significantly benefited from the re-exportation of gold, diamonds, coltan, timber, and coffee, and commodity sales significantly improved the country's balance of payments. Uganda is often cited as an economic success story in Africa, a model of economic growth and a country committed to poverty reduction, but there has been little scrutiny by international financial institutions (IFIs) regarding the role of its illegal exploitation of resources in the DRC in bolstering its economy. The U.N. Panel reported in 2001:

[T]he illegal exploitation of gold in the Democratic
Republic of the Congo brought a significant
improvement in the balance of payments of Uganda.
This in turn gave multilateral donors, especially the
IMF, which was monitoring the Ugandan treasury
situation, more confidence in the Ugandan economy …
[illegal exploitation of resources in the DRC] brought
more money to the treasury through various taxes on
goods, services and international trade … A detailed
analysis of the structure and the evolution of the fiscal
operations reveals that some sectors have done better
than others, and most of those tend to be related to the
agricultural and forestry sector in the Democratic
Republic of the Congo.

This problem has not been publicly acknowledged by the IFIs. Thomas
Dawson, the director of the IMF's External Relations Department,
wrote in June 2002, "in recent years, the Ugandan government's
economic policies have proven quite successful in containing inflation
and promoting strong economic growth …The IMF has fully supported
this program with advice and lending." In a September 2003 review of
Uganda's performance under the Poverty Reduction Strategy Paper
(PRSP) process, the IMF and World Bank praised the country for its
export-led growth. Although the report raised concerns about human
rights and the humanitarian situation in northern Uganda, it was silent
on the country's role in the DRC. Overall, it found that "the staffs of
the Bank and Fund consider that, based on the PRSP annual progress
report, Uganda's efforts toward implementation of the poverty
reduction strategy provide adequate evidence of its continued

commitment to poverty reduction, and therefore the strategy remains a sound basis for Bank and Fund concessional assistance."

The U.N. panel mentioned above also found that Rwanda, which has no diamond reserves of its own, began to export diamonds after it became involved in the war. It found that the Rwandan military financed its involvement in the DRC through commercial exploitation of resources, shareholding in businesses operating in the DRC, payments from the rebel group RCD-Goma, and taxation and protection payments from businesses operating in Rwandan-controlled areas in the DRC. Most of the revenues generated from these activities are opaque and off-budget. Uganda has been more brazen and has kept this revenue on-budget, even though the source of that revenue is considered to be illegal exploitation of another country's resources; funds are brought in through formal channels and openly included as a source of government revenue. The panel of experts further concluded that the nature of combat in the DRC was intertwined with control over resources. It noted in 2001:

> Current big battles have been fought in areas of major economic importance, towards the cobalt- and copper-rich area of Katanga and the diamond area of Mbuji Mayi. Military specialists argue that the Rwandan objective is to capture these mineral-rich areas to deprive the Government of the Democratic Republic of the Congo of the financial sources of its war effort. Without the control of this area, the Government of the Democratic Republic of the Congo cannot sustain the

war. This rationale confirms that the availability of
natural resources permits the continuation of the war
…. In view of the current experience of the illegal
exploitation of the resources of the eastern Democratic
Republic of the Congo by Rwanda and Uganda, it could
also be thought that the capturing of this mineral-rich
area would lead to the exploitation of those resources.
In that case, control of those areas by Rwanda could be
seen primarily as an economic and financial objective
rather than a security objective for the Rwandan
borders.

The Ugandan Government established the Porter Commission on May
23, 2001 to look into the allegations of Ugandan involvement in illegal
exploitation of Congolese resources.The final report was produced in
November 2002, but only made public in 2003. The report exonerated
the Ugandan government and its army of official involvement in such
exploitation up to 2002. The Commission did, however, support the
U.N. panel's findings in relation to senior Ugandan military officials.The
Commission strongly recommended further investigation of diamond
smuggling, stating that there was a link between senior Ugandan army
members, known diamond smugglers, and a Ugandan business.

Despite these activities, no punitive measures have been taken against
either Rwanda or Uganda. Nor have international financial institutions
demanded audits or other scrutiny of the sources of the countries'
contentious revenues.

317

What Can be Done

The international community should be more consistent in demanding that governments manage their resources soundly, and it should insist on compliance with arms embargoes against known abusers. International financial institutions, the U.N. Security Council, governments, and companies all have important roles to play in pressing for transparency. Each of these actors has taken some steps recently, but many current proposals either depend on voluntary compliance by the government in question or are too limited to be fully effective in promoting greater transparency and accountability.

To its credit, the IMF has been a forceful proponent of such measures in Angola and Liberia. Human Rights Watch does not take a position on the work of the international financial institutions per se but can and does examine the positive or negative impact their activities can have on human rights. Whatever one thinks of the IMF's economic prescriptions, its efforts to promote transparency in Angola and Liberia have been an important source of leverage for those interested in human rights improvements in the country. It has so far refused to enter into a program with the Angolan government until more transparency is evidenced. In Liberia, which has had its IMF voting rights and related privileges suspended, the fund has insisted that greater transparency in the use of timber and maritime revenues will be a key component of any future cooperation with the government.

However, the IMF has been inconsistent regarding transparency globally. As noted above, the IMF has been silent on Uganda's role in the DRC. It has pressed the issue with most of Africa's oil-producing countries but less so in Sudan. Even though there is considerable controversy over the government's use of its oil revenue and control over the country's southern oil fields has led to widespread human rights abuses. It has been less forceful with oil-rich Kazakhstan. The IMF urgently needs to adopt a consistent strategy to promote transparency and accountability in order to address ongoing and potential conflicts throughout the world.

The World Bank has also been moving towards a consistent approach on transparency. A two-year-long review by the World Bank assessing its role in the extractive industries has largely concluded that the bank should consistently address these issues. The Chad-Cameroon pipeline has promising transparency measures built in to it, but it is too early to tell whether they will be consistently enforced. The bank is also providing technical assistance to countries like Angola in order to help them better manage revenue. Recently, the bank approved financing for the Baku-Tbilisi-Ceyhan pipeline and has required government disclosure of oil revenues as a condition of financing. But it is less forceful in Central Asia or in Uganda on these issues. By requiring audits, accurate public disclosure of revenues and expenditures, the public in resource-rich countries could have an opportunity to exercise oversight over governments' use of public funds.

Third-party governments also have a critical role to play, particularly where institutions such as the IMF and World Bank have no leverage. Oil-producing governments often generate far more revenue than IFIs can provide, and many of those governments choose not to enter into programs with them. For example, Nigeria, Venezuela, Equatorial

Guinea, Angola, and Kazakhstan do not have formal IMF programs. The U.K. government has led the Extractive Industries Transparency Initiative (EITI). The EITI is a voluntary effort that would allow for the publication of such data by both governments and companies. It involves governments, companies, IFIs, and NGOs. But as a voluntary initiative, it is wholly reliant on opaque governments to cooperate. Unless there is forceful diplomatic pressure on governments and commitment by the sponsoring governments, such as the U.K., this mechanism may not yield the desired level of transparency in countries where management of revenues has been most problematic. While some governments have been quick to support voluntary measures, there is a real need for mandatory measures and constant diplomatic pressure to promote transparency.

Companies also have a role to play. They should voluntarily endeavor to publish their payments to governments. Royal Dutch/Shell has begun to do this in Nigeria, but many companies resist voluntary disclosure out of fear of antagonizing host governments. The Publish What You Pay campaign is an NGO-led effort to make such disclosure mandatory. Although corporate disclosure without government disclosure may not yield full transparency, it would definitely enhance transparency. At a minimum, disclosure would allow interested parties to determine different sources of revenue in order to begin to determine how it is spent. However, no government has embraced mandatory disclosure at this writing. The International Finance Corporation (IFC), the private-sector lending arm of the World Bank, is considering mandatory disclosure as part of its loan agreements with extractive industry companies.

Perhaps the most important aspect of responsibly managing revenue is ensuring that it takes place regardless of whether a country is at peace, preparing for war, or engaged in conflict. Although the war in Sierra Leone is over, the misuse of diamond revenue and related corruption still means that the population is not experiencing the full benefits of its country's natural wealth. Nigeria's oil-producing Niger Delta may not be at conflict or war in the technical sense of those words; It is nonetheless anarchic and riddled with violence that stems from the fact that oil revenue has not benefited communities in the oil producing regions. Under successive dictatorships, billions of dollars of oil revenue were diverted into private hands. Moreover, oil theft and black-market sales drain tens of millions of dollars from public coffers. Such theft cannot occur without some official acquiescence because of the scale of the operations involved. Those revenues are also used to arm and equip private actors who engage in violence, in part to maintain control over those resources.

Sanctions need better monitoring and enforcement. UNITA was able to profit from illicit diamond revenue while sanctions were in force. Charles Taylor flouted longstanding arms embargoes and was not deterred until the U.N. Security Council enhanced monitoring of sanctions busting and increased enforcement of the embargoes. The international community should adopt a rigorous approach toward monitoring and enforcement of sanctions wherever a conflict takes place. A positive development is the use of investigative panels to monitor misuse of resources and sanctions busting in Angola, the Democratic Republic of Congo, Liberia, and Sierra Leone. The international community may want to consider a permanent roster of

321

experts that can investigate these issues throughout the world, rather than ad hoc panels.

When governments actively break sanctions or embargoes, or illegally exploit the resources of a third country, the Security Council's treatment of Liberia provides a model. Security Resolution 1343 was the first time that the council imposed sanctions on one country for its refusal to comply with sanctions on another. The Liberia sanctions were essentially designed to assist the peace process in Sierra Leone. They fully achieved this objective. The diamond embargo in particular resulted in an almost complete cessation of the trade in illicit diamonds from Sierra Leone to Liberia and helped realign the trade axis to Freetown. In conjunction with sanctions, IFIs should require audits of questionable commodity flows, which they are already empowered to do by their existing mandates, and should push for compensation of or repayment to countries from which resources have been illegally extracted.

Conclusion

When unaccountable, resource-rich governments go to war with rebels who often seek control over the same resources, pervasive rights abuse is all but inevitable. Such abuse, in turn, can further destabilize conditions, fueling continued conflict. Factoring the greed of governments and systemic rights abuse into the "greed vs. grievance" equation does not minimize the need to hold rebel groups accountable, but it does highlight the need to ensure that governments too are transparent and accountable. Fundamentally, proper management of revenues is an economic problem, and that is why the role of IFIs is so important. But it is an economic problem that also has political dimensions and requires political solutions. Political will and pressure, including targeted U.N. sanctions where appropriate, can motivate opaque, corrupt governments to be more open and transparent. Where such pressure is lacking, as in Liberia prior to enforcement of sanctions, continued conflict, rights abuse, and extreme deprivation of civilians all too commonly are the result.

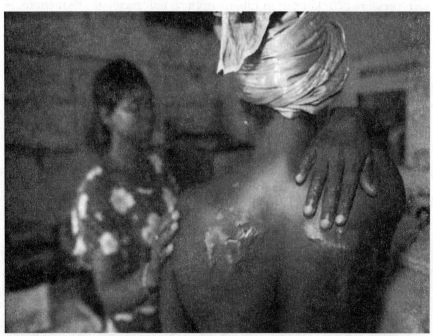
A woman receives psychological and medical treatment in a clinic to assist rape victims in Freetown. In January 1999, she was gang-raped by seven rebels in her village in northern Sierra Leone. After raping her, the rebels tied her down and placed burning charcoal on her body. © 1999 Corinne Dufka/Human Rights Watch

In War as in Peace: Sexual Violence and Women's Status

By LaShawn R. Jefferson

More than ten years after the commencement of wars in the former Yugoslavia, and almost a decade after the Rwandan genocide—conflicts notorious for attacks on women and girls—combatants continue to use sexual violence as a tactic of war to terrorize and control civilian populations. Sexual violence targeting women and girls has been used in all recent conflicts, including in the former Yugoslavia, Sierra Leone, India (Kashmir), Rwanda, Sri Lanka, the Democratic Republic of Congo (DRC), Angola, Sudan, Côte d'Ivoire, East Timor, Liberia, Algeria, the Russian Federation (Chechnya), and northern Uganda.

Rape has always meant direct physical harm, trauma, and social ostracism for the victim. Now, it may also be a death sentence for many women. Women are increasingly, and sometimes deliberately, being infected with HIV through wartime rape. By disrupting normal economic activity and destroying bases of economic support, armed conflict also puts women at risk for trafficking and at greater risk for having to engage in "survival" sex or sexual bartering, through which many women are becoming infected with HIV.

Although there has been increasing international attention to sexual violence in armed conflict, two essential features have persisted. First, it is routinely used on a large scale in most wars against women (though

325

much less frequently, men and boys too are sometimes targeted for sexual attack). Second, perpetrators of sexual violence continue to enjoy near complete impunity. Over the past decade, the number of successful prosecutions has been paltry compared to the scale of the crimes.

At the start of the 21st century, with some of the most horrific known examples of sexual violence during armed conflict taking place before our very eyes, we have to ask why wartime rape recurs with such alarming predictability. Why are women so consistently targeted for this specific type of assault? Ultimately, can wartime sexual violence be prevented?

Several critical factors make sexual violence in conflict resistant to eradication. First, women's subordinate and unequal status in peacetime renders them predictably at risk for sexual violence in times of war. Second, increasing international exposure and public outrage about rape in conflict have failed to translate into vigorous investigation and prosecution of perpetrators, a necessary element in any serious effort to deter such violence. Finally, inadequate services for survivors of wartime sexual assault reflects official disregard for the harm women and girls suffer in the course of conflict and suggests a lack of commitment to facilitating rape survivors' reintegration into society.

Treatment of Women in Times of "Peace"

Sexual violence has continued to be systematic and unrelenting in part because of state failure to take seriously, prevent, and prosecute routine and widespread discrimination and violence against women during times of "peace."

Women throughout the world face systemic attacks on their human rights and chronic, routinized and legal discrimination and violence, much of it justified through cultural and religious arguments. Even where discrimination is prohibited, it often persists in practice. By any reasonable measure, state failure to uphold women's rights as full and equal citizens sends an unmistakably clear message to the broader community that women's lives matter less, and that violence and discrimination against them is acceptable.

The discrimination and violence women endure is targeted at them in part or in whole because of their sex. In both law and practice, women are subordinate and unequal to men. Women are frequently denied their right to equality before the law; their right to substantive equality; their rights to freedom of movement, association, and expression; and equal access to education, work, and healthcare.

The state often plays a crucial and complicit role in permitting discrimination and violence targeting women and girls. For example, governments have abysmal records of prosecuting domestic and sexual violence against women. Since government statistics are so poor, it is debatable which of the two is less vigorously prosecuted.

Although most states fail to protect women as equal citizens on myriad fronts, state failure is particularly noteworthy with regard to the prevention and prosecution of sexual assault. In most countries, rape goes largely unreported. When it is reported, prosecutions are rarely successful and are sometimes determined by whether the victim was a virgin. Biased judicial officials disregard the testimony of women with sexual experience outside of marriage. Evidentiary standards disadvantage women. Moreover, in some countries, a victim's failure to convince the state that she has a credible claim of rape can be converted into an admission of out-of-wedlock sex, and the state can prosecute her for adultery.

Many states fail to uphold women's right to sexual autonomy and bodily integrity in peacetime. Many women are legally unable to protect themselves from unwanted sex. States have enacted marital exemption clauses to rape. Some states still allow a rapist to marry the rape victim in order to escape punishment. Some states obstruct women's access to divorce. States permit customary and other practices—such as widow "cleansing," forced marriage, and wife inheritance—to flourish, even though they are predicated on the rape of women.

In far too many countries, the honor of a community or family is still closely tied to control of the sexual activity of women and girls. Male family members often put a premium on female virginity, "purity," or sexual inexperience. Consequently, combatants the world over know that targeting women and girls both inflicts grave harm on individuals *and* symbolically assaults the larger community (or ethnic group or nationality) to which the female victims belong. Until this fundamental fact changes, women and girls will always be at risk.

A principal impetus to sexual violence (whether in peace or wartime) is sexual subordination and deriving sexual gratification from sexually harming another. Such subordination is both an important motivation for the attack and an obstacle to subsequent prosecution—in part because women are still greatly stigmatized for the violence that is inflicted on them. Sexual violence is the only crime for which the community's reaction is often to stigmatize the victim rather than prosecute the perpetrator.

Many men are accustomed to enforcing gender norms and stereotypes through physical violence. They interact in violent ways (actual and threatened) with women without sanction, and sometimes with community and government support. Such violence is often culturally, sometimes legally, sanctioned.

This is the backdrop against which rape and other forms of gender-based violence in armed conflict must be understood. It is a continuation—and a significant worsening—of the various discriminatory and violent ways that women are treated in times of peace.

The following cases from armed conflicts in the DRC and Sierra Leone illuminate the link between wartime sexual violence and other forms of gender-based violence and women's subordinate status in peacetime.

Sexual violence against women has been a pervasive and alarming feature of armed conflict in eastern DRC. Tens of thousands of women and girls have been assaulted. Most of the forces involved in the conflict—combatants of the Rassemblement congolais pour la démocratie (RCD), Rwandan soldiers, the Mai-Mai, armed groups of Rwandan Hutu, and Burundian rebels of the Forces for the Defense of Democracy (Forces pour la défense de la démocratie, FDD) and Front for National Liberation (Front pour la libération nationale, FNL)— frequently and sometimes systematically rape women and girls. All parties to the conflict have been implicated. There is no sign of abatement. In early November 2003, the United Nations reported that in new fighting in eastern DRC thousands of women and girls had been tortured and raped.

Well before conflict broke out in the DRC, women and girls were second-class citizens. The law and social norms defined the role of women and girls as subordinate to men. The Congolese Family Code expressly subordinates women in the family by requiring them to obey their husbands, who are recognized as the head of the household. Reflecting the community's sense that educating boys is more important than educating girls, a higher percentage of boys attend school than girls. Some male household heads "resolve" rape cases involving their daughters or sisters by accepting money payment from the perpetrator or his family, or by arranging to have the perpetrator marry the victim, thus underscoring the notion that rape was a crime against the perceived "owner" of the victim.

In Sierra Leone's armed conflict, sexual violence was committed on a much larger scale than the highly visible amputations for which Sierra Leone became notorious. Thousands of women and girls of all ages, ethnic groups, and socioeconomic classes were subjected to widespread and systematic sexual violence, including individual and gang rape. Rapes were perpetrated by both sides, but mostly by the rebel forces of the Revolutionary United Front (RUF), the Armed Forces Revolutionary Council (AFRC), and the West Side Boys, a splinter group of the AFRC.

Like women in the DRC, Sierra Leonean women faced widespread discrimination in practice, law, and custom before armed conflict erupted—each compounding and reinforcing the other, to women's enormous disadvantage. Although the constitution formally contains a guarantee of sex equality, provisions permitting discrimination in adoption, marriage, divorce, and inheritance, among other areas, nullify this guarantee. The constitution thus legitimizes and codifies women's subordinate and second-class status. In addition, under customary and Islamic law, the two systems under which most women are married, women have distinctly subordinate status. Notably, a married woman is often considered a minor and as such can be represented by her husband, who has the right to prosecute and defend actions on her behalf.

Further, married women in Sierra Leone had lost significant control over their sexual autonomy well before the war began. Under customary law, a wife can only refuse to have sexual intercourse with her husband if she is physically ill, menstruating, or breast-feeding. She can also refuse intercourse during the day, in the bush, or during Ramadan. Physical violence against women is widespread is Sierra Leone, and under customary law, a husband has the right to "reasonably chastise his wife by physical force." Men who were accustomed to exercise control over women's bodies in times of peace continued to do so with extreme brutality during the civil war.

In Sierra Leone, a complicated constellation of rape laws in the statutory system ensures minimal prosecution of rape. In some communities, the only type of rape that is treated as a serious crime is that of a virgin. Even in such cases, the punishment for rape in local courts often involves fines or "virgin money," payable to the victim's family. The emphasis continues to be on the injury to family honor and, to the extent the injury to the girl is considered, the emphasis is on her status as a virgin.

During armed conflict, combatants routinely abduct women—for long and short periods of time—and force them to become "wives," essentially obliging women to cook, clean, wash clothes, and have sex (and often as a consequence to bear children), all of which are stereotyped, gender-specific forms of labor. Such relationships, of course, mimic relationships during peacetime, especially peacetime situations in which forced marriage and expectations of free female labor are common practice. This stereotyped perception of women

332

persists in wartime and puts them at great risk for abduction and violence.

For example, in Sierra Leone, the RUF and other rebel units regularly abducted women and girls, occasionally for combat, but most often for forced sex and slave labor. In eastern DRC, combatants abducted women and girls and held them for periods up to a year and a half, forcing them during that time to provide both sexual service and undertake gender-specific work. Women and girls were obliged to carry out domestic labor, such as finding and transporting firewood, cooking, and doing laundry for the men who held them captive and sexually assaulted them.   During Rwanda's genocide, militia members held some women in forced "marriages." These women not only were raped, but militia members held them and forced them to do household work, including cooking and cleaning. In Algeria's civil war, armed Islamist groups abducted women and girls from local villages, often times raped them, killed most, and held others in captivity to do cooking and other household work. Colombia's guerrilla and paramilitary forces recruit female child combatants, some of whom are pressured to have sexual relations with commanding officers and forced to use contraception. In northern Uganda, teenage girls are forced into sexual slavery as "wives" of Lord's Resistance Army commanders, who subject them to rape and other sexual violence, unwanted pregnancies, and the risk of sexually transmitted diseases, including HIV/AIDS.

The male demand for female labor to perform female household chores persists during armed conflict. These patterns of social dominance and deeply engrained gender-specific roles get violently expressed in wartime and too often lead to women's abduction and enslavement during armed conflict.

This level of social conditioning and gender stereotyping can be addressed through education and through measures to ensure equality and respect for women's human rights. Such behavior must be punished through international—and one day local—prosecution.

Prevention

Many wars are foretold in some way. Rarely does a war erupt overnight. If wars can be anticipated, so can the fact that women will be victims of sexual violence during the fighting. National governments, the U.N., civil society, and regional actors must do more during peacetime, in periods when hostilities are mounting, and during the early stages of armed conflict to prevent sexual violence. Better training of combatants is a necessary first step.

Such training should include better and more regular instruction of combatants not only on protections generally due to civilians under international humanitarian law (IHL), but also the specific prohibitions against sexual violence.

Improved and more rigorous training and education on IHL will unlikely reach many of the less organized rebel groups increasingly participating in wartime rape, but it will reach more organized rebel groups and will affect a core group of uniformed soldiers and officers under state authority. Soldiers in the field should receive timely, clear, consistent, and regular training and reinforcement on the illegality and unacceptability of sexual violence in conflict, and should act as examples to other, nonregularized combatants.

Although it is doubtful that many of those who commit sexual assault in conflict and use it to their strategic ends are unaware of its illegality, governments are not relieved of their responsibility to continue to attempt to prevent sexual violence. Governments should disseminate information on its prohibition and signal a serious commitment to investigate and punish all humanitarian law violations, including sexual violence.

As civilians are likely to take up arms and participate in combat when the rule of law collapses or in times of civil war, better and broader education of civil society on IHL will also decrease the use of rape in conflict. Governments should engage in broad, grass-roots dissemination and education campaigns (radio, television, print media, internet) with as many components of civil society as possible to educate them about prohibitions under IHL, particularly the prohibitions against the use of sexual violence.

Training and deploying civil society monitors in times of war is potentially a significant deterrent and can aid post-conflict accountability efforts. Civil society monitors at all levels of society should be trained in the basics of international human rights and humanitarian law. As monitors, they can act as witnesses to violations and document them for future trials and other accountability mechanisms. Nongovernmental organizations (NGOs) with interest and relevant experience would be good candidates for this. This training should also benefit women by reinforcing what should always be the case—that sexual violence is a crime that should be prevented and punished even during peacetime.

International Investigation and Prosecution as Deterrence

To date, sexual violence in armed conflict has been prosecuted primarily at the international level—through ad hoc courts created by the U.N. Security Council (the International Criminal Tribunal for the former Yugoslavia, ICTY, and the International Criminal Tribunal for Rwanda, ICTR) and mixed or hybrid courts (such as the Sierra Leone Special Court). Prosecution of sexual violence is an important indication of commitment to improved accountability for gender-specific crimes in conflict. It is also an important expression of commitment to deterring future crimes of this nature.

Although both the ICTY, established in 1993, and the ICTR, established in 1994, began strongly, their commitment seems to have waned after a number of important initial convictions. The present record is disappointing, given the high hopes that women's rights activists, female survivors of sexual violence, and others had held for the tribunals.

Both tribunals contributed groundbreaking international jurisprudence on sexual violence and gender-based crimes in armed conflict. However, both have been plagued by weak investigations and neither has had an effective long-term prosecution strategy that acknowledges the degree of wartime sexual violence suffered by women. Barring dramatic advances before the expiration of their respective mandates in 2010, in terms of sexual violence prosecutions each criminal tribunal risks being remembered for what it missed doing, rather than for what it achieved.

The ICTY was established to prosecute persons for serious violations of international humanitarian law, including grave breaches of the Geneva Conventions, war crimes, and crimes against humanity committed in the territory of the former Yugoslavia since 1991. Rape of women by combatants as a strategy of war featured prominently in the wars in the former Yugoslavia, up to and including the 1998-99 Kosovo conflict.

The women's human rights community the world over applauded the creation of the ICTY. They believed that the exercise of the ICTY's mandate and the public revelation and subsequent documentation of the widespread use of rape in wars in the former Yugoslavia would significantly erode the historic impunity afforded sexual violence in armed conflict. Activists hoped that the ICTY would pursue cases of sexual violence in conflicts in the former Yugoslavia as vigorously as, and on equal terms with, other crimes committed during the wars.

Yet, the ICTY—like its sister institution, the ICTR—has failed to meet expectations for establishing accountability for sexual violence in the former Yugoslavia. To its credit, it has indicted at least 27 individuals for crimes that involved either rape or sexual assault. (In perhaps its most famous recent case, the ICTY is trying former Serbian President Slobodan Milosevic for command responsibility for war crimes, including acts of sexual violence, in Kosovo.)

Though the ICTY's record on prosecution is underwhelming, several of its cases have nevertheless broken new ground in jurisprudence on sexual violence under international law. In one landmark case, in February 2001, the ICTY convicted Dragoljub Kunarac, Radomir Kovac, and Zoran Vukovic for rape, torture, and enslavement. The three received sentences of twenty-eight, twenty, and twelve years, respectively. These cases marked the first time in history that an international tribunal had indicted individuals solely for crimes of sexual violence against women. The ICTY ruled that rape and enslavement were crimes against humanity, another international precedent. The tribunal found that the defendants had enslaved six of the women. Most important, although two of the women were sold as chattel by Radomir Kovac, the ICTY found that enslavement of the women did not necessarily require the buying or selling of a human being. Such jurisprudence is the exception, not the rule.

Like the ICTY, the ICTR has failed to give priority to sexual violence cases after its initial landmark decisions involving rape. Although NGOs and U.N. agencies report that tens of thousands of women were sexually assaulted during the Rwandan genocide, the ICTR to date has

handed down only one conviction involving sexual assault that has
survived appeal.

Established to prosecute persons responsible for genocide and other
serious violations of IHL, the ICTR issued a verdict in September 1998
that convicted former mayor Jean-Paul Akayesu for individual criminal
and command responsibility on nine counts of genocide, crimes against
humanity, and war crimes. The verdict was the first handed down by the
Rwanda Tribunal; the first conviction for genocide by an international
court; the first time an international court had punished sexual violence
in a civil war; and the first time that rape was found to be an act of
genocide when it was committed with the intent to destroy a particular
group targeted as such.

Despite its promising start, the ICTR has been a weak vehicle for
providing redress for sexual violence crimes committed against women
during the 1994 genocide. Although at this writing there were more
than a dozen cases pending that include charges of sexual violence, there
had been only two convictions—that of Jean-Paul Akayesu and a later
conviction of Alfred Musema, which was subsequently overturned on
appeal in November 2001.

Even the Akayesu decision did not come without a fight. The ICTR
initially was reluctant to indict Akayesu for rape. When Akayesu was first
charged in 1996, the twelve counts in his indictment did not include
sexual violence—despite the fact that Human Rights Watch and other
rights groups had documented widespread rape during the genocide,

particularly in areas under his control. A lack of political will among some high-ranking tribunal officials, as well as faulty investigative methodology by some investigative and prosecutorial staff, in part explains this initial omission. It was only after local and international women's rights activists protested the absence of rape charges against Akayesu, including by submitting an amicus curiae brief to the ICTR urging it to bring charges of rape and other crimes of sexual violence against Akayesu, did the tribunal amend the indictment.

More generally, the ICTR's effectiveness in investigating and prosecuting sexual violence has been hampered by a number of factors, including lack of financial resources, poor staff training, lack of political will, poor witness protection, weak investigations, and a general perception by investigators that rape cases are too hard to prove in court.

In 2001, in response to complaints by local and international NGOs about a lack of political will to prosecute sexual violence, the ICTR amended many of its indictments to include sexual violence charges. In meetings and letters, NGOs have expressed concerns that indictments have been hastily amended to include gender-based violence charges without substantial evidentiary support, and that this strategy will undermine the tribunal's long-term effectiveness regarding the prosecution of sexual assault.

Whether cases of sexual violence are prosecuted at the local or international levels, programs to protect victims and witnesses at all stages are critical. Sexual violence prosecutions by the ICTY and the ICTR have been hampered or abandoned because female witnesses have felt that their testimony would put them at risk. In particular, they fear that their identities would be revealed and that their families would suffer retaliation and stigma.

Effective witness and victim protection programs are a cornerstone to successful prosecution. Women victims of sexual violence in the former Yugoslavia have refused to testify for fear that their identity would become known and they and their families would face reprisals. Female rape victims who have testified before the ICTR in Arusha have reported returning home to Rwanda to find that their testimony, including details of their rapes, are known by people in their home areas. Other rape survivors who have testified before the ICTR returned home to face anonymous threats and other harassment as a result of their testimonies on rape. After such incidents, some Rwandan NGOs threatened to boycott the ICTR and discourage women from testifying if the ICTR did not improve its mechanisms for protecting their identity and safety.

It remains to be seen how effectively other international or mixed courts will investigate and prosecute sexual violence. However, the Special Court for Sierra Leone appears to be taking its mandate on sexual violence seriously. The court, which will try a limited number of perpetrators from all warring groups who bear the greatest responsibility for serious violations of IHL committed from November 1996 onward, has a mandate for three years. Investigating and prosecuting crimes of sexual violence have been an integral part of the investigative and prosecutorial strategy from the beginning of court operations in July 2002. As such, crimes of sexual violence—including rape, sexual enslavement, abduction or forced labor—form part of ten out of the total of thirteen indictments issued to date. The court has on staff two full-time gender crimes investigators and has conducted gender sensitivity training for all members of the investigations team.

The establishment of the International Criminal Court (ICC) in July 2001 (whose treaty came into force on July 1, 2002) holds the promise of establishing meaningful accountability for gender-based crimes against women in armed conflict. Women's rights activists in many countries hailed the creation of the Court, particularly those who have worked tirelessly for years to ensure that the ICC would be an effective and strong vehicle for accountability for wartime violence against women. Its statute criminalizes sexual and gender violence as war crimes and crimes against humanity. Accordingly, the definitions of war crimes and crimes against humanity include rape, sexual slavery (including trafficking of women), enforced prostitution, forced pregnancy, enforced sterilization, other forms of grave sexual violence, and persecution on account of gender.

In addition to this critical area of codification, the ICC's statute includes measures to facilitate better investigation of gender-based crimes and better care of female witnesses. It provides procedural protections for witnesses and victims, has rules of evidence to protect victims of sexual violence, requires the appointment of advisers with legal expertise on sexual and gender violence, and facilitates victims' direct participation in the court's proceedings.

In July 2003, the ICC prosecutor announced that he was following developments in the Ituri province in eastern DRC very closely. As noted above, the conflict there has included widespread and systematic rape, as well as other forms of sexual violence against women and girls.

Post-conflict Social Reintegration

How governments treat survivors of sexual violence in the aftermath of conflict is a critical measure of their seriousness in addressing the crime and of their commitment to preventing future abuses.

Justice and accountability for female victims of sexual violence in armed conflict is not merely a matter of international or local prosecution but should include a focus on programs and services to address the psychological and physical injuries to victims and to assist their reintegration into the broader community. Too often in post-conflict settings female survivors of sexual assault are left with little community support, insufficient economic means to sustain themselves (and often children who are the product of rape), and profound physical and psychological trauma.

Communities often blame women and girls abducted by members of warring factions for what happened to them. When conflict ends, the women and girls often do not return home for fear of being rejected by their families and typically find little support and certainly no specially designed programs to address their needs. As such, many are left with no other option but to remain with the very rebel or militia "husband" who abducted and most often raped them.

Because of the persistent stigma attached to sexual violence victims in most of the world, many women are discouraged from ever coming forward to seek help. Women victims of rape often face ostracism by their families, intimate partners, and communities (in the worst cases they become victims of "honor crimes"); if they are married, they risk being divorced or otherwise abandoned by their husbands; and if they are not married, they risk never becoming so (and therefore living as outcasts from their communities). Those infected by HIV can expect even more discrimination and stigma from their families and communities. Many survivors of sexual violence will unnecessarily suffer and die in silence, absent well-designed programs and community efforts to urge them to come forward for assistance.

It would be a gross injustice if women survived sexual violence in armed conflict only to have to endure similar abuses in peacetime. Governments committed to the recovery of sexual violence survivors must undertake efforts to improve women's human rights in all aspects of their lives and eradicate discrimination against them. To this end, governments need to focus specific efforts on protecting women's sexual autonomy, in part by reviewing laws and customary practices to eliminate all impediments to women's equal and autonomous sexual decision-making. This means, in part, ending forced marriage; eradicating discriminatory nationality laws; decriminalizing adult, consensual sex; ending wife inheritance; ending widow "cleansing"; criminalizing spousal rape; ending inheritance and property rights discrimination against women; reviewing personal status laws and customs and guaranteeing women equal rights in the family; ending all harmful customary practices that subordinate women sexually; and vigorously condemning, investigating, and prosecuting all forms of violence against women, in particular sexual violence.

Post-conflict recovery for sexual violence survivors also requires the establishment of educational and work programs to enable them to become economically self-sufficient. Access to economic opportunities is critical because, first, women survivors of sexual violence are very likely to be the primary caretakers of their own children and other relatives; and second, many women may be in desperate need of medical attention for treatment of HIV-related and other illnesses, and to stave off full-blown AIDS. Women must be given the means to provide for themselves and their dependents and thus to avoid the need to exchange sex for basic goods, services, or shelter. Economic autonomy better positions women to refuse unwanted sex and reclaim their bodily integrity.

Sexual violence victims need services to address the extensive physical and psychological consequences of sexual assault. They frequently suffer long-term physical and emotional scarring. Many survivors of sexual violence confront unwanted pregnancies, debilitating gynecological problems, and untreated sexually transmitted diseases, including HIV. Post-traumatic stress syndrome and other lasting psychological consequences of assault plague women survivors and can obstruct their full and productive reintegration into civil society. In a post-conflict setting, it is critical that individual governments and the international community work quickly to reconstitute healthcare services and establish mechanisms to improve rape survivors' access to these services. This accessible care should include counseling, information, and treatment for a range of STDs, including HIV.

In this context, making post-exposure HIV prophylaxis (PEP) easily available to female survivors of sexual violence could save many lives. PEP, a standard policy for rape and sexual assault survivors in many countries, is an affordable four-week treatment with antiretroviral drugs that can prevent HIV disease in persons raped by an HIV-positive perpetrator. Where it already exists as a service in peacetime, it should be possible to preserve in wartime. Where it does not exist already, it should be a priority for donors concerned about the impact of sexual violence in war.

Doctors Without Borders (Médecins Sans Frontières), the humanitarian medical aid agency, has been providing PEP as part of its package of care for sexual violence survivors in emergency settings, including in DRC and Congo-Brazzaville, demonstrating that this is a feasible intervention in conflict settings. U.N. agencies are also currently reviewing the inclusion of PEP in reproductive health kits provided in emergency settings.

National governments should work with NGOs and other actors in civil society to help sexual violence survivors re-integrate into society and, if they wish, seek redress. For example, in DRC, local human rights and women's NGOs have joined forces and started to document abuses against women and girls more systematically. The Coalition against Sexual Violence in South Kivu was formed in December 2002 as an advocacy platform. Local churches are involved in providing spaces for rape survivors to discuss their trauma, as part of the recuperation process.

Women should be active participants in the rebuilding of civil society—and not just in traditionally "female" spheres, such as those involving children, health, or welfare. U.N. Security Council Resolution 1325 on Women, Peace, and Security, adopted in October 2000, recognizes the important role women can and should be playing in pre and post-conflict societies, as a means to prevent conflict in the first place and as a means to achieve sustainable peace once conflict has ended and ensure women's greater participation in government. Governments should look to this resolution for guidance, and should actively undertake efforts to have women participate fully in the planning and implementation of the reconstruction of civil society, as full and equal partners at all levels of decision-making.

Focusing post-conflict efforts on promoting civil, political, economic, cultural, and social rights for all women will invariably improve the prospects of many survivors of sexual violence. The same efforts will improve women's status more generally and render them less at risk for violence in times of war.

The End of Sexual Violence Against Women in Armed Conflict

One of the greatest challenges is to prevent sexual violence against women in the first instance. This can be achieved by making concerted efforts in at least three arenas. First, there must be heightened respect for women's human rights in all aspects of their lives. Failure to address sex discrimination as a significant underlying cause of sexual violence will ensure that present and future generations of women continue to be at risk for sexual violence. Second, there must be significantly improved compliance with the provisions of IHL during armed conflicts. Key methods include regular training and education of soldiers and other combatants regarding international legal protections for civilians, specifically prohibitions against rape and other forms of gender-based violence. Finally, there must be vigorous condemnation, investigation, and prosecution of gender-specific crimes against women in times of peace as well as war.

Serb returnees to Croatia, Smiljana and Pavao Cakic, in front of their occupied house, Popovic brdo, April 2003. © 2003 Davar Kovacevic

Legacy of War: Minority Returns in the Balkans

By Bogdan Ivanisevic

In the territories that comprise the former Yugoslavia—notably Croatia, Bosnia and Herzegovina (hereafter Bosnia), and Kosovo—the failure of international and domestic efforts to promote the return of refugees and displaced persons has left substantially in place the wartime displacement of ethnic minorities. The Balkan experience offers an important lesson for other post-conflict situations: unless displacement and "ethnic cleansing" are to be accepted as a permanent and acceptable outcome of war, comprehensive and multi-faceted return strategies—with firm implementation and enforcement mechanisms—must be an early priority for peace-building efforts. Post-war efforts in the former Yugoslavia make clear that when these elements are present, minority return progresses; when they are absent, return stalls.

In all parts of the former Yugoslavia affected by ethnic wars during the 1990s, persons displaced by war from areas in which they now comprise an ethnic majority were able to return to their homes fairly soon after the end of hostilities. The true measure of effectiveness of the return policies pursued by national authorities and the international community, however, is the extent to which minorities have been able to return. By that measure return has been far less successful. Most minority members are still displaced, and it is increasingly evident that, even if the conditions for return improve in the future, most will not return to their homes.

In most areas of return, nationalistic politicians remained in power during the crucial immediate post-war period and either used that power to hinder the return of minorities, or did precious little to facilitate it. There was no physical security for prospective returnees, and they were unable to repossess their occupied homes or to have destroyed homes reconstructed. Rather than enhance prospects for reconciliation and return by bringing to justice war crimes perpetrators irrespective of their ethnicity, authorities directed their prosecutorial zeal against minorities, including returnees. The international community proved unable or unwilling to counteract this obstructionism.

By the time the authorities, under pressure from the international community or with its direct involvement, finally began to improve the security and housing situation for returnees, the willingness to return had faltered. Having spent months and years living elsewhere, the refugees and displaced persons had already become acclimated to their new environment. At the same time, return to the place of pre-war residence promised discrimination in employment, education, and law enforcement. Given a choice between local integration and return under such conditions, many opted for the former.

Only a resolute response from the international community could have opened a way for successful minority returns. For the most part such resoluteness has been missing. The international community has been too tolerant of the excuses made by governments in the region to justify their failure to return properties to pre-war occupants. International peacekeepers in Bosnia and Kosovo too often showed themselves unwilling to confront the extremists responsible for ethnically motivated violence against minorities or to arrest high-ranking war crimes suspects.

Although inadequate policies made many refugees and displaced persons lose interest in returning to their homes, the international community and national authorities should do their utmost to assist those who do want to return or they run the risk of providing succor to those who believe that the forcible expulsion of a population is a legitimate objective of war. The following analysis sets out the obstacles to minority returns in the former Yugoslavia, current initiatives to facilitate return, and recommendations on the way forward.

How Many are Still Displaced

Between 300,000 and 350,000 Croatian Serbs left their homes during the 1991-95 war in Croatia, mostly for Serbia and Montenegro and Bosnia. The majority remain refugees. The total number of returns registered by the Croatian government as of July 2003 was 102,504. The actual number of returnees is significantly lower because, after a short stay in Croatia, many depart again for Serbia and Montenegro or Bosnia.

In the period 1995-99, the nationalistic Croatian Democratic Union of the late president Franjo Tudjman enacted laws and carried out policies with the clear intention of preventing the return of Serb refugees. In January and February 2000, parties and candidates with a professed commitment to democracy and human rights defeated the nationalists in parliamentary and presidential elections, and it appeared that the conditions for return would improve significantly. In reality the new authorities have been slow to amend the returns policy, and the overall conditions for return have barely improved.

By the end of the 1992-95 war in Bosnia, 1.2 million people had found refuge abroad and more than a million others were internally displaced. The Dayton-Paris Peace Agreement, which ended the war, guaranteed the return of all refugees and internally displaced persons. Between 1996 and July 2003, the United Nations High Commissioner for Human Rights registered 965,000 returns of refugees and displaced persons to their pre-war homes, while more than a million remain displaced. Of those who have returned, some 420,000 returned to the areas in which their ethnic group—Bosniac (Bosnian Muslim), Serb, or Croat—is a minority.

The large-scale return of refugee and displaced Bosnian minorities began only in 2000, after the Office of the High Representative (OHR) in Bosnia (created under the Dayton-Paris Peace Agreement in December 1995 to oversee implementation of the civilian aspects of the agreement) introduced well-devised property legislation and international agencies took a more robust approach toward local officials who had obstructed returns. The breakthrough also resulted from a series of arrests between 1998 and 2000 of persons indicted for war crimes by the International Criminal Tribunal for the former Yugoslavia (ICTY). While the number of minority returns was 41,000 both in 1998 and 1999, in 2000 the number rose to 67,500, in 2001 to 92,000, and in 2002 reached a peak with 102,000 returns. In the first eight months in 2003, some 34,100 minorities returned. In comparison to the same period in the previous year, the figure represents a 50 percent drop. Rather than suggesting a dramatic aggravation of the conditions for return, however, the decrease reflects the narrowing of the pool of persons willing to return, eight or more years after they had fled their homes.

In Kosovo, approximately 230,000 Serbs, Roma, and others not of Albanian ethnicity have fled since the end of the 1999 NATO war and the pullout of Serbian police and Yugoslav soldiers from the province. Only about 9,000 minority members have returned since 1999, about half of them Serbs and half Roma. Precarious security conditions remain the chief obstacle to return. The situation is similar in Serb-controlled northern Kosovo, only with reversed roles, with ethnic Albanians unable to return.

Obstacles to Return

Obstacles to the return of minorities have been similar in most parts of the former Yugoslavia. It has taken years for the security situation to become conducive to minority return. Some areas of return, notably Kosovo, remain unsafe. Those who do wish to return frequently find that their homes are occupied, yet administrative bodies and courts have often failed to evict temporary occupants, or proceeded slowly in doing so. The limited government funds available for reconstruction of damaged and destroyed properties have mainly benefited members of the majority ethnic group. By the time other obstacles for minority return in the former Yugoslavia began to soften, international donors had shifted their focus elsewhere. Discrimination has also played a role in discouraging return. Judiciaries have been eager to prosecute minorities on war-crime charges and reluctant to bring to justice

355

suspects from the majority. Local public enterprises have failed to employ returning minorities.

It is clear that political will on the part of local authorities can have a significant impact on minority return. Experience shows that when leaders engage in efforts to facilitate return, the situation on the ground improves. For example, the largest number of returns to mixed communities in Kosovo has been in the Gnjilane municipality, where ethnic Albanian officials have distinguished themselves by unequivocally condemning anti-Serb violence and encouraging dialogue between local Albanians and the prospective Serb returnees.

Security Impediments

Violence, harassment, and threats, coupled with police failure to arrest perpetrators, have frustrated the efforts of refugee and displaced minorities in the former Yugoslavia to return to their homes. The problem is particularly stark today in Kosovo, where Serbs and Roma are the primary targets. The vast majority of post-war ethnically motivated murders and other serious crimes in the province remain unpunished. By failing to deter organized violence from the very beginning, the international military and civilian missions in Kosovo have contributed to its proliferation, and set off a spiral of impunity that continues to feed extremism on both sides of the ethnic divide. In comparison to the period 1999-2001, the number of life-threatening attacks against minority communities declined in 2002-03, but this was at least in part due to reluctance of fearful Serbs to venture out of their enclaves into majority Albanian areas—hardly a sign of improved ethnic relations.

In Bosnia, security concerns remained a major impediment to return years after the conclusion of hostilities. A 1999 survey co-sponsored by the United Nations High Commissioner for Refugees (UNHCR) found that 58 percent of displaced persons and refugees who indicated a preference to sell, exchange, or lease their properties in Bosnia said that they would return to their former homes if the local authorities guaranteed their safety or if their pre-war neighbors returned. In recent years, however, security conditions have significantly improved. The breakthrough resulted in large part from the NATO-led Stabilization Force (SFOR) arrests of a dozen ICTY indictees in the critical areas of Prijedor (western parts of Republika Srpska) and Foca (eastern part of Republika Srpska) between 1998 and 2000. Despite an improved situation overall, however, incidents directed against minorities still occur. In 2002 and 2003 the incidents included use of arms and explosive devices, as well as attacks on religious shrines and cemeteries.

By 2003, physical attacks against returnees in Croatia, already rare in comparison to Kosovo and Bosnia, had all but disappeared. However, in certain areas, including Benkovac, Zadar, Gospic, and Petrinja, Serbs continue to be concerned about their safety, due to general hostility from local populations or authorities.

357

Impunity for War Crimes and Discriminatory Prosecutions

It is clear that the failure to bring to justice war crime suspects, including those indicted by the ICTY, has weakened minorities' resolve to return and live as neighbors with their wartime foes. Where prosecutions have been carried out, authorities have taken a selective approach, prosecuting minorities in far greater numbers than members of the majority and sending a message to minorities that they are not equal citizens in the country of return. Rather than promoting reconciliation, ethnic bias in war crimes prosecutions has perpetuated the ethnic divide and deterred return.

While Croatia's cooperation with the ICTY with respect to provision of documents has earned it a passing grade from the international community, the government has nonetheless failed to hand over Ante Gotovina, a Croatian Army general indicted for crimes against Croatian Serbs between July and November 1995. The government claims that, since July 2001, when the ICTY prosecutor issued the indictment against Gotovina, the police have been unable to track him down. ICTY prosecutor Carla del Ponte and the Croatian press, however, have persuasively argued that Gotovina is at liberty in Croatia.

Croatia has demonstrated far more enthusiasm for the domestic prosecution of Croatian Serbs for war crimes. More than 1,500 have been indicted, often on ill-founded charges. The arrest of returning Serb refugees on war crimes charges has been particularly problematic. Although most arrests of Serb returnees ended in dropped charges or acquittals, the threat of arrest and prolonged detention has deterred the return of other refugees. At the same time, Croatian courts have dealt with only a handful of war crimes against ethnic Serbs, usually resulting in acquittals and absurdly low sentences. The Lora trial from 2002, and trial for crimes in Paulin Dvor, ongoing at this writing, dramatically exposed the absence of adequate witness protection measures in Croatia, as frightened key witnesses declined to offer relevant testimony or even show up in court.

The authorities in Bosnia's Republika Srpska have yet to arrest a single individual indicted by the ICTY or to try any Bosnian Serb on war crimes charges. A dozen war crimes trials are ongoing in Bosnia's other entity, the Federation of Bosnia and Herzegovina, where Bosniacs (Bosnian Muslims) and Bosnian Croats are in the majority. Trials have often been marred by the reluctance of witnesses to testify, the absence of effective witness protection mechanisms, poor case preparation, and weak cooperation with other judiciaries in the region.

The justice system established by the international community in Kosovo has done little to hold individual perpetrators accountable and break entrenched perceptions of collective guilt. Kosovo's judiciary has been unable to bring to justice those responsible for anti-Albanian crimes, and this failure alienated and radicalized many Kosovo Albanians. At the same time, Kosovo Albanian prosecutors and judges manifested an ethnic bias at the expense of local Serbs, thus alienating the Serb minority.

In the four years since the end of the war, only four people have been found guilty of war crimes against Kosovo Albanians by a final judgment delivered by the Kosovo courts, three of them Kosovo Serbs and the other an ethnic Albanian. A dozen other Serbs have been prosecuted on war crimes charges in cases with Albanian prosecutors and investigating judges, and tried by trial panels consisting of Albanian judges alone—or sometimes with an international judge in the minority. Monitors from the Organization for Cooperation and Security in Europe (OSCE) and human rights organizations reported serious due process violations, as well as apparent or actual bias on the part of Kosovo Albanian judges and prosecutors. Most of these trials resulted in guilty verdicts, but the Kosovo Supreme Court, with an international-majority panel eventually quashed the verdicts. By June 2003 Kosovo courts had still not brought a single indictment for war crimes committed against ethnic Serbs.

The unwillingness of Serbian authorities to bring to justice those responsible for war crimes committed in 1998 and 1999 in Kosovo also has impeded the return of Kosovo Serbs. Since 2000, Serbian courts have tried only four Kosovo-related war crimes cases, only one of which dealt with mass killings of Kosovo Albanians. There has been no investigation into the killings in Gornje Obrinje, Racak, Suva Reka, Mala Krusa, Cuska, Dubrava prison, Izbica, Slatina, Meja, Vucitrn, and Bela Crkva, each involving dozens of victims. In the eyes of Kosovo Albanians, the failure to prosecute betrays a continuing disrespect for Albanian victims and Serbs' refusal to confront the past. As a result prospects for reconciliation remain dim and the return of minority Serbs to Kosovo has been indirectly hampered.

Occupied Homes

Most minority refugees and displaced persons have not been able to repossess their occupied homes, nor have they received alternative housing or monetary compensation. Repossession concerns both privately owned houses and so-called socially owned apartments. The latter are apartments previously owned by the state or state enterprises, in which hundreds of thousands of families lived in pre-conflict Yugoslavia. The right to use a socially owned apartment—frequently referred to as the right of tenancy—was a real property right, and had many of the attributes of ownership, though holders of tenancy rights could not sell the right and the state could terminate their rights in certain narrow circumstances. During the war and immediately afterward, authorities in Croatia and in Bosnia terminated the tenancy rights of tens of thousands of displaced minorities. In Kosovo, former tenancy rights holders are in a better position because they had been allowed to purchase their apartments and many had become full owners before the 1999 war.

Since the end of the war, Croatia has prevented virtually all Croatian Serbs who lost tenancy rights from reoccupying their apartments or receiving substitute housing. Successive Croatian governments have refused to recognize lost tenancy rights as an issue requiring resolution. Serb homeowners have fared better, repossessing 14,430 out of 19,270 homes abandoned during the war. More than 5,000 homes, however, remain occupied by Croats. Government efforts to return these homes to their owners have been limited to providing alternative accommodation for Croat temporary occupants, either by constructing new homes or purchasing homes from Serbs who do not wish to return.

However, these methods require substantial state funding, and the government's ability to provide it has been limited, leading to substantial delays. In the meantime, many Serbs have grown disillusioned and decided to sell their houses.

In Bosnia, the principal role of the internationally appointed High Representative in the repossession process resulted in much higher repossession rates. As of August 2003, the rate for privately owned properties and socially owned apartments had been around 88 percent. Unlike Croatia, former tenancy rights holders in Bosnia have been able to repossess their pre-war apartments. This difference well illustrates the importance of political will. In Croatia, authorities have favored the Croat majority and left tens of thousands Serb families dispossessed. In Bosnia, an ethnically neutral international administration devised legislation and set in motion practices that helped tenancy rights holders repossess their homes. Nonetheless most of those who repossess their pre-war homes in Bosnia then sell, exchange, or rent the property, rather than moving back in, preferring to remain in their new area rather than return to their former homes. This is particularly true in cities.

Associations of displaced Serbs from Kosovo claim that up to two-thirds of Serb properties in Kosovo are occupied. Funding for agencies responsible for property repossession continued to be insufficient long after the 1999 war. As a result, housing authorities as of early 2003 had issued decisions on only 1,856 claims for repossession of properties, some 8 percent of the total claims registered at that time.

Access to Reconstruction Assistance

Slow and often discriminatory reconstruction of damaged and destroyed homes and properties is another huge obstacle to return. While the government in Croatia has done impressive work in reconstructing the damaged or destroyed houses of ethnic Croats, reconstruction assistance to returning Serbs began only at the end of 2002, seven years after the end of the war.

Unequal aid allocation also impacts reconstruction in Kosovo, where Albanians have had better access to funding. For example, in the municipality of Klina, more than half of the Albanian houses had been reconstructed as of the end of 2002, contrasted with only 6-7 percent of Serb-owned houses. In Bosnia, funding constraints rather than discrimination have proved the main impediment to reconstruction assistance. UNHCR and OHR estimate that, at the beginning of 2002, reconstruction funding was available for 20 percent of 66,500 devastated properties whose owners had expressed an interest in returning.

Discrimination in the Enjoyment of Social and Economic Rights

Discrimination against minorities in Croatia, Bosnia, and Kosovo persists in various forms. In most areas of return, virtually no minority returnees are employed in public services and institutions, such as health centers, schools, child-care centers, post offices, courts, police, power-supply companies, customs services, or the local administration. Limited opportunities for employment are often aggravated by

363

employment discrimination. Educational policies have also hindered return in Bosnia and in Kosovo, with access to schooling for returnee children often limited to schools with ethnically or linguistically biased curricula and textbooks. Few parents have been willing to send their children to such schools. To avoid them, parents have often kept children in the displacement community, housing the children with relatives or with one parent who remained behind for the purpose; other families have opted not to return at all. In some parts of the former Yugoslavia, discrimination against returnees also affects their enjoyment of social services, pension rights, and health care.

Shared Responsibility of Local and International Actors

The multitude of actors involved in returns-related activities often makes it difficult to identify those responsible for impeding minority returns. Local authorities in the areas of return are often even more nationalistic than the central government, and central governments are only too willing to point to local opposition as the explanation for ill-functioning returns policies. The substantial international presence in Bosnia and Kosovo, both military and civilian, can also serve as pretext for local actors to leave hard decisions and hazardous actions— including war crimes arrests and the prevention of inter-ethnic violence—to foreigners. Nonetheless, it is safe to conclude that all actors—international and domestic—bear some of the responsibility for the limited success of minority return in the region.

In Croatia, rates of ethnic Serb return since the end of the war have depended primarily on policies of the national government. While the pre-2000 government blocked return, the government constituted after the 2000 elections has tolerated it within certain limits, defined by the government's fear of alienating broad sectors of the nationalistic electorate. The role of the international community in promoting the return of refugees has taken the form of political conditionality linked first to Croatia's membership in the Council of Europe, and more recently to its desire to join the European Union and to the ongoing presence of an OSCE monitoring mission in Croatia. The limited involvement of the international community and its unwillingness fully to exercise what leverage it did possess has enabled successive Croatian governments to discriminate against Serbs and impede returns.

In Bosnia, return-related responsibilities have been shared by international agencies on the ground and the local authorities. The Office of the High Representative has had a key role in return activities. The High Representative imposed relevant legislation and removed from their posts numerous Bosnian officials who obstructed its implementation—but such robust practices began only three years after the war, by which time many among the displaced had already lost faith in returning. The contribution of domestic actors in Bosnia has consisted mainly in implementation of housing legislation by municipal housing commissions. Nonetheless, the key for continued return of minorities is in the hands of the Bosnian politicians. The willingness of displaced Bosnians to return depends largely on how they anticipate and experience reception in the areas of return. The role of Bosnian politicians in fostering a climate and policies conducive to return cannot be substituted by any outside actor.

In Kosovo, responsibility for return of minorities is shared by a number
of actors. The Special Representative of the United Nations Secretary-
General (SRSG) who heads the United Nations Interim Administration
in Kosovo (UNMIK), has the main executive authority, legislative
power in certain areas, as well as veto power over legislative acts of the
Kosovo Assembly. UNMIK includes an international police force. The
NATO-led Kosovo Force (KFOR) conducts peacekeeping activities.
Provisional institutions of self-government include the Assembly and
ten ministries. In addition to elected municipal assemblies and
administrations, since October 2000 UNMIK local community officers
have operated to enhance the security of minorities and to assist them in
access to public services. The unwillingness of UNMIK and KFOR to
confront local actors involved in forcing out minorities created a climate
of impunity in Kosovo which has been difficult to overcome,
notwithstanding subsequent international efforts to facilitate return.

In Kosovo, the government of Serbia and Montenegro has maintained
parallel judicial, administrative, health, and educational institutions in
Serb municipalities in the north and in enclaves in the center and the
south. Such an approach has thwarted integration of Kosovo Serbs into
economic and social life in the province, a necessary condition for
sustainable return.

Recent Initiatives to Improve Minority Return

Addressing Insecurity

In Kosovo insecurity remains the key obstacle to return, and persists to some extent in Bosnia. In Croatia, security for returnees is no longer a significant obstacle. There are some recent signs that UNMIK is taking a tougher stance on crimes against minorities in Kosovo. In uncharacteristic moves in October and November 2003, UNMIK arrested six Albanian suspects for the murder of four Serbs earlier in the year. It remains to be seen whether these arrests mark a definitive departure from what had been UNMIK's passive approach to crimes against non-Albanians.

In Bosnia and in Kosovo, the international community has relied on creating a multi-ethnic structure for the municipal police as a means for improving both the perception and the reality of security for minorities. The results have been modest at best. Despite commitment by international agencies and Bosnian officials in both the Federation and Republika Srpska that local police forces should reflect the pre-war ethnic balance, the numbers of minority officers remain small. The most recent U.N. report stated that by May 2002 only 16 percent of the targeted 28 percent in the Federation were minorities, while only 5 percent of the force in Republika Srpska were minorities compared to a 20 percent target. In Kosovo, minorities comprised 16 percent of the Kosovo Police Service in October 2003. However, minority police are barely present in the areas with an Albanian majority, and it is precisely in those areas where obstacles to return are greatest.

Accountability for War Crimes

The Chief State Prosecutor in Croatia formally instructed local prosecutors in June 2002 to review pending war crimes cases and drop charges where evidence against the suspects was insufficient. Possibly as the result of the state-wide review, the number of arrests of Serbs fell from 59 in 2001 to 28 in 2002. In addition, half of the arrested Serbs were provisionally released during pre-trial proceedings. In 2002 and 2003 the authorities also began prosecuting ethnic Croats for war crimes against Serbs. Still, the number of arrested, tried, and convicted Serbs remains far higher than that of ethnic Croats.

The past year saw modest signs of improvement in Bosnia in the process of establishing accountability for war crimes. An all-Bosnian State Court came into existence in January 2003. Some of the deficiencies present in earlier war crimes prosecutions before local courts are expected to be remedied when the court's humanitarian law chamber becomes operative in 2004. At this writing, Republika Srpska was also expected to begin its first war crimes trial against Serb indictees by the end of 2003, in a case of the abduction and disappearance of Roman Catholic priest Father Tomislav Matanovic in September 1995.

The most controversial development in Kosovo during 2003 was the July 16 conviction of former Kosovo Liberation Army commander Rustem Mustafa and three collaborators for illegally detaining and torturing eleven ethnic Albanians and one Serb, and executing six Albanians suspected of collaborating with the Serb regime, during the 1998-99 conflict. The men received sentences ranging from five to seventeen years. The convictions caused deep resentment among

Kosovo Albanians and triggered a wave of violent attacks against UNMIK. In June, the departing UNMIK chief Michael Steiner promulgated a new criminal code for Kosovo, giving more powers to international prosecutors to investigate atrocities and other serious crimes, and providing for more effective witness protection.

Property Repossession and Reconstruction

Repossession of property remains a major impediment to return in Croatia and Kosovo, while insufficient reconstruction assistance hinders returns in Croatia and Bosnia. The Croatian cabinet recently adopted laws and decrees purportedly aimed at providing housing for dispossessed tenancy rights holders. Legislation adopted in July 2002 stipulates that the government will provide alternative accommodation in "areas of special state concern" (areas controlled by Serb rebels during the 1991-95 war) to Croatian citizens without apartments or houses in Croatia or other parts of the former Yugoslavia. However, in its first year of implementation, not a single Serb former tenancy right holder is known to have obtained housing by virtue of the law. In June 2003, the cabinet adopted a decree enabling individuals returning to places outside areas of the special state concern to rent or purchase government-built apartments at below-market rates. Even the purchase rates stipulated by the June 2003 decree, however, will be beyond the financial means of most prospective returnees, and other forms of reparation or compensation for past dispossession remain unavailable to them.

Resolution of property claims finally made limited progress in Kosovo in 2003. As of September 2003, housing authorities had issued decisions on 31 percent of claims for restoration and confirmation of residential property rights (in contrast to only 8 percent at the start of the year). However, temporary occupants were slow to vacate the properties, and effective enforcement mechanisms were lacking. As of September, the number of actual repossessions still barely exceeded 2 percent of all claims.

After having reconstructed more than 100,000 Croat houses in the second half of 2002, the Croatian government has started to reconstruct Serbs homes with state funds. Then-Deputy Prime Minister Goran Granic stated in mid-June 2003 that 75 percent of the houses to be reconstructed during 2003 are Serb-owned. All reconstruction is scheduled to be completed by 2006.

In Bosnia, foreign funding for reconstruction continues to diminish, a trend which began in late 1990s. In Kosovo, the funding available for reconstruction of Serb homes has been sufficient, possibly because of the low number of those who are seriously considering return in light of safety concerns.

Tackling Discrimination

The efforts of the High Representative and other international agencies in Bosnia are shifting from property repossession toward combating discrimination and further integrating Bosnian political and social structures. The policies are intended to stimulate return of those whose ethnicity has made them feel like second-class citizens. In 2003, the most significant effort toward ending discrimination was directed at ending segregation in public education. Minority children have been able to share school buildings with majority children since 2000, but classes, curricula, and teaching staff, and even shifts in some cases, remained separate. On August 8, 2003, the educational authorities of Republika Srpska, Federation BH, ten Federation cantons, and the independent district of Brcko, signed an agreement on Common Core Curriculum, which incorporates the curricula of all entities and cantons. Pursuant to the agreement, schools which until recently functioned as "two schools under one roof" are to register as single legal bodies with one school director and one school board. The agreement, if implemented, should give a decisive blow to segregation in Bosnian schools, while leaving room for separate studying of the so-called "national subjects" that reflect the cultural distinctiveness of each constituent people.

In December 2002 the Croatian parliament enacted the Constitutional Law on the Rights of National Minorities. Under the law, the state has to ensure proportional representation of minorities in the administration and the judiciary at state, county, and municipal levels. However, the obligation to ensure proportional representation does not extend to public institutions, such as schools, universities, and hospitals, or to the police. Given the history of persistent discrimination against Serbs in post-war Croatia, the lack of legal obligation to pursue adequate minority representation in public institutions and enterprises does not augur well for a marked increase in the employment of Serb returnees.

In Kosovo, UNMIK has enacted regulations on the minimum employment of minorities in central institutions and public enterprises, but the 10 percent figure achieved by October 2003 remains far below the targeted 18 percent. In contrast to Croatia and Bosnia, however, the low level of minority participation in Kosovo is more often caused by the unsafe environment and limited freedom of movement for potential employees than by employment discrimination as such.

Recommendations

In territories of the former Yugoslavia, insecurity, limited tenancy rights, failures of justice, and discrimination are the central barriers to return of refugees and displaced people. While some of the basic preconditions for return in Bosnia—including physical safety and the ability to repossess pre-war homes—have been satisfied, there is still wide room for improvement in the reconstruction of houses. The continued failure to arrest ICTY indictees and to pursue domestic prosecutions of war crime suspects have also created a climate less than hospitable to return. Croatia has yet to start resolving the tenancy rights issue or to bring Croat war criminals to justice, and its long-term commitment to the reconstruction of Serb homes is an open question. In Kosovo, improved security is a precondition for addressing all return-related problems. In all parts of the former Yugoslavia, effective measures to combat employment discrimination have to be devised and implemented. Only when all these changes are in place will minority refugees and displaced persons have a fair chance to opt between return and a permanent integration in their current place of residence. For the changes to materialize, both domestic actors and the international community will have to redouble their efforts to facilitate minority return.

To adequately address security problems in Kosovo, the international community must maintain pressure on local political leaders to promote ethnic tolerance. KFOR and UNMIK must themselves marshal the political will necessary to pursue full accountability for ethnic violence and create measures to effectively coordinate criminal investigations. Local police should strengthen patrols in areas in which returnees report security problems or an increased sense of insecurity. UNMIK should speed up the recruitment of minority police officers in ethnically mixed areas, and all Kosovo Police Service members who show ethnic bias in the conduct of their activities should be disciplined or dismissed. In Bosnia, the European Union Policing Mission (EUPM) should robustly discipline and dismiss local police officers who obstruct efforts to resolve inter-ethnic violence and discrimination against ethnic minorities.

In all parts of the former Yugoslavia, cooperation with the ICTY and domestic war crimes prosecutions should be significantly improved. Croatia should arrest indicted Ante Gotovina and surrender him to the custody of the ICTY, and Serbia and Republika Srpska authorities should do the same with respect to the two dozen Serb indictees who live in those areas. Most importantly, authorities should show a greater commitment to bringing to justice and fairly trying war crimes suspects irrespective of their ethnic origin. Cooperation between states in war crimes prosecutions should include providing requested documents and allowing access to all witnesses sought by the court. Governments in the territory of the former Yugoslavia should facilitate testimony of witnesses from other jurisdictions, including by videoconference. The legislation providing for witness protection measures in Croatia, Bosnia, and Kosovo should be vigorously implemented, and Serbia should enact a detailed witness protection law. Legislation criminalizing intimidation of or threats to witnesses and other participants in the proceedings should be adequately enforced.

There is a pressing need for enhanced international support for accountability efforts in the former Yugoslavia. International donors should assist domestic judiciaries with technical and financial support for effective war crimes prosecution; allocate sufficient funds for effective implementation of witness and victim protection measures; and assist in out-of-region relocations of those in need of protection. NATO-led SFOR remains the only credible force in Bosnia able to arrest the wartime leader of Bosnian Serbs, Radovan Karadzic, and should do so. The international community should also put pressure on the authorities in Serbia and Montenegro to cooperate with war crime investigations in Kosovo, in particular by handing over suspects to UNMIK.

Croatia should vigorously implement the July 2002 legislative changes addressing property repossession, and introduce and implement rules that would remove the many remaining obstacles to effective repossession. In particular, Croatia should reconsider its existing policies on cancelled tenancy rights. It should give original tenancy rights holders an opportunity to repossess apartments which have not been privatized by subsequent occupants, and, where the apartments have already been sold, it should help them to obtain property of equivalent value or financial compensation. In Kosovo, the housing authorities should substantially speed up repossession procedures.

In all parts of the former Yugoslavia, evictions of temporary occupants often have been accompanied by the looting and destruction of the property by the outgoing occupants. Governments should enact legislation making such targeted looting and destruction a separate criminal offense and prosecute those responsible. Housing authorities should include a notice or warning to temporary occupants about the criminal sanctions for looting or destruction of property.

Finally, authorities in all parts of the former Yugoslavia should closely monitor employment practices in state institutions and enterprises. Pertinent ministries should intervene in cases in which discrimination on ethnic grounds is apparent and develop a proactive strategy for recruitment and hiring of qualified minority candidates. Discriminatory practices for minority returnees in government positions and state-owned enterprises should end, and authorities should ensure fair employment opportunities.

Right Side Up: Reflections on the Last Twenty-Five Years of the Human Rights Movement

By Reed Brody

The human rights movement has come a long way since Human Rights Watch was founded twenty-five years ago. In almost every nook and cranny of the globe, activists raise the banner of human rights to support their demands for respect and dignity. Thanks to this movement, by the end of the last century human rights had become one of the world's dominant ideologies, tirelessly proclaimed by governments. Although the movement was unable to stop genocide in Iraq, Rwanda, and Yugoslavia, and massive killings elsewhere, it was beginning to impose a moral element in international relations with a force unprecedented in modern history. The movement was a factor in democratic transformations in Eastern Europe, Latin America, and parts of Africa and Asia.

Yet the human rights movement now faces serious challenges. In particular, the horrific attacks of September 11, 2001, aimed at the heart of American power, have unleashed a reaction that threatens to wipe away many gains under the cover of an endless "war on terror." As this campaign unfolds, protagonist governments again relegate human rights to second-class status, just as they did before and during the Cold War, while others opportunistically invoke the war on terror to justify internal repression. In the face of these challenges, the movement must demonstrate that the promotion of fundamental rights is essential to security and an indispensable tool in the fight against terrorism.

***

"Human rights activists, after years of being ignored or disdained as
cranks, are riding a wave of popularity because of President Carter's
focus on the rights issue. They say the experience is at once exhilarating
and unsettling. 'Human rights is suddenly chic,' says Roberta Cohen,
executive director of the International League for Human Rights. 'For
years we were preachers, cockeyed idealists or busybodies and now we
are respectable.'"

So began a 1977 New York Times article on the human rights
movement. Later that year, Amnesty International would win the Nobel
Peace Prize in acknowledgement of its already considerable
achievements. The following year, Human Rights Watch would be
founded. Today, human rights, and the human rights movement, are a
fundamental part of the international political landscape.

In the past twenty-five years, a vast new array of groups—national and
international—have breathed life into the Universal Declaration of
Human Rights and other norms adopted after World War II. The
banner of human rights is raised throughout the world—by Tibetan
monks and Ecuadorian plantation workers, by African women's groups
and gay and lesbian activists in the United States. A United Nations high
commissioner for human rights is the official champion of the Universal
Declaration. The United States and the European Union, among others,
have by legislation made respect for human rights a factor in bilateral
relationships. Most countries have domestic human rights commissions

377

or human rights ombudsmen. Human rights education is part of the curriculum in more than sixty countries. Most countries have ratified most of the major human rights treaties. An International Criminal Court is gearing up to investigate some of the worst atrocities, while the movement has already ensnared such emblems of brutality as Augusto Pinochet and Slobodan Milosevic.

The human rights movement itself has become more inclusive, a substantial mosaic that includes large professional INGOs (international nongovernmental organizations) as well as thousands of regional, national, and local organizations working on issues ranging from self-determination to the rights of children, and from access to HIV medicines to the right to water.

As the movement expands, previously neglected issues, particularly those dealing with economic and social rights, have moved into the mainstream. Indeed, there has been a growing convergence in the work of groups dedicated to promoting economic and social development on the one hand, and those protecting human rights on the other. Many development organizations are shifting from needs-based, welfare oriented and humanitarian approaches to rights-based approaches to development. Human rights groups once focused largely on civil and political issues such as political imprisonment and torture. But increasingly we are addressing the underlying social and economic causes of these violations or championing economic and social rights issues, such as education, health, and housing.

Women's rights, once kept at the margins, has become a driving force in the human rights movement since women's groups took the 1993 United Nations World Conference on Human Rights in Vienna by storm and won full recognition that "women's rights are human rights." Among other things, the focus on women's rights has helped broaden the core human rights concepts of "violation" and "violator," directing the movement away from an exclusive focus on state actions to examine the culpability of state inaction in the face of known abuses by private actors.

The different layers of the movement complement each other. There are what we might call primary organizations or movements of people struggling to claim rights for their own members, such as some civil rights groups in the United States, many women's organizations, the Landless Workers Movement in Brazil, and the like. There are groups seeking to promote rights by creating the building blocks of a rights-respecting society—a free press, an independent judiciary, education in human rights and tolerance, and civilian control of the military. And there are national and international groups, from groups such as the Colombian Commission of Jurists to Human Rights Watch, which monitor respect for human rights norms and mobilize pressure to prevent or end abuse.

The movement has also become considerably more sophisticated in its advocacy. From the early letter-writing campaigns invented by Amnesty International, the movement has evolved to include campaigners, organizers, lobbyists, and media experts. The leading INGOs now have researchers on the ground connected by e-mail with advocacy offices at the United Nations and in major capitals, putting us in a strong position to affect international decisions as they are being made. Some monitoring groups, such as Human Rights Watch, target advocacy at powerful governments—such as the United States and the European Union—treating them sometimes as partners in pressing for change, sometimes as surrogates for their abusive allies who are more impervious to democratic criticism, (and, of course, sometimes as perpetrators of abuses themselves). We are of course mindful of Ian Martin's salient warning that "the human rights movement cannot be happy in working through the existing power relationships in an unequal world, nor can it even be neutral in its attitude to them." Yet applying the methodology of "naming and shaming" not only to abusive governments but also to their international allies, when it is done with the support of our own partners in the affected country, has made the movement a much more powerful force with which to reckon.

After the Cold War

For years after Human Rights Watch's founding, the Cold War provided both an incentive for governments to use human rights as a weapon and an obstacle to those seeking principled international cooperation to advance human rights. The United States was eager to raise the banner of human rights in its ideological war with the Soviet Union and its allies, even as it covered up abuses (when it did not directly sponsor them) in authoritarian regimes that it aided, ostensibly as bulwarks against communism. The eastern bloc, for its part, rejected criticism of its rights record as impermissible "interference in the internal affairs" of sovereign countries and paralyzed the United Nations human rights machinery.

Even during the Cold War, however, human rights mobilization helped lead to many important accomplishments, playing no small role in the end of *apartheid* in South Africa and the move towards democratic governance in much of Latin America. The Helsinki process—which triggered the creation of Helsinki Watch, the forerunner of Human Rights Watch—created the framework for individuals both within and outside of the Soviet bloc to challenge repressive governments, ultimately leading to the collapse of a Soviet system that in practice denied fundamental human rights.

The end of the Cold War seemed to bring a new consensus around the human rights ideal. The dissidents of the Soviet bloc who had created the human rights movement there, and for whom the international movement had campaigned, were not only free but in some cases were swept into power. A movement towards multi-party democracy took hold in Africa. Latin America completed its transformation from the era of U.S.-backed military dictatorships. In some Asian countries such as the Philippines and South Korea, human rights movements also helped usher in democratic change. A new democratic majority—now including many countries of Eastern Europe and Latin America—unlocked the potential of the United Nations Commission on Human Rights, which in the early 1990s finally unlocked the potential of the United Nations to take human rights seriously and, in some cases, even adopt something close to the activist role that Eleanor Roosevelt might have envisioned.

Most importantly, the principle of state sovereignty steadily yielded in the face of human rights pressure. In 1993, the United Nations World Conference on Human Rights in Vienna decisively put the sovereignty defense to rest by proclaiming that the "promotion and protection of all human rights is a legitimate concern of the international community." The way a state treated its people was indeed everyone's business. In the face of challenges from supporters of cultural relativism and "Asian values," the Vienna conference also emphatically declared that the "universal nature of these rights and freedoms is beyond question."

Human rights became, in the words of Michael Ignatieff, the "dominant moral vocabulary in foreign affairs," even if, in practice, they were often trumped by inconsistent economic and security goals. With the rhetoric of human rights ascendant, and television and the internet carrying instantaneous reports of abuse, the free hand of governments to act in the perceived interests of ruling elites was, perhaps more than any other time in recent history, constrained by an informed and active civil society. Richard Falk rightly recognized that "during the decade of the 1990s, the movement towards an international human rights consensus was initiating a normative revolution in international relations that was beginning to supersede realist calculations of power and status in the political imagination of observers and policymakers."

Yet even in this supposed golden decade of the 1990s, the human rights movement could not stop genocides in the former Yugoslavia and Rwanda, crimes against humanity in East Timor and Chechnya, or the killing of millions of civilians in armed conflict in central Africa. (Indeed, as we were meeting in Vienna to celebrate the triumph of human rights, the slaughter in Bosnia continued unabated only a few hundred miles away). Half of our planet's six billion people still live in poverty, 24 percent in "absolute poverty." Two billion of the human rights movement's clients do not have access to health care; one-and-a-half billion have no access to drinking water.

In a world in which intolerance and extremism are on the rise, in which millions die in armed conflict, in which poverty and misery are rampant, some are tempted to ask, as David Rieff has, whether improved norms have accomplished anything "for people in need of justice, or aid, or mercy, or bread?" Have they "actually kept a single jackboot out of a single human face?"

One should not confuse gloom about the current course of human events with scepticism about the value of the human rights endeavour or the accomplishments of the movement, however. It is certainly true that norms alone will not stop a tyrant or an extremist faction bent on genocide, and that is where the human rights movement, like many others, must confront the difficult question of military intervention to stop atrocity. (I think that most of my colleagues would agree that recourse to force is not only legitimate but also morally imperative in the face of genocide or equivalent atrocity. However there remains deep disagreement on how that force is to be authorized or employed). But while dictators may not be constrained by norms, open democracies are, as long as they are supported by an engaged civil society. Between the relatively surgical nature of the bombing of Iraq and Serbia and the carpet-bombing of Laos and Cambodia, not to mention the destruction of Hiroshima or Dresden, there is more than an evolution in the kindness of generals. Similarly, it is more difficult to imprison a Nelson Mandela for twenty-five years or a Chia Thye Poh from Singapore for twenty-three years. What was common practice fifty or twenty-five years ago is simply not acceptable today.

Norms empower activists and victims, by creating benchmarks, by legitimising their demands, by establishing, in the words of the Universal Declaration of Human Rights, "a common standard of achievement for all peoples and all nations." In a host of areas, ranging from the rights of women to the trend away from the death penalty, the process of developing norms and then mobilizing for their enforcement has indeed achieved concrete results.

Participating in the Pinochet case in the British House of Lords in 1998, I was struck at how the human rights movement had come of age. Not only were lofty proclamations like the United Nations Convention against Torture finally being applied in a concrete case, they were being applied in the case of the man whose sneering face behind the dark sunglasses had come to symbolized ruthless dictatorship, and whose repressive tactics twenty-five years earlier had unleashed the very forces—human rights activism and international conventions—which would lead to his arrest and to those hearings. Pinochet sent hundreds of thousands of articulate Chileans into exile. They, together with an outraged world opinion, swelled the ranks of groups like Amnesty International, which in turn pressed for the adoption of the Convention against Torture that would allow for the arrest of the ex-dictator.

September 11

At the height of its strength, however, the human rights movement was confronted with a new challenge that threatened, and still threatens, to undo much of what it had achieved. Looking out from our office conference room on the morning of September 11, 2001, Human Rights Watch staff watched as two hijacked airplanes destroyed the World Trade Center. These crimes against humanity, aimed at the heart of American power, have unleashed a reaction that threatens to wipe away many gains under the cover of an endless "global war on terror." The campaign against terrorism has seen the erosion of the rule of law rather than its enforcement. Human rights have been undermined at the very time they most need to be upheld.

Around the world, many countries cynically attempted to take advantage of the war on terror to intensify their own crackdowns on political opponents, separatists, and religious groups, or to suggest they should be immune from criticism of their human rights practices. Many states have responded to the indiscriminate violence of terrorism with new laws and measures that themselves fail to discriminate between the guilty and the innocent. Numerous countries have passed regressive anti-terrorism laws that expand governmental powers of detention and surveillance in ways that threaten basic rights. There has been a continuing spate of arbitrary arrests and detentions of suspects without due process. In some places, those branded as terrorists have faced assassination and extra-judicial execution.

One of the most worrying developments has been the renewed debate over the legitimacy of torture. Even if torture had continued to be

385

widespread around the world, until recently it had become almost axiomatic that no country admits to condoning torture. Torture is the ultimate degradation, the unspeakable medieval act that we had banished from acceptable practice. Torture was one of Amnesty International's first battles and thanks to the movement, torture has been considered the emblematic barbarity that was no longer permissible under any circumstances. It is the torturer who, a U.S. court noted in the Filártiga case, had supplanted the pirate of yore as "an enemy of all mankind." It was for torture, not mass killings, that Pinochet was stripped of his immunity. Yet now we see, particularly in the United States, important voices suggesting that torture can be a proper tool in the fight against terrorism. Indeed, there have been serious charges that detainees captured in Afghanistan have been beaten and subject to what are known as "stress and duress" techniques by U.S. officials or handed over to third countries where they are likely to be tortured, charges which the Bush administration has failed squarely to address.

At the inter-governmental level, concern for human rights has taken a back seat to lining up allies in the terror war, effectively giving free passes to newfound as well as more established strategic allies. This year at the Commission on Human Rights in Geneva, no government was willing to table a resolution critical of China, while Russia easily beat back a resolution on Chechnya despite its on-going atrocities there.

These developments led Michael Ignatieff to ask, after September 11, "whether the era of human rights has come and gone."

There is no doubt that the human rights movement faces a new challenge. The gloves have come off. We should not cling to the illusion that without the support of an organized citizenry the United States (or any other powerful country) will make human rights the "soul of [its] foreign policy," to use President Jimmy Carter's words.

In this new era, the movement must demonstrate that the promotion of human rights internationally is not just an ethical value but is also an essential tool in the fight against terrorism. Kofi Annan pointed the way in his September 2003 address to the General Assembly: "We now see, with chilling clarity, that a world where many millions of people endure brutal oppression and extreme misery will never be fully secure, even for its most privileged inhabitants." While terrorists themselves are not likely to be mollified by policy changes, we must act on the evidence that support for terrorism feeds off repression, injustice, inequality and lack of opportunity. As Richard Falk has said, "The message of extremism is not nearly as likely to resonate as broadly and nearly as menacingly if its animating grievances are not widely shared in the broader affected community." Where there is democracy and equality, where there is hope, where there are peaceful possibilities for change, terrorism is far less likely to gain popular support. Global security is thus enhanced by the success of open societies that foster respect for the rule of law, promote tolerance, and guarantee people's rights of free expression and peaceful dissent.

In the United States, where the shock waves of September 11 are most naturally felt, the resulting fears have been exploited by the Bush administration to press a radical roll-back of constitutional rights. The human rights movement is striving to persuade Americans that, while the government has to be empowered to take those measures which are reasonable and necessary to reduce the very real threat of terrorism, the requirements of security can and must be reconciled with the blessings of liberty. In one of the most chilling warnings by a sworn defender of the constitution, U.S. Attorney General John Ashcroft told Congress that "to those who scare peace-loving people with phantoms of lost liberty, my message is this: Your tactics only aid terrorists, for they erode our national security and diminish our resolve. They give ammunition to America's enemies, and pause to America's friends." Though it is an uphill battle, the movement is responding with the words of Benjamin Franklin, one of the U.S.'s founding fathers, that "they who would give up an essential liberty for temporary security, deserve neither liberty nor security."

These difficult times demand that the human rights movement reach its full potential to mobilize individuals and groups. This means completing the unfinished task of integrating all its parts, of developing mutually beneficial relations between international and national human rights groups. We have come a long way since a Central American activist complained to me that the movement followed the "maquila" model in which northern groups exploited the south's "raw material" of abuses and then pressed for rich governments to condition aid to poor countries. But we are still struggling to find ways in which national and local front-line groups can overcome their difficulties in access to funding, international media, and expertise in order to better participate in defining the international rights agenda. This is not just politically correct rhetoric. As Bahey El Din Hassan, Director of the Cairo Institute for Human Rights Studies, has pointed out, for example, only by empowering Arab partners to help define the agenda can international NGOs help them counter the perception that human rights are a western imposition. The movement must come to grips with the fact it is weakest precisely where support for terrorism is greatest, in the Middle East and west Asia.

In order to reach our full strength, we must create a synergy between the human rights movement and those campaigning for social and economic justice. Even if our agendas are not always a perfect fit, we need to join our voices around the key issues that unite us. Many of our signal successes as a movement, such as the creation of an International Criminal Court and the anti-apartheid struggle, came about when we joined forces with wider constituencies. The International Campaign to Ban Landmines, for instance, of which Human Rights Watch was a founder, unites a massive coalition of 1,300 human rights, humanitarian, children, peace, disability, veterans, medical, humanitarian mine action, development, arms control, religious, environmental, and women's groups in over 90 countries. In awarding the Nobel Peace Prize to the Campaign and its lead coordinator, Jody Williams, the Nobel Committee cited the uniqueness of an effort that made it "possible to express and mediate a broad wave of popular commitment in an unprecedented way."

I have no doubt that an overwhelming majority of people in our world support the human rights ideal. Our unfinished task is to mobilize that majority into a force too powerful to be resisted.

Appendix: 2003 Human Rights Watch Publications

Reports by Country

Afghanistan:

"Killing You is a Very Easy Thing for Us:" Human Rights Abuses in Southeast Afghanistan, 07/03, 101pp.

Algeria:

Truth and Justice on Hold: The New State Commission on "Disappearances," 12/03, 30pp.

Time For Reckoning: Enforced Disappearances and Abductions, 02/03, 84pp.

Angola:

Struggling Through Peace: Return and Resettlement, 08/03, 29pp.

Forgotten Fighters: Child Soldiers in Angola, 04/03, 26pp.

Armenia:

An Imitation of Law: The Use of Administrative Detention in the 2003 Armenian Presidential Election, 05/03, 24pp.

Azerbaijan:

Azerbaijan: Presidential Elections 2003, 10/03, 20pp.

Bangladesh:

Ravaging the Vulnerable: Abuses Against Persons at High Risk of HIV Infection, 08/03, 51pp.

Bhutan:

"We Don't Want to Be Refugees Again:" A Briefing Paper for the Fourteenth Ministerial Joint Committee of Bhutan and Nepal, 05/03, 22pp.

Brazil:

Cruel Confinement: Abuses Against Detained Children in Northern Brazil, 04/03, 51pp.

Burundi:

Everyday Victims: Civilians in the Burundian War, 12/03, 64pp.

Civilians Pay the Price of Faltering Peace Process, 02/03, 21pp.

Cambodia:

Don't Bite the Hand that Feeds You: Coercion, Threats, and Vote-Buying in Cambodia's National Elections, 07/03, 22pp.

World Report 2004

The Run-Up to Cambodia's 2003 National Assembly Election: Political Expression and Freedom of Assembly Under Assault, 06/03, 15pp.

Serious Flaws: Why the U.N. General Assembly Should Require Changes to the Draft Khmer Rouge Tribunal Agreement, 4/03, 12pp.

Canada:

Abusing The User: Police Misconduct, Harm Reduction and HIV/AIDS in Vancouver, 05/03, 25pp.

Chile:

Discreet Path to Justice?: Chile, Thirty Years After the Military Coup, 09/03, 16pp.

China:

Locked Doors: The Human Rights of People Living with HIV/AIDS in China, 09/03, 95pp.

Colombia:

"You'll Learn Not to Cry:" Child Combatants in Colombia, 09/03, 168pp.

Colombia's Checkbook Impunity, 09/03, 13pp.

Côte D'Ivoire:

Trapped Between Two Wars: Violence Against Civilians in Western Côte D'Ivoire, 08/03, 55pp.

Croatia:

Broken Promises: Impediments to Refugee Return to Croatia, 09/03, 61pp.

Democratic Republic of Congo:

Ituri: "Covered in Blood:" Ethnically Targeted Violence in Northeastern DR Congo, 07/03, 57pp.

Egypt:

Security Forces Abuse of Anti-War Demonstrators, 11/03, 40pp.

Charged With Being Children: Egyptian Police Abuse of Children in Need of Protection, 02/03, 79pp.

El Salvador:

Deliberate Indifference: El Salvador's Failure to Protect Worker's Rights, 12/03, 98pp.

Eritrea:

The Horn of Africa War: Mass Expulsions and The Nationality Issue (June 1998-April 2002), 01/03, 64pp.

Ethiopia:

Lessons in Repression: Violations of Academic Freedom, 01/03, 52pp.

India:

Compounding Injustice: The Government's Failure to Redress Massacres in Gujarat, 07/03, 70pp.

Small Change: Bonded Child Labor in India's Silk Industry, 01/03, 88pp.

Indonesia:

Aceh Under Martial Law-- Muzzling the Messengers: Attacks and Restrictions on the Media, 11/03, 33pp.

A Return to the New Order? Political Prisoners in Megawati's Indonesia, 07/03, 23pp.

Without Remedy: Human Rights Abuse and Indonesia's Pulp and Paper Industry, 01/03, 91pp.

Iraq:

Off Target: The Conduct of the War and Civilian Casualties in Iraq, 12/03, 154pp.

Hearts and Minds: Post-War Civilians Deaths in Baghdad Caused by U.S. Forces, 10/03, 72pp.

Climate of Fear: Sexual Violence and Abduction of Women and Girls in Baghdad, 07/03, 16pp.

Basra: Crime and Insecurity Under British Occupation, 06/03, 24pp.

Violent Response: The U.S. Army in Al-Falluja, 06/03, 19pp.

The Mass Graves of Al-Mahawil: the Truth Uncovered, 05/03, 15pp.

Flight From Iraq: Attacks on Refugees and Other Foreigners and their Treatment in Jordan, 05/03, 22pp.

Forcible Expulsion of Ethnic Minorities, 03/03, 34pp.

Cluster Munitions a Foreseeable Hazard in Iraq, 03/03, 6pp.

Iraqi Refugees, Asylum Seekers, and Displaced Persons: Current Conditions and Concerns in the Event of War, 02/03, 25pp.

International Humanitarian Law Issues in a Potential War in Iraq, 02/03, 14pp.

Israel/Occupied Territories:

The Roadmap: Repeating Oslo's Human Rights Mistakes, 5/03, 14pp.

Briefing to the 59th Session of the UN Commission on Human Rights on the Human Rights Situation in Israel and the Occupied Territories, 02/03, 4pp.

Kazakhstan:

Fanning The Flames: How Human Rights Abuses are Fueling the AIDS Epidemic in Kazakhstan, 05/03, 54pp.

World Report 2004

Kenya:

Double Standards: Women's Property Rights Violations, 03/03, 51pp.

Kenya's Unfinished Democracy: A Human Rights Agenda for the New Government, 12/02, 27pp.

Liberia:

Weapons Sanctions, Military Supplies, and Human Suffering: Illegal Arms Flows to Liberia and the June-July 2003 Shelling of Monrovia--A Briefing Paper for the U.N. Security Council, 11/03, 32pp.

Greater Protection Required for Civilians Still at Risk, 09/03, 5pp.

The Regional Crisis and Human Rights Abuses in West Africa--A Briefing Paper for the U.N. Security Council, 06/03, 10pp.

Macedonia:

Solutions for Macedonia's Roma Refugee Problem, 12/03, 25pp.

Mexico:

Justice in Jeopardy: Why Mexico's First Real Effort to Address Past Abuses Risks Becoming Its Latest Failure, 07/03, 30pp.

Nepal:

Trapped by Inequality: Bhutanese Refugee Women in Nepal, 09/03, 76pp.

The Netherlands:

Fleeting Refuge: The Triumph of Efficiency Over Protection in Dutch Asylum Policy, 04/03, 33pp.

Nigeria:

The Warri Crisis: Fueling Violence, 12/03, 31pp.

Renewed Crackdown on Freedom of Expression, 12/03, 40pp.

The "Miss World Riots:" Continued Impunity for Killings in Kaduna, 07/03, 33pp.

Testing Democracy: Political Violence in Nigeria, 04/03, 39pp.

The O'odua Peoples Congress: Fighting Violence with Violence, 02/03, 58pp.

Nigeria at the Crossroads: Human Rights Concerns in the Pre-Election Period, 01/03, 15pp.

Russia:

To Serve Without Health? Inadequate Nutrition and Health Care in the Russian Armed Forces, 11/03, 40pp.

Russia's "Spy Mania:" a Study of the Case of Igor Sutiagin, 10/03, 20pp.

Spreading Despair: Russian Abuses in Ingushetia, 09/03, 28pp.

Briefing Paper to the 59th Session of the UN Commission on Human Rights on the Human Rights Situation in Chechnya, 04/03, 8pp.

Situation of Ethnic Chechens in Moscow, 02/03, 8pp.

Into Harm's Way: Forced Return of Displaced People to Chechnya, 01/03, 27pp.

Rwanda:

Preparing for Elections: Tightening Control in the Name of Unity, 05/03, 16pp.

Lasting Wounds: Consequences of Genocide and War for Rwanda's Children, 03/03, 80pp.

Saudi Arabia:

The Criminal Justice System in the Kingdom of Saudi Arabia, 05/03, 9pp.

Sierra Leone:

"We'll Kill You If You Cry:" Sexual Violence in The Sierra Leone Conflict, 01/03, 75pp.

South Africa:

Truth and Justice: Unfinished Business in South Africa, 02/03, 12pp.

Sudan:

Sudan, Oil, and Human Rights, 11/03, 772pp.

Togo:

Borderline Slavery: Child Trafficking in Togo, 04/03, 85pp.

Tunisia:

Human Rights Lawyers and Associations Under Siege in Tunisia, 03/03, 8pp.

Turkey:

Turkey and War in Iraq: Avoiding Past Patterns of Violation, 03/03, 11pp.

A Human Rights Agenda for the Next Phase of Turkey's E.U. Accession Process, 01/03, 10pp.

Uganda:

Just Die Quietly: Domestic Violence and Women's Vulnerability to HIV, 08/03, 77pp.

Abducted and Abused: Renewed Conflict in Northern Uganda, 07/03, 73pp.

Stolen Children: Abduction and Recruitment in Northern Uganda, 03/03, 24pp.

Ukraine:

Women's Work: Discrimination against Women in the Ukrainian Labor Force, 08/03, 52pp.

World Report 2004

Negotiating The News: Informal State Censorship of Ukrainian
Television, 03/03, 47pp.

United Kingdom:

An Unjust "Vision" for Europe's Refugees: Commentary on the U.K.'s
"New Vision" Proposal for the Establishment of Refugee Processing
Centers Abroad, 06/03, 17pp.

United States:

Ill-Equipped: U.S. Prisons and Offenders with Mental Illness, 10/03,
224pp.

Injecting Reason: Human Rights and HIV Prevention for Injection
Drug Users--California: A Case Study, 09/03, 61pp.

Non-Discrimination in Civil Marriage: Perspectives from International
Human Rights Law and Practice, 07/03, 5pp.

Briefing Paper on U.S. Military Commissions, 06/03, 9pp.

Incarcerated America, 04/03, 5pp.

The Legal Prohibition Against Torture, 03/03, 7pp.

Uniform Discrimination: The "Don't Ask, Don't Tell" Policy of the U.S.
Military, 01/03, 54pp.

Uzbekistan:

From House to House: Abuses By Mahalla Committees, 09/03, 37pp.

Persecution of Human Rights Defenders in Uzbekistan, 05/03, 10pp.

Deaths in Custody in Uzbekistan, 04/03, 12pp.

Venezuela:

Caught in the Crossfire: Freedom of Expression in Venezuela, 05/03, 20pp.

Vietnam:

New Documents Reveal Escalating Repression, 04/03, 20pp.

New Assault on Rights in Vietnam's Central Highlands: Crackdown on Indigenous Montagnards Intensifies, 01/03, 25pp.

Zimbabwe:

Not Eligible: The Politicization of Food in Zimbabwe, 10/03, 52pp.

Under a Shadow: Civil and Political Rights in Zimbabwe, 06/03, 17pp.

More Than A Name: State-Sponsored Homophobia and Its Consequences in Southern Africa, 05/03, 310pp.

Worldwide:

Landmine Monitor Report 2003: Toward A Mine-Free World, 08/03, 826pp.

Landmine Monitor Report 2003: Executive Summary, 08/03, 95pp.

In the Name of Counter-Terrorism: Human Rights Abuses Worldwide, 3/03, 25pp.

World Report 2004

Reports by Theme

Arms Issues:

Off Target: The Conduct of the War and Civilian Casualties in Iraq, 12/03, 154pp.

Weapons Sanctions, Military Supplies, and Human Suffering: Illegal Arms Flows to Liberia and the June-July 2003 Shelling of Monrovia--A Briefing Paper for the U.N. Security Council, 11/03, 32pp.

Landmine Monitor Report 2003: Toward A Mine-Free World, 08/03, 826pp.

Landmine Monitor Report 2003: Executive Summary, 08/03, 95pp.

Small Arms and Human Rights: The Need for Global Action--A Briefing Paper for the U.N. Biennial Meeting on Small Arms, 07/03, 22pp.

Cluster Munitions: Measures to Prevent Explosive Remnants of War and to Protect Civilian Populations--Memorandum to Delegates to the Convention on Conventional Weapons, 03/03, 7pp.

Cluster Munitions a Foreseeable Hazard in Iraq, 03/03, 6pp.

International Humanitarian Law Issues in a Potential War in Iraq, 02/03, 14pp.

Children's Rights Issues:

Policy Paralysis: A Call for Action on HIV/AIDS-Related Human Rights Abuses Against Women and Girls in Africa, 12/03, 38pp.

"You'll Learn Not to Cry": Child Combatants in Colombia, 09/03, 150pp.

"Killing You Is a Very Easy Thing for Us": Human Rights Abuses in Southeast Afghanistan, 07/03, 101pp.

Climate of Fear: Sexual Violence and Abduction of Women and Girls in Baghdad, 07/03, 17pp.

Forgotten Fighters: Child Soldiers in Angola, 04/03, 26pp.

Cruel Confinement: Abuses Against Detained Children in Northern Brazil, 04/03, 63pp.

Fleeting Refuge: The Triumph of Efficiency Over Protection in Dutch Asylum Policy, 04/03, 32pp.

Lasting Wounds: Consequences of Genocide and War for Rwanda's Children, 04/03, 80pp.

Borderline Slavery: Child Trafficking in Togo, 04/03, 79pp.

Stolen Children: Abduction and Recruitment in Northern Uganda, 03/03, 31pp.

Charged With Being Children: Egyptian Police Abuse of Children in Need of Protection, 02/03, 87pp.

Suffering in Silence: Human Rights Abuses and HIV Transmission to Girls in Zambia, 01/03, 121pp.

Small Change: Bonded Child Labor in India's Silk Industry, 01/03, 85pp.

"We'll Kill You If You Cry": Sexual Violence in the Sierra Leone Conflict, 01/03, 75pp.

World Report 2004

Gay, Lesbian, Bisexual, Transgender Issues:

Non-Discrimination in Civil Marriage: Perspectives from International Human Rights Law and Practice, 07/03, 5pp.

More Than A Name: State-Sponsored Homophobia and Its Consequences in Southern Africa, 05/03, 310pp.

Uniform Discrimination: The "Don't Ask, Don't Tell" Policy of the U.S. Military, 01/03, 54pp.

HIV/AIDS Issues:

Policy Paralysis: A Call for Action on HIV/AIDS-Related Human Rights Abuses Against Women and Girls in Africa, 12/03, 38pp.

Locked Doors: The Human Rights of People Living with HIV/AIDS in China, 09/03, 95pp.

Injecting Reason: Human Rights and HIV Prevention for Injection Drug Users--California: A Case Study, 09/03, 61pp.

Ravaging the Vulnerable: Abuses Against persons at High Risk of HIV Infection in Bangladesh, 09/03, 51pp.

Just Die Quietly: Domestic Violence and Women's Vulnerability to HIV in Uganda, 08/03, 77pp.

Fanning the Flames: How Human Rights Abuses are Fueling the AIDS Epidemic in Kazakhstan, 06/03, 51pp.

More Than A Name: State-Sponsored Homophobia and Its Consequences in Southern Africa, 05/03, 310pp.

Abusing the User: Police Misconduct, Harm Reduction and HIVAIDS in Vancouver, 05/03, 28pp.

Double Standards: Women's Property Rights Violations in Kenya, 03/03, 54pp.

Refugee Issues:

Solutions for Macedonia's Roma Refugee Problem, 12/03, 25pp.

The International Organization for Migration (IOM) and Human Rights Protection in the Field: Current Concerns, 11/03, 19pp.

Broken Promises: Impediments to Refugee Return to Croatia, 09/03, 61pp.

Trapped by Inequality: Bhutanese Refugee Women in Nepal, 09/03, 76pp.

An Unjust "Vision" for Europe's Refugees: Commentary on the U.K.'s "New Vision" Proposal for the Establishment of Refugee Processing Centers Abroad, 06/03, 17pp.

"We Don't Want to Be Refugees Again:" A Briefing Paper for the Fourteenth Ministerial Joint Committee of Bhutan and Nepal, 05/03, 22pp.

Flight From Iraq: Attacks on Refugees and Other Foreigners and their Treatment in Jordan, 05/03, 22pp.

Fleeting Refuge: The Triumph of Efficiency Over Protection in Dutch Asylum Policy, 04/03, 32pp.

Iraqi Refugees, Asylum Seekers, and Displaced Persons: Current Conditions and Concerns in the Event of War, 02/03, 25pp.

The Horn of Africa War: Mass Expulsions and The Nationality Issue (June 1998-April 2002), 01/03, 64pp.

World Report 2004

Women's Rights Issues:

Trapped by Inequality: Bhutanese Refugee Women in Nepal, 10/03, 77 pp.

From House to House: Abuses by Mahalla Committees, 09/03, 36pp.

Trapped Between Two Wars: Violence Against Civilians in Western Côte d'Ivoire, 08/03, 54pp.

Ravaging the Vulnerable: Abuses Against Persons at High Risk of HIV Infection in Bangladesh, 08/03, 51pp.

Struggling through Peace: Return and Resettlement in Angola, 08/03, 33pp.

Women's Work: Discrimination Against Women in the Ukrainian Labor Force, 08/03 52pp.

Just Die Quietly: Domestic Violence and Women's Vulnerability to HIV in Uganda, 08/03, 77pp.

Abducted and Abused: Renewed Conflict in Northern Uganda, 07/03, 73 pp.

Compounding Injustice: The Government's Failure to Redress Massacres in Gujarat, 07/03, 70pp.

Climate of Fear: Sexual Violence and Abduction of Women and Girls in Baghdad, 07/03, 77pp.

Killing You is a Very Easy Thing For Us: Human Rights Abuses in Southeast Afghanistan, 07/03, 101 pp.

Fanning the Flames: How Human Rights Abuses are Fueling the AIDS Epidemic in Kazakhstan, 06/03, 53pp.

Borderline Slavery: Child Trafficking In Togo, 04/03, 79pp.

Stolen Children: Abduction and Recruitment in Northern Uganda, 03/03, 24pp.

Double Standards: Women's Property Rights Violations in Kenya, 03/03, 54pp.

"We'll Kill You If You Cry": Sexual Violence in the Sierra Leone Conflict, 01/03, 77pp.